The Salesman's Paradox

"How to actually sell without selling."

Joseph D. Poltor, PsyM

Table of Contents

Part One: Unleashing Your Inner Sales Power

1. The Essence of "The Sell": Unlocking Potential — 6
2. The Purpose of This Journey: Your Path to Greatness — 8
3. Understanding the Buying Impulse: Cracking the Code — 11
4. Breaking the Salesperson Stereotype: Shattering Myths — 14
5. Passion for Your Product: Love What You Sell — 17
6. Success Through Genuine Help: Transforming Lives — 19

Part Two: The Psychology of Selling

7. Mental Jiu-Jitsu: Mastering Minds and Winning Hearts — 25
8. Understanding and Engaging Personality Types: Adaptive Strategies — 27
9. Identifying and Overcoming Blindspots: Seeing Clearly — 33
10. Building Authentic Rapport: Creating Unbreakable Bonds — 36
11. The Art of Mirroring for Influence: Subtle Power Moves — 39
12. Energy Dynamics: Harnessing Invisible Forces — 42
13. The Decision Maker's Role: Targeting the Right Influences — 45
14. Catering to Ego Needs: The Secrets of Flattery — 48
15. Overcoming Desperation in Sales: Staying Confident and Calm — 52
16. Setting Ambitious Goals: Dream Big, Achieve Bigger — 55
17. Cultivating Genuine Enthusiasm: Infectious Positivity — 57
18. Reading Posture and Micro-Expressions: Hidden Signals — 59
19. Leading Clients to YOUR Desired Outcomes: Power of Guidance — 66
20. Becoming the Inspirational Guide: Being the Wizard — 70
21. The Power of Storytelling: Captivate Your Audience — 73
22. Owning the Sale: They Came to YOU — 75
23. Balancing Want VS. Needs — 78
24. Buyer's Remorse: Ensuring Satisfaction — 81
25. Staying Humble: Learning from Everyone — 83
26. The Power of Strategic Dismissal: Commanding Respect — 86
27. Leveraging Cialdini's Six Principles: Influence and Persuasion — 89

28. Harnessing the Power of Testimonials: Social Proof	93
29. Delivering Exceptional Customer Service: Delight and Retain	96
30. Handling Objections with Grace: Turning No into Yes	100
31. Transparency as a Success Strategy: Building Trust	103
32. Obnoxious Optimism: Creating Silver Lining	106
33. The "Can Do" Mentality: Unwavering Belief	109
34. Believing in Yourself: Confidence is Key	113
35. Building a Strong Support System: Your Success Network	117
36. The Importance of Rest and Recuperation: Recharge to Excel	121
37. Positive Thinking for Success: Mind Over Matter	124
38. Recognizing and Avoiding Self-Sabotage: Your Worst Enemy	127
39. The "It is what it is" Principle: Acceptance and Growth	130
40. Exploring Neurolinguistic Programming: Mind Mastery	135
41. Introduction to Psychodynamic Marketing: Deep Influence	141
42. Enhancing the Mind Through Physical Fitness: Body and Brain	145
43. Creating Urgency with Limited Offers: Timely Temptation	149
44. Compounding Interest in Leads: Building Momentum	153
45. Embracing F.I.T. - Fortitude, Integrity, Temperance: Core Values	157
46. Comparing Positivity vs. Misery: Choose Joy	161
47. If You've Done Your Best, Don't Worry that was Your Best	164
48. The 4-Square Checklist for Success: Your Roadmap	167
49. Eating the Frog: Tackling Tough Tasks First	170
50. The Culture of Truly Loving Your Team	172
51. Self-Care and Recognizing Burnout: Stay Balanced	174
52. The Power of Inception in Sales: Planting Ideas	176
53. Dealing with Different Generations in Sales: Tailored Approaches	178

Part Three: The Sales Game - Tactical Execution

54. Preparing and Researching for Success: Be Ready, Be Smart	182
55. Effective Lead Generation Strategies: Fill Your Funnel	184
56. Understanding Your Client Base: Know Your Audience	188
57. Mastering the Art of Prospecting: Finding Gold	190

Part Four: Mastering Marketing

58. Innovative Lead Generation Techniques: Creative Approaches	193
59. Education-Based Marketing Strategies: Teach to Sell	203
60. Retargeting for Results: Staying Top of Mind	206
61. Shotgun Marketing: Broad Reach, Big Impact	209
62. Crafting Captivating Sales Copy: Words that Win	212
63. Mastering Socials Marketing & Perception: Digital Dominance	216

Part Five: Conquering Adversity and Thriving in Sales

64. Thriving Amidst Competition: Stand Out, Stay Ahead	220
65. Breaking Through Sales Stigmas: Changing Perceptions	222
66. Navigating Outside Influences: Steering Through Storms	224
67. Balancing Needs vs. Wants: The Ultimate Solution	226

Part Six: The 5 E's of "The Sell" - The Exact Process

68. E1 – Creating an Impactful **Entry**: First Impressions	231
69. E2 – **Extraction** of Valuable Information: Deep Understanding	235
70. E3 – **Engaging** with Purpose: Meaningful Interactions	238
71. E4 – Generating **Excitement**: Building Anticipation	240
72. E5 – Delivering a Memorable **Ending**: The Perfect Close	242

Part Seven: Mastering Productivity and Peak Performance

73. 30/30/30/10 Rule Meets Pareto's 80/20 Principle	246
74. Minimizing Time Wasting: Maximize Productivity	249
75. The Work Environment: Happy Place, High Performance	251
76. Fighting the Good Fight: Upholding Integrity through Adversity	255
77. Maximizing Productivity with a 4-Hour Workday: Work Smarter	258

Part Eight: Conclusion - Your Ultimate Sales Transformation

78. Comprehensive Review of Key Concepts: Your Toolkit	262
79. Conclusion: Your Path to Sales Mastery: Journey's End	265
80. Additional Resources for Continued Learning: Keep Growing	267

Book One - Introduction

"I'm not sure if you've ever thought about it like this but one of the best things about reading a book is that it is typically a culmination of a man's life's work. Everything he knew, everything he cared about and everything he wanted is in those pages. It's his life's legacy put on paper to be passed on to you. I think that's beautiful."

Acknowledgements

"I'd like to thank my family for always being there for me and supporting me through my out of the box thinking and failing forward over and over again. It took a long time to get to where we are now. My wife Sheree, my daughters - India, Sophia and Saleha and of course our puppy - SargyPargyPuddinPie. I have had a few notable mentors - Reggie G., Phil H., and John W., all who made a significant impact on the person, salesman and trainer I am today. Also, thank you to everyone who has ever taught me anything, helped me with anything, challenged me or just made me better in any way. And the books, I am the type to constantly try to improve and grow so I have read hundreds of self-help books, watched seminars, listened to audios, took classes and anything else I can do to be better. There is so much value out in the world, I hope this book becomes a strong resource of that value for you.

Essence of "The Sell"

Imagine the transformative power of a sale—a scenario where a nervous job applicant, moments before his interview, finds solace in a box of girl scout cookies he bought from you and your daughter. As he nervously waits, he reaches for a caramel chocolate coconut delight, and the hiring manager notices. Those cookies trigger memories of her daughter's scout days, sparking a connection. She sees ambition and innocence in him, and he nails the interview. Those cookies, sold by you, became more than a snack; they sparked a ripple effect that launched his career, leading to promotions, a home, a growing family, and dreams fulfilled.

This is the essence of "The Sell"—a transformative process where your product isn't just a transaction but a catalyst for change in someone's life. Whether you're selling homes, recruiting talent, or promoting new ideas, your role as a salesman goes beyond mere persuasion. It's about nurturing desires, instilling confidence, and showing how your offering can shape a brighter future. Throughout this book, my goal is to elevate your salesmanship to a mastery level. "The Sell" isn't confined to boardrooms or showroom floors; it permeates every interaction, every decision we make. It's convincing your boss, negotiating with clients, or even convincing yourself to pursue your dreams despite doubt. Internally, it's that voice urging you forward or holding you back. Right now, it might be nudging you to dive deeper into this book or dismiss it as another self-help gimmick. Listen closely; that voice of encouragement, faint as it may be, is the one that leads to success.

Let me share more about myself—I've spent over two decades mastering sales, from winning top accolades in real estate and recruiting to training sales teams nationwide. My journey through sales and psychology has shown me that closing a deal isn't the pinnacle; it's understanding human motivations and forging lasting connections that makes any job worth doing. I began my working life as a waiter, where sales skills were as essential as delivering food. Since then, I've navigated the highs and lows of the real estate market, succeeding even during economic downturns. My master's degree in psychology deepened my understanding of the sales process from a psychological perspective, culminating in my integrative project titled "Psychodynamic Marketing," which you'll find at the end of this book.

Why am I sharing this? Because I've seen too many talented salespeople struggle. They focus on the close when the journey—the relationship built, the trust earned—is what truly matters. Sales isn't just a career; it's a gateway to financial freedom and lifestyle flexibility. Imagine working fewer hours, earning more, and having the freedom to prioritize family or personal interests. By delving into the concepts laid out in this book, you're equipping yourself not just with sales techniques but with a mindset for success. Whether you're a seasoned pro or starting out, embracing "The Sell" means embracing a path where helping others and achieving personal fulfillment align seamlessly.

Purpose of this Journey

The purpose of this book is to transform you from an average or below-average salesperson into a top producer. Whether you're new to sales or have decades of experience, this book will provide the tools and insights you need to elevate your sales game to new heights. Top producers constantly seek to hone their craft, and by picking up this book, you've already taken the first step toward becoming one of them. I'm pouring my heart and soul into this book because I have wisdom in this area that should be shared. By mastering these concepts, you will take control of your life and accomplish your dreams.

"The Sell" is happening all around us in many ways, shapes, and forms. Once you understand it and learn to control the sales outcome, you can have almost anything. Imagine being able to talk your way in and out of any situation—how beneficial would that be for you? What could that mean for your future? Take a moment to think about this concept. Please, always be sure to use this knowledge to help others and improve their lives, do not use it to manipulate or coerce. This book is valuable for beginners, seasoned salespeople with decades of experience, and everyone in between. The key to success is diving into the concepts, understanding, and implementing them. Highlight, take notes, and ensure you fully grasp what's being conveyed. Understanding isn't enough; implement daily until you can teach these concepts. Teaching helps you comprehend why these principles work. Like using a computer, you don't need to know how every component works, just how to use it. This book will give you more than the basics. Aim to master these concepts and fuel your desire for success in "The Sell."

You picked this book to become better, right? We all can improve and learn from anything if we keep an open mind. Some concepts may be new or seem eccentric, but trust in the value of these pages, backed by decades of experience and research. This book is broken into several sections, each designed to build your expertise step by step. In **Book One: Introduction to Sales Mastery**, we start by exploring **What is "The Sell"?** and the purpose of this journey. You'll learn **Why Do People Buy?** and how to **Break the Salesman Stereotype**, transforming your approach to sales. We'll ignite your **Passion for Your Product** and demonstrate how **Success Through Genuine Help** can transform your career.

In **Book Two: The Psychology of Selling**, we'll delve deep into the mental aspects of sales. You'll master **Mental Jiu-Jitsu: Mastering Minds and Winning Hearts** and understand the importance of **Personality Types, Yours and Theirs**. We'll cover how to engage with different personalities, identify and overcome blindspots, and build authentic rapport. You'll learn the art of mimicking for influence, harness energy dynamics in sales, and target the decision maker effectively. We'll also explore **Catering to Ego Needs**, overcoming desperation, setting ambitious goals, and cultivating genuine enthusiasm.

The next chapters will guide you through **Reading Posture and Micro-Expressions**, leading clients to desired outcomes, and becoming the inspirational guide—**Being the Wizard**. You'll harness the power of storytelling, balance wants vs. needs, and manage buyer's remorse. Staying humble, leveraging Cialdini's six principles, and delivering exceptional customer service will also be covered. Handling objections with grace, transparency, optimistic persistence, and believing in yourself are key themes. Building a strong support system, understanding the importance of rest, and embracing positive thinking for success are vital for your journey.

Book Three: The Sales Game focuses on practical strategies. You'll learn **Preparing and Researching for Success**, effective lead generation strategies, understanding your client base, and mastering the art of prospecting. In **Book Four: Mastering Marketing**, we'll explore innovative lead generation techniques, education-based marketing strategies, retargeting for results, shotgun marketing, and crafting winning sales copy. You'll master social media marketing and perception, ensuring you reach your audience effectively. **Book Five: Overcoming Challenges** will help you thrive amidst competition, break through sales stigmas, navigate outside influences, and balance needs vs. wants.

In **Book Six: The 5 E's of "The Sell"**, you'll learn the essential steps of a successful sales process. We'll cover **E1 – Creating an Impactful Entry**, **E2 – Extracting Valuable Insights**, **E3 – Engaging with Purpose**, **E4 – Generating Excitement**, and **E5 – Delivering a Memorable Ending**. Each step is crucial for guiding your clients and ensuring a successful sale. **Book Seven: Efficient Work Practices** will teach you to implement the 30/30/30/10 rule, minimize time wasting, cultivate a positive work environment, recognize and avoid toxicity, and maximize productivity with a 4-hour workday. Finally, in **Book Eight: Review and Conclusion**, we'll provide a comprehensive review of key concepts and a conclusion that ties everything together. We'll also offer an additional resources list to fuel your ongoing desire for success in "The Sell."

As you embark on this journey, remember that the purpose of this book is not just to make you a better salesperson, but to help you become a better person. Sales is a craft you can hone, develop, master, teach, understand, and live. As your understanding grows, be proud—you're becoming stronger. Motivating you to level up is a step toward greater success! Keep an open mind as you delve into these concepts, and always remember that our ultimate goal is to help others. Use the knowledge gained from this book to improve lives, build lasting relationships, and achieve personal and professional fulfillment. You have the potential to become a sales master, and this book is your guide to unlocking that potential. Let's embark on this journey together and transform your approach to sales, one chapter at a time.

Buying Impulse: Cracking the Code

Have you ever stopped and actually asked yourself this question? Why do people buy? Why do we do anything that we do? Take a second and reflect on the question, then I'll give you my perspective and we'll dig a bit deeper. When I shop for something, it tends to be out of perceived necessity. Maybe necessity isn't as great of a term as I want. I don't need those donuts from Dunkin' Donuts, but I am hungry and need to eat. I don't need that new piece of workout equipment, but working out makes me feel better. I have a computer that works, but if I had a faster one, maybe I'd be more productive, so that should be a good purchase, right? Let's dig into that a little bit more. I'm hungry and I need to eat; I could go home and make something for breakfast or I could stop for that delicious bacon, egg, and cheese bagel that's seemingly always on special. There is convenience in not having to make my own breakfast sandwich. It's promoted as a deal, so I believe I am doing something good for my pocket (even though I clearly am not) and I am satisfying my basic need for food. Also, if the sandwich is always on deal, isn't that just the actual price? Regardless, I pick this up regularly and I feel good about my decision. From this transaction, we could deduce that I need to eat something, this sandwich is convenient, and I am attracted to the deal.

But there's more to it than just convenience and necessity. Do you ever buy to impress others, to stand out, or to cater to your ego? Why else? Do you buy solely out of necessity, or do you prefer name brands over generic? Why? These are all questions that we must explore to get a true meaning of why we, as humans, buy things. Think about the last time you bought something special—maybe a luxury item or a high-end gadget. What was the driving force behind that purchase? Often, it's not just about the product itself but about what it represents. Buying a luxury car, for example, isn't just about transportation. It's about status, achievement, and the feeling of success. It's about the emotions that the purchase evokes and the story it tells about you. Humans are emotional beings, and our purchases often reflect our deepest desires and fears. We buy things that make us feel good, things that make us feel safe, and things that we believe will improve our lives. This is why understanding the psychology of selling is crucial. When you understand what drives people to buy, you can tailor your approach to meet their emotional needs.

Let's consider another scenario: buying clothes. Do you buy clothes just to cover your body, or do you buy them to express your personality, to fit in with a certain group, or to stand out? Fashion is a powerful form of self-expression, and the clothes we choose to wear can say a lot about who we are and how we want to be perceived. When you sell clothing, you're not just selling fabric; you're selling confidence, identity, and a sense of belonging. The same goes for technology. Why do people line up for the latest smartphone when their current one works perfectly fine? It's not just about the new features; it's about being part of the cutting edge, having the latest and greatest, and the excitement of new possibilities. It's about the anticipation and the status that comes with owning the newest tech.

Understanding these deeper motivations allows you to connect with your clients on a more profound level. It's not enough to know what people buy; you need to understand why they buy. This knowledge will enable you to address their true needs and desires, making your sales approach more effective and meaningful. Do you ever buy gifts for loved ones? Think about why you choose certain gifts. It's not just about the item itself but about the thought and emotion behind it. You want to show appreciation, love, and care. The gift represents your feelings and the relationship you have with the recipient. When you sell gifts, you're helping people express their emotions and strengthen their relationships. Even in the world of everyday purchases, there's a story. Take groceries, for instance. You might choose organic produce over conventional because you care about health and wellness, or maybe you're concerned about the environment. Each purchase decision is a reflection of your values and priorities.

So, why do people buy? It's a complex web of emotions, desires, and needs. People buy to feel good, to solve problems, to express themselves, to belong, to stand out, to celebrate, to cope, and to fulfill their dreams. As a salesperson, your role is to tap into these motivations and show how your product or service aligns with them. Throughout this book, we'll explore various aspects of why people buy and how you can leverage this understanding to enhance your sales techniques. We'll delve into the psychology of selling, learning how to read your clients, build rapport, and connect with their deeper motivations. You'll discover how to transform a simple transaction into a meaningful exchange that satisfies both parties. Remember, every sale is an opportunity to make a positive impact on someone's life. By understanding why people buy, you can become a more empathetic, effective, and successful salesperson. Let's embark on this journey together and unlock the true potential of "The Sell."

Salesman's Stereotype & Shattering Myths

Salespeople often face negative stereotypes. The image of the pushy, aggressive, and manipulative salesperson is pervasive, undermining the profession's credibility and the trust customers place in it. However, modern sales professionals are transforming this outdated image by adopting ethical practices, focusing on building relationships, and providing genuine value to their clients. This chapter explores strategies to break the salesman stereotype and establish a reputation as a trusted advisor.

To break the salesman stereotype, it's essential to understand the origins of the negative traits associated with salespeople. The traditional stereotype of a salesperson is someone who prioritizes their own commission over the customer's needs, uses high-pressure tactics to close deals, misleads or exaggerates the benefits of a product or service, and disregards customer satisfaction after the sale is made. These behaviors harm the salesperson's reputation and damage customer trust and loyalty. Building trust through integrity is the foundation of transforming this perception. When customers believe a salesperson is honest and transparent, they are more likely to engage and build a long-term relationship. Demonstrating integrity involves providing accurate information about your products or services, being upfront about any limitations or potential drawbacks, and avoiding making promises you can't keep. Ethical selling practices are crucial: prioritize the customer's best interests, avoid manipulative or deceptive tactics, and ensure that the products or services you offer genuinely meet the customer's needs. Consistency in your actions and communication is also vital—follow through on commitments and promises, and maintain a high standard of professionalism at all times. Remember, trust is like a stapler; once it's broken, it's hard to put back together again without leaving a mark.

Modern sales success relies on building strong, lasting relationships instead of focusing on one-time transactions. Relationship-based selling emphasizes understanding and meeting the customer's needs, fostering loyalty, and encouraging repeat business. Active listening is key: pay attention to what the customer is saying, ask open-ended questions to understand their needs and concerns, and show empathy and understanding in your responses. Personalization is also essential—tailor your approach to each customer based on their unique needs and preferences, use customer data and feedback to offer personalized solutions, and demonstrate that you value them as individuals, not just as potential sales. Follow-up and aftercare are crucial components of relationship-based selling. Check in with customers after the sale to ensure they are satisfied, provide ongoing support and address any issues promptly, and offer additional value through advice, resources, or updates relevant to their needs.

Breaking the stereotype involves showing that you are more than just a salesperson—you are a trusted advisor who provides real value. This can be achieved by educating customers: share your knowledge and expertise to help customers make informed decisions, provide insights and advice that are beneficial even if they don't lead to an immediate sale, and host workshops, webinars, or create content that addresses common customer challenges. Adding value beyond the sale is also important: offer solutions that enhance the customer's experience with your product or service, be a resource for related needs, guiding customers to other trusted providers if necessary, and show that you are committed to their long-term success, not just the initial purchase. Delivering exceptional customer service is another critical aspect of providing genuine value. Respond promptly and effectively to customer inquiries and issues, go the extra mile to exceed customer expectations, and foster a positive experience that encourages customers to recommend you to others.

Authenticity in sales means being true to yourself and your values while genuinely caring about your customers. Authentic salespeople build stronger connections and earn more trust. To embrace authenticity, be yourself—don't try to fit into the traditional mold of a salesperson. Let your personality shine through in your interactions and build your sales style around your strengths and values. Show genuine interest in your customers' needs, interests, and goals. Engage in conversations that go beyond just the sale and demonstrate that you care about their success and well-being. Maintain integrity by staying true to your ethical principles, even when it's challenging. Avoid compromising your values for the sake of a sale and earn respect through your consistent, principled behavior.

Breaking the stereotype also means committing to continuous improvement and staying informed about best practices in the industry. This involves investing in ongoing education and training to enhance your skills, staying updated on industry trends and new technologies, and learning from successful sales professionals and mentors. Seek feedback from customers and colleagues to identify areas for improvement and use feedback constructively to refine your approach. Be open to change and adapt based on feedback. Reflect regularly on your sales interactions and outcomes, identify what worked well and what could be improved, and set goals for personal and professional growth.

Breaking the salesman stereotype requires a commitment to ethical practices, building genuine relationships, providing real value, and embracing authenticity. By focusing on these principles, you can transform the perception of sales from a manipulative endeavor to a noble profession centered on trust and mutual success. This shift not only enhances your reputation but also leads to more sustainable and rewarding sales outcomes. Embrace these strategies, and you'll not only become a better salesperson but also a trusted advisor and valued partner in your clients' success.

Passion/Love for Your Product

Passion for your product is one of the most powerful tools a salesperson can possess. Loving what you sell goes beyond mere enthusiasm; it translates into genuine belief, authenticity, and a compelling narrative that resonates with customers. Remember earlier when we saw how selling something as trivial as cookies could change someone's life? This chapter delves into why loving your product is essential and how it can elevate your sales performance.

When you truly believe in your product, your authenticity shines through in every interaction. Customers can sense when a salesperson is genuinely passionate, and this sincerity helps build trust. Authenticity means you aren't just reciting a sales pitch; you are sharing a product you believe in, making your message more compelling and credible. Consider the difference between two salespeople: one who couldn't care less and is merely going through the motions, and another who is genuinely excited about what they are selling. The latter's enthusiasm is infectious, creating a positive experience that draws customers in and builds a stronger, trust-based relationship.

Loving your product naturally leads to a deeper understanding of its features, benefits, and nuances. This comprehensive knowledge allows you to answer questions confidently, provide detailed insights, and tailor your sales approach to meet the specific needs of each customer. When you are passionate about your product, you are more likely to stay informed about updates, industry trends, and customer feedback, all of which enhance your expertise and ability to serve your clients effectively. Every product has a story, and when you love your product, you become an enthusiastic storyteller. Sharing the journey of the product, from its inception to its impact on customers, can create an emotional connection that goes beyond mere functionality. A compelling narrative can transform a standard sales pitch into an engaging story that resonates with customers, highlighting the product's value and the positive change it can bring to their lives.

In sales, objections are inevitable. However, when you are passionate about your product, you can address these objections with conviction and confidence.

Your belief in the product helps you remain positive and persistent, turning potential roadblocks into opportunities for deeper engagement. By sharing personal anecdotes and success stories, you can demonstrate how the product has benefited others, helping to alleviate concerns and build trust. A salesperson who loves their product is more likely to go the extra mile to ensure customer satisfaction. This dedication enhances the overall customer experience, fostering loyalty and encouraging repeat business. Your enthusiasm can create a positive atmosphere that makes customers feel valued and appreciated, leading to stronger relationships and long-term success.

Passion for your product fuels motivation and resilience. In the face of challenges and setbacks, your belief in what you are selling provides the drive to persevere. This intrinsic motivation helps you stay committed to your goals, continually improve your skills, and maintain a positive attitude. Loving your product makes your work more enjoyable and fulfilling, reducing burnout and increasing your overall job satisfaction.

As a sales leader, your passion for the product can inspire and motivate your team. When you model genuine enthusiasm and belief, it sets a positive example for others to follow. This contagious passion can create a cohesive, motivated team that shares a common purpose and is dedicated to achieving collective success. Imagine the energy in a room where everyone is genuinely excited about what they are offering—it's like having a team of superheroes ready to save the day.

Loving your product is not just about enthusiasm though; it's about authenticity, deep knowledge, and a genuine belief in the value you offer. This passion translates into trust, compelling storytelling, effective objection handling, and an enhanced customer experience. It fuels your motivation and resilience, inspires your team, and ultimately leads to greater sales success. By embracing and sharing your love for your product, you can transform your sales approach and build lasting, meaningful relationships with your customers. So, next time you talk about your product, remember, you're not just selling a thing, you're sharing a piece of yourself—like a dad sharing a corny joke. What did the grape say when it got stepped on? Nothing, it just let out a little wine. Now, go out there and let your passion shine!

Truly Helping Equals Success

In the world of sales, success is often measured by numbers—quotas met, deals closed, revenue generated. However, true success in sales goes beyond mere transactions; it lies in the genuine desire to help others. This chapter explores why adopting a mindset of true service and assistance not only enhances your sales career but also leads to profound personal fulfillment.

At the heart of successful salesmanship lies trust. When customers perceive that your primary goal is to solve their problems and meet their needs rather than merely making a sale, trust naturally develops. Trust forms the bedrock of strong, lasting relationships, essential for repeat business and referrals. By focusing on helping your customers achieve their goals, you establish yourself as a trusted advisor rather than a pushy salesperson. Sales is not just about one-time transactions; it's about cultivating relationships that endure, that become friendships, that earn you the spot of subject matter expert in their eyes. When you prioritize helping your clients succeed, you invest in long-term partnerships. These relationships evolve beyond initial sales interactions into collaborations where you become instrumental in your clients' success stories. Your commitment to their well-being fosters loyalty and turns satisfied customers into advocates who champion your services to others.

Effective selling begins with understanding the distinction between what customers need and what they want. Needs are fundamental—problems to be solved, challenges to be overcome. Wants are desires and preferences that enhance the customer experience. By focusing on uncovering and addressing both needs and wants, you demonstrate a comprehensive understanding of your clients' objectives. This approach not only increases the value you provide but also positions you as a strategic partner invested in their success. Sales is fundamentally about solving problems. When you approach each client interaction with a mindset of service, you seek to understand their pain points deeply. This understanding enables you to tailor solutions that address their specific challenges effectively. By offering solutions that add tangible value and deliver measurable results, you differentiate yourself from competitors who may prioritize closing deals over customer satisfaction.

Your reputation as a sales professional is built on how well you serve your clients. When you consistently prioritize their needs and deliver exceptional service, your reputation as a trusted expert grows. This positive reputation precedes you, opening doors to new opportunities and referrals. As clients recognize the genuine care you provide, they are more likely to choose you over competitors, regardless of price. Beyond financial success, true fulfillment in sales comes from knowing you've made a positive impact on others' lives. Helping clients achieve their goals fosters a sense of purpose and satisfaction that transcends monetary rewards. Professionally, this commitment to service drives continuous improvement and personal growth. As you refine your skills in understanding client needs and delivering effective solutions, you become a more proficient and respected salesperson. The path to success in sales is paved with genuine care and a steadfast commitment to helping others succeed. By prioritizing your clients' needs, fostering trust, and delivering value-driven solutions, you not only achieve sales targets but also build a fulfilling career rooted in meaningful relationships and personal growth. Embrace the ethos of true service, and success will naturally follow.

This principle is probably one of the most important principles of the entire book. If you understand the depth of this, feel it in your bones and wake up every day doing everything you can to just accomplish the message of this chapter, you will be successful, both personally and professionally.

Part Two

The Psychology of Selling

The Psychology of Selling

*Onto arguably the most **exciting** aspect of this book, the psychology. In this section, I hope that your mind awakens to some extraordinary opportunities. If you are the type that is an avid lifelong learner, you want to master your craft and are intrigued by life's beauty, this section is going to put a smile on your face. I hope that you take the time to really consider each of these topics and how they may impact your life and your sales ability. I want you to be awestruck by what you find, I want you to be enthusiastic about employing these tactics and feel accomplished with the mastery of them.*

While there may be some abstract or even esoteric ideologies in the coming pages, the intent here is very real and practical. It's implausible to categorize some of the psychological phenomena into anything but abstract. Please learn it, consider it, enjoy it, and take your sales ability beyond your current realm of what's possible in the art that is our work. Consider the beauty of "the sell" and its applicability in every situation. Think about each one of these topics and how you could have applied it to a previous situation. Think about situations where you have unknowingly used these tools and how you could have better used them now that they are consciously exposed. You got this book to become better at sales, but I hope you are seeing how it can help you become better at life.

The psychology of selling encompasses a wide range of fascinating and impactful concepts. We will delve into understanding personality types and how interacting with different personality types can enhance your sales approach. Each personality type has unique traits and behaviors, and by recognizing these, you can tailor your communication and selling strategies to better resonate with each individual. We'll explore the concept of mental jiu-jitsu—mastering minds and winning hearts through subtle and strategic interactions. This involves using psychological tactics to gently guide your clients towards making favorable decisions, all while maintaining their trust and respect. The art of mimicking, for instance, is a powerful technique where you subtly mirror your client's body language and speech patterns to build trust and rapport.

Understanding energy dynamics in sales is another crucial aspect. The energy you project during your interactions can significantly influence the outcome of a sale. Positive, confident energy can create a welcoming and persuasive atmosphere, while negative energy can deter potential clients. We'll discuss how to harness and direct your energy effectively to create the desired impact. Another fascinating topic; identifying and overcoming blind spots in your selling approach is essential for continuous improvement. Blind spots are the unconscious biases and behaviors that can hinder your sales performance. By becoming aware of these and addressing them, you can refine your approach and avoid potential pitfalls.

Surprisingly, the decision maker's role in the sales process cannot be overstated. It's vital to identify who holds the decision-making power (it's not necessarily who you are talking with) and tailor your approach to address their specific needs and concerns. This ensures that you are engaging the right person with the right message, increasing your chances of success. Catering to ego needs is another psychological tactic that can be highly effective in sales. Everyone has an ego, and by recognizing and validating your client's ego, you can create a sense of importance and appreciation. This builds a stronger connection and makes your client more receptive to your message.

Overcoming desperation is a key psychological hurdle. Desperation can be sensed by clients and can undermine your credibility and confidence. We'll explore techniques to maintain composure and project confidence, even in challenging situations. Setting ambitious goals and cultivating genuine enthusiasm are vital for maintaining motivation and drive. When you are passionate about your product and your work, this enthusiasm naturally translates into your interactions, making your pitch more compelling.

Reading posture and micro-expressions is a skill that can provide valuable insights into your client's thoughts and feelings. By paying attention to subtle cues, you can adjust your approach in real-time to better align with your client's needs and emotions. Leading clients to desired outcomes involves guiding them through the decision-making process in a way that feels natural and unforced. This requires a deep understanding of their motivations and concerns, as well as the ability to present your product as the optimal solution. Embracing the role of the inspirational guide, or as I like to call it, being the wizard, allows you to position yourself as a trusted advisor, someone who's been there, created success and who genuinely cares about their success. By demonstrating this level of commitment and expertise, you can foster a deeper connection and inspire greater loyalty.

As we dive into these concepts, I encourage you to think about each one and how it could have applied to previous situations. Reflect on times when you have unknowingly used these tools and consider how you could have better utilized them with conscious awareness. This journey through the psychology of selling is not just about becoming better at sales; it's about becoming a better, more insightful, and empathetic person. By mastering these psychological tactics, you will not only enhance your sales performance but also enrich your personal interactions and relationships. So, get ready to explore the fascinating world of sales psychology, and let your mind awaken to the extraordinary opportunities that lie ahead.

Mental Jiu-Jitsu

Do you know much about Brazilian Jiu-Jitsu? It's a martial art focused on overcoming your opponent with the least amount of effort possible. In the gym, you have sparring partners with whom you grapple at full force to become better at the art. Both you and your sparring partner engage back and forth with one move to a counter until one of you overcomes the other by submitting them, also known as forcing them to quit before you break their joints or suffocate them. Many consider Jiu-Jitsu comparable to human chess, with numerous theories and processes to achieve victory. While in a competition, you may not care for your partner and couldn't care less if you hurt them; in class, you want to work hard but also don't want to injure your sparring partner because you are friends and don't want to hurt each other. Injuring them negatively impacts your training because you have fewer people to train with.

Think of your client as a sparring partner. You don't want to hurt them in "the sell" because you want them to be happy and help you become better. When you try to out-Jiu-Jitsu a client in the mental grappling of sales, they may leave feeling outdone or with a bruised ego and may not be willing to bring you more business through referrals or more of their business. What you want is a fun and challenging mental Jiu-Jitsu match that leaves you the winner but also leaves them feeling satisfied and happy with their decision due to how well you have worked together. You want them to feel like they are your teammate and you came together to get the result both of you wanted.

In Jiu-Jitsu, it is best to have a game plan from the beginning of the match, but you must be able to pivot instantly to another move or strategy. The similarities continue when you start to think about passing the guard in Jiu-Jitsu. One of the primary focuses of the Jiu-Jitsu match is to get past the legs of the sparring partner or past his guard so that you can begin to apply pressure to his upper body. When his guard is strong, he is able to keep you at a distance. In sales, when the psychological guard is up, there is little you can say or do to encourage the sale until you have developed some rapport and trust to get the sparring partner to lower his guard. Once the guard has been passed, you have to control the movement and posture of the opponent. This is similar in that once a client has let their guard down and welcomed you in, it is time to help them come to the decision that your product or service is in their best interest. This is a control of their posture and movement within "the sell." Now that you are in control of the conversation (with strong rapport), it is time to look for opportunities to seal the deal and execute your finishing moves. Perhaps, as you look for that perfect submission, they counter with an objection, so you have to adjust, pressure in, and overcome, awaiting your ability to finish the job. Once you have successfully overcome the objection, you wordsmith your way to a successful ending. That's it, the deal is sealed, you're proud of yourself, you're proud of your partner, the bell rings, you thank each other, you both have won in your own ways and it's time to start again.

They say most of Jiu-Jitsu is creating a dilemma for your training partner. Do you turn this way and give up your back so I can choke you, or do you turn that way so that I can armbar you? Well, in sales, the client is already coming to you with a dilemma in hand. Do they continue with their current problems, or do we come together in understanding how our product or service will alleviate the pain that they are currently going through? How do I build trust and rapport as fast as possible so that they lower their guard? Now that the guard is down, how do I tactfully apply pressure and lead the conversation to the end result that gets the client on this side and out the door with this product or service? How do I pivot and overcome objections, then return to the tactful pressure that leads to an ideal finish? This is how "the sell" is very similar to the martial art of Brazilian Jiu-Jitsu and how you could consider it the art of Mental Jiu-Jitsu.

Just like in Brazilian Jiu-Jitsu, where you sometimes get twisted into unexpected positions, remember: even if your sales strategy gets tangled, keep your cool. After all, what's a Mental Jiu-Jitsu artist's favorite submission? A happy customer! Keep rolling, stay flexible, and enjoy the dance of the deal.

Understanding Personality Types

What do you know about personality types? Understanding personality types in sales is like having a master key that unlocks doors to better communication, deeper relationships, and greater success. This chapter dives deep into the fascinating world of personality types, detailing how to recognize your own personality, identify those of your clients, engage each one effectively, and why all this matters immensely in the sales process. Our personalities shape how we perceive the world, make decisions, and interact with others. In the realm of sales, understanding both your own personality and that of your clients can dramatically improve your ability to connect, build trust, and close deals. Think of it in terms of mental jiu-jitsu, where knowing your opponent's strengths and moves allows you to engage more effectively and achieve victory.

Before you can effectively engage others, you need to understand yourself. Knowing your own personality type helps you leverage your strengths, recognize your weaknesses, and adapt your approach accordingly. The most commonly used framework for understanding personality types is the Myers-Briggs Type Indicator (MBTI). This model categorizes personalities into 16 types based on four dimensions:

- **Introversion (I) vs. Extraversion (E):** Do you gain energy from solitude or social interactions?
- **Sensing (S) vs. Intuition (N):** Do you focus on concrete details or abstract concepts?
- **Thinking (T) vs. Feeling (F):** Do you make decisions based on logic or emotions?
- **Judging (J) vs. Perceiving (P):** Do you prefer structured plans or spontaneous actions?

For example, if you are an ENTJ (Extraverted, Intuitive, Thinking, Judging), you might excel in leadership and strategic planning but may need to be mindful of not coming across as too dominating.

To discover your personality type, you can take an MBTI test on various online platforms that provide a comprehensive analysis of your personality type. Reflect on your behavior in different situations, how you make decisions, and what environments you thrive in. Seek feedback from colleagues, friends, and family for their insights into your personality traits.

Understanding your clients' personality types requires keen observation and active listening. Here's a deeper dive into the four main personality categories, how to identify them, and how to engage with them effectively:

1. **The Analyst (INTJ, INTP, ENTJ, ENTP):** Analysts are logical, strategic, independent, and analytical. They are often precise, love data, and enjoy discussing theories and ideas. They ask a lot of questions and prefer in-depth information. Engage them by providing detailed data and logical arguments. Be prepared with facts and be concise. Analysts appreciate well-researched and evidence-based discussions.
2. **The Diplomat (INFJ, INFP, ENFJ, ENFP):** Diplomats are empathetic, idealistic, creative, and people-focused. They are usually warm, enthusiastic, and keen to talk about values and emotions. They often seek harmony and consensus. Build rapport through personal connection and shared values. Highlight how your product aligns with their vision and values. Use stories and testimonials to create an emotional connection.
3. **The Sentinel (ISTJ, ISFJ, ESTJ, ESFJ):** Sentinels are practical, reliable, organized, and detail-oriented. They prefer structured environments, are detail-focused, and value tradition and stability. They often ask practical, detail-oriented questions. Emphasize reliability and efficiency. Provide clear, structured information and examples. Highlight the practical benefits and how your product solves their specific problems.
4. **The Explorer (ISTP, ISFP, ESTP, ESFP):** Explorers are spontaneous, adventurous, flexible, and hands-on. They are energetic, love new experiences, and prefer action over theory. They are often charismatic and enjoy engaging discussions. Keep the conversation dynamic and engaging. Highlight the innovative and exciting aspects of your product. Offer interactive demos or trials to let them experience the product firsthand.

Once you've identified your client's personality type, the next step is to tailor your engagement approach. Analysts appreciate thoroughness and evidence-based discussions, so be logical, concise, and well-prepared. Diplomats value personal connections and shared goals, so be empathetic, enthusiastic, and visionary. Sentinels appreciate clear, practical, and structured information, so be organized, reliable, and straightforward. Explorers enjoy dynamic and interactive discussions, so be energetic, flexible, and engaging. Different personality types perceive and process information uniquely. Analysts might see a product's potential through its technical specs, while Diplomats might envision its impact on their lives. Sentinels might value its reliability, and Explorers its novelty. Understanding these differences is crucial for building trust, enhancing communication, increasing conversion rates, and fostering long-term relationships.

Imagine becoming a chameleon, able to adapt and blend into any environment with ease. This adaptability in understanding and engaging with different personality types is your superpower in sales. By mirroring and adapting to your clients' personalities, you create a sense of familiarity and trust, making them more open to your message. This ability to be flexible and versatile in your approach will set you apart from the competition and make you an invaluable asset to your clients. Research in psychology and sales science supports the importance of understanding personality types. Studies have shown that sales professionals who adapt their approach based on the client's personality type are significantly more successful. For instance, a study published in the Journal of Applied Psychology found that salespeople who tailored their communication style to match their clients' personalities closed 30% more deals than those who didn't. Implementing personality-based selling involves training and development to help your sales team understand and recognize different personality types. Utilize CRM tools to track and analyze client interactions and personality insights. Encourage regular reflection on client interactions and adapting strategies based on feedback and results.

Consider the real-life example of pitching to an INTJ CEO. Understanding his analytical nature, the presentation focused on data, return on investment, and long-term strategic benefits. The logical, well-structured approach was appreciated, leading to a decision to move forward. Or the ENFJ HR manager, where the conversation centered around employee well-being and company culture. Sharing success stories about how the product improved employee satisfaction resonated deeply, leading to a successful sale. Sales is not a one-size-fits-all process. Embrace the diversity of personality types, both yours and your clients', to create meaningful and impactful interactions. By recognizing and adapting to different personalities, you not only enhance your sales effectiveness but also foster trust, satisfaction, and loyalty. Believe in the power of understanding and engaging with different personalities, and watch your sales soar to new heights.

Mastering the art of engaging different personality types is a game-changer. It's not just about understanding who you're dealing with; it's about adapting your approach to meet their unique needs and preferences. Now let's guide you through strategies to effectively engage various personality types, how to start meetings on a neutral note, what to do if the conversation veers off course, and how to maintain control, especially with dominant Type A personalities.

Imagine stepping into a sales meeting without preconceived notions, ready to adapt and flow like a skilled Jiu-Jitsu player. Approaching in neutral means setting aside assumptions and staying open to cues from your client. Begin by asking open-ended questions such as, "What are your main goals with our product?" or "Can you share some challenges you're facing?" These questions not only provide valuable insights but also show your genuine interest in understanding their needs. As you listen, observe their body language and tone of voice to gather clues about their personality type. This initial neutrality sets the stage for a tailored, effective interaction.

Engaging different personality types effectively starts with recognizing their distinct traits and preferences. For analytical types, focus on detailed data and logical arguments. They appreciate thoroughness and evidence-based discussions. Avoid emotional appeals and stick to facts and figures. For empathetic and people-focused individuals, build rapport through personal connection and shared values. Use stories and testimonials that resonate emotionally. Highlight how your product aligns with their vision and values, creating a strong emotional bond. Practical and detail-oriented clients appreciate reliability and efficiency. Provide clear, structured information and examples, emphasizing how your product solves their specific problems. Use straightforward language and offer detailed plans, timelines, and practical benefits in your follow-ups. Energetic and adventurous clients, on the other hand, thrive on dynamic and engaging conversations. Highlight the innovative and exciting aspects of your product. Use lively, creative language and offer interactive demos or trials to let them experience the product firsthand.

Even with careful planning, meetings can sometimes veer off course. If the conversation strays, gently steer it back to the main topic by acknowledging the tangent and connecting it to the core discussion. For example, you might say, "That's an interesting point. Let's explore how it relates to the main issue we're discussing." Use open-ended questions to redirect the focus to the client's needs and goals. Periodically summarize key points to maintain clarity and direction. "To summarize, we've discussed X, Y, and Z. Let's now look at how our solution addresses these points." If they're not at the same place in "the sell" with you, ask questions about if you are on track or if they can further explain. It's easy enough to say, "I want to make sure I am fully on track so that I can give you all of the information you need to make a sound and strong decision." Staying calm and patient helps manage deviations without escalating tensions.

Dealing with Type A personalities requires a strategic approach to maintain control. Start the meeting with a clear agenda and objectives, such as, "Today, we're going to cover A, B, and C." This sets clear expectations and boundaries. Be assertive without being aggressive, using confident body language and a firm tone. Guide the conversation with focused questions like, "Can we delve into this point further?" Reinforce the boundaries of the meeting politely but firmly, ensuring the discussion stays on track.

Imagine, you as the chameleon, seamlessly adapting to different environments and personalities. This adaptability is your superpower in sales. By mirroring and adjusting to your clients' personalities, you create a sense of familiarity and trust, making them more open to your message. This ability to be flexible and versatile in your approach will distinguish you from the competition and make you an invaluable asset to your clients. Engaging different personality types effectively requires a blend of observation, adaptation, and strategic communication. By understanding and respecting the unique characteristics of each personality type, you can create a more productive and positive interaction.

You need to think about this adaptability in understanding and engaging with different personality types as your sales superpower, simple as that. It's a vital skill that sets you apart from your competition. By mirroring and adapting to your clients' personalities, you create a sense of familiarity and bond, making them more open to your message. This ability to be flexible and versatile in your approach will set you apart from the rest and make you the invaluable asset you aim to be. And remember, just like in Brazilian Jiu-Jitsu, sometimes it's the subtle moves that make the biggest impact. So, why don't martial arts students make good comedians? Because they always get caught in the punchline! Alright, I'm done, now, go out there and grapple with those sales like the true master you are, adapting and flowing with every interaction to achieve victory.

Blindspots: Seeing Clearly

Understanding and acknowledging our blindspots can be a challenging yet crucial aspect of personal growth and professional development. Our ego often blinds us to our imperfections, leading us to believe that we are flawless and immune to oversight. However, embracing the concept of blindspots requires humility and a willingness to accept that there are areas where we can improve. To truly grasp the concept of blindspots, we must first accept that no one is perfect. Blindspots are aspects of ourselves or our behavior that we are unaware of or choose to ignore. This self-awareness is foundational to personal and professional growth, especially in sales where perception and communication play pivotal roles. The beauty of understanding blindspots is that it allows us to evolve continuously, adapting to new challenges and refining our skills.

Let me share a personal anecdote that vividly illustrates this point. During a sales seminar I was conducting, I engaged passionately with the audience, captivated by my own delivery. Unbeknownst to me, my use of colorful language, which some found inappropriate, was noticed by a perceptive colleague. Despite receiving assurances that my language wasn't offensive, I decided to apologize and adjust my approach. This small shift in behavior significantly enhanced the seminar's atmosphere, earning admiration and engagement from the participants. This experience underscored the importance of feedback in uncovering blindspots. Initially resistant to change, I realized that addressing my blindspot not only improved my professionalism but also deepened my connection with the audience. It taught me that acknowledging and correcting blindspots can transform potential negatives into opportunities for growth and connection. In sales, identifying blindspots is essential because they can hinder our ability to serve clients effectively. Clients rely on us to provide solutions and guidance, expecting us to operate at the highest levels of professionalism. By addressing blindspots, we demonstrate our commitment to excellence and client satisfaction.

Learning from feedback is a pivotal step in uncovering and addressing blindspots. The incident with my seminar highlighted how feedback, even when uncomfortable, can be a powerful tool for personal and professional growth. When we open ourselves to constructive criticism, we gain insights that help us refine our approach, making us more effective and relatable. Let's examine some common blindspots that may affect sales professionals. Conflict avoidance is a significant one. Are there times when you avoid addressing issues that need attention? Addressing conflicts promptly can lead to better outcomes for you and your clients. Another common blindspot is speaking out of turn. Sometimes, speaking out impulsively can jeopardize relationships or derail conversations. I suffer from this still but I acknowledge it and make a conscious effort to be as tactful as possible in the professional environment. Understanding when to speak and when to listen is crucial in maintaining professionalism.

In my journey as a leader, I have encountered numerous challenges that tested my perceptions and reactions. Initially resistant to feedback, I learned the value of restraint and strategic thinking. For instance, what seemed like favoritism in hiring decisions often had underlying strategic reasons that became clear with time and perspective. This evolution in understanding helped me make more informed and balanced decisions. Recognizing and addressing blindspots is not just about self-improvement; it's about becoming a more effective salesperson and leader. Embracing feedback, humility, and self-awareness allows us to continuously evolve and better serve our clients. By proactively identifying and correcting blindspots, we pave the way for deeper connections, improved outcomes, and sustained success in sales.

Imagine being able to see what others can see in you, the good and the areas needing improvement. Embracing this journey is like polishing a diamond; the more you refine yourself, the more you shine. This process not only makes you a better salesperson but also a better human being. Each step you take towards recognizing and addressing your blindspots brings you closer to mastery in your craft. Consider the practical steps you can take to uncover and address your blindspots. Start by seeking feedback from colleagues, mentors, and clients. Honest, constructive feedback can provide invaluable insights into areas you may have overlooked. Reflect on your interactions and decisions regularly. Ask yourself what went well, what could have been better, and what you can learn from each experience. This continuous reflection helps you stay aware of your blindspots and make necessary adjustments.

In the fast-paced world of sales, it's easy to become so focused on targets and outcomes that we forget the importance of personal growth. Yet, it is this very growth that can lead to more meaningful and sustained success. By acknowledging our blindspots and working to improve them, we not only enhance our professional capabilities but also build stronger, more authentic relationships with our clients. They see us not just as salespeople, but as trusted advisors (our ultimate goal) committed to their success.

As you embark on this journey of self-discovery, remember that it's okay to have imperfections. What matters is your willingness to address them and your commitment to continuous improvement. Embrace the feedback, welcome the growth, and watch as your sales career and personal life reach new heights. After all, it's not about being perfect; it's about being better every single day. Why did the car salesman go to the optometrist? Because he kept missing his blindspots! Sorry again, I just want to keep throwing these zingers out there every once in a while. Just like spotting those blindspots while driving can prevent an accident, recognizing and addressing your personal blindspots can prevent professional pitfalls. So, let's polish those rough edges and shine brighter than ever before.

Before we move on, one of the wildest blindspots that I used to have was the way I interacted with Middle Eastern Muslims. I became an adult in the era of 9/11 and the media shaped my perception of the Muslim faith. It wasn't until some years ago when I went to Thailand with my wife for vacation when we stayed on Koh Lanta, an island which was 90% Muslim that I found out how amazingly loving, nice and caring the people of the Muslim faith can be. I still regret my unconscious bias toward that faith for the decade or so that I had it and the way to bettering myself is by acknowledging and working towards being a better person. You're not like me though, you're better, you're reading this book to help you on your path to become the best you can be.

Authentic Rapport - Unbreakable Bonds

The power of rapport is the power of influence. Rapport can be regarded as the strongest influential point for the success of a sale. Have you ever heard the saying, "He could sell a ketchup popsicle to a woman in white gloves?" That idiom is based on rapport being built to the point where the woman would do anything that the salesman wanted. Having rapport with someone isn't just a natural occurrence; it is something you can manufacture. It starts in the first 7-10 seconds when you meet someone. That's when the initial impression begins forming. You don't want to be intimidating, but you also don't want to appear to be a pushover. I have heard it described as approaching in neutral and being the wizard. I am sure there are plenty of ways to describe the best initial impression approach, but I want you to think about it as if you are their nonchalant superhero. You are here to help them, you know it, and they know it, but you are still as humble as can be about it. The best thing you can do before meeting someone is to have an interpersonal conversation with yourself. Reassure yourself that you are there to help them and that you have something they need. If you didn't have something they needed, they wouldn't have agreed to have the conversation with you.

Let's talk about a couple of other things that I did before having someone come into my office. The first thing I always did, regardless of how busy I was, would be to have them sit in the waiting room and take a look at some of my testimonials. Testimonials are reviews that I gathered throughout years of being a salesman. This helps to lower the guard of the client because they can see twenty, thirty, fifty, even a hundred other people who have dealt with you and cared enough to let others know about their experience. According to a study by BrightLocal, 87% of consumers read online reviews for local businesses in 2020, with 79% trusting them as much as personal recommendations. This highlights the power of testimonials in building trust and credibility. I highly recommend gathering testimonials if you are not currently, but we'll go more into this in the future chapters. At one point, I had an admin assistant greet and sit my guests for me, which further added to the legitimacy of the interaction, but it isn't necessary.

After a few minutes of cleaning up my desk (you need to actually clean your desk, close your computer, create a space where you can focus 100% Ton the client) and after the client had read over some of the reviews, I would invite them into a warm and open office that highlighted my successes, education, and even my adorable family. They would sit, and then I would sit with a smile. I would also offer water or something of inherent value. I assume you have experienced this or that this is a similar path to how your meetings begin. Let's think about what all just transpired in a matter of moments. By asking them to sit and wait for me, I subtly showed that I am in charge of the conversation. By having them read over my testimonials, they are more inclined to trust and allow us to build rapport. By entering my office and seeing the awards, degrees, and pictures, they believe that I am relatable yet successful and able to help with their problem. My office is clean and professional, and my desk shows that this time is for them. By waiting for them to sit before I do, I am again in command of the conversation, and lastly, by offering them something of value, such as water, they are inclined to reciprocate the gesture of giving something to me, which will end up being their business.

The psychology of these interactions is profound. When you ask a client to wait and observe your accolades, you are subtly reinforcing your credibility and expertise. This not only sets the stage for a productive conversation but also eases any initial apprehensions they might have. A study by Harvard Business Review found that people are more likely to comply with requests from those they perceive as experts (Cialdini, 2001). The display of testimonials and personal achievements creates an environment of trust and reliability, making them more comfortable and open to discussing their needs and how you can meet them. Furthermore, the ambiance of your office plays a crucial role. A warm, welcoming space that reflects your professional journey and personal life strikes a balance between professionalism and relatability. Clients want to know they are dealing with someone competent and approachable. By showcasing your achievements and personal side, you make a powerful impression that you are not just a salesperson but someone they could and should trust.

Offering a small token, such as water, might seem trivial, but it's a significant gesture. It humanizes the interaction and creates a sense of reciprocity. According to a study by the University of Zurich, acts of kindness, even as small as offering a drink, increase the likelihood of cooperative behavior and trust in social interactions. This simple act can soften the client's defenses and build a subtle yet profound connection. When they accept your offer, they are psychologically primed to return the favor, which in this context means engaging positively with your proposal. The key to mastering rapport is consistency and authenticity. Each step, from the initial greeting to the conclusion of the meeting, should reflect genuine interest and a sincere desire to help. When you approach each interaction with this mindset, you build a foundation of trust that is hard to break. This trust becomes the cornerstone of your influence, allowing you to guide the conversation and ultimately close the sale.

Building rapport is like planting a seed. It requires patience, care, and attention to grow. Every gesture, every word, every smile adds to the nurturing environment that allows this seed to flourish into a strong, trusting relationship. So, take the time to perfect your approach, be mindful of your actions, and watch as your ability to build rapport transforms your sales interactions. According to the Journal of Personal Selling & Sales Management, building rapport with customers significantly impacts sales performance and customer satisfaction. By understanding the power of rapport and implementing these strategies, you can create a strong, trusting relationship with your clients. This foundation of trust and credibility will not only help you close more sales but also build lasting relationships that lead to repeat business and referrals. Embrace the power of rapport and watch your sales career soar.

Art of Mirroring for Control

Sales is more than just a transaction; it's an intricate dance of energies, emotions, and subtle cues. One of the most powerful yet often overlooked techniques in this dance is the art of mirroring, also known as mimicking. By subtly mirroring your client's body movements, you can create a harmonious atmosphere, establish deeper rapport, and guide the energy in the room to your advantage. This chapter delves into the esoteric art of mirroring, revealing its profound impact on the sales process. Mirroring, in essence, is the act of subtly reflecting the body language, posture, and even speech patterns of your client. This technique taps into a fundamental aspect of human psychology: our innate tendency to connect with those who are similar to us. When done skillfully, mirroring creates a sense of familiarity and trust, setting the stage for a more receptive and positive interaction.

The effectiveness of mirroring is rooted in neuroscience. Mirror neurons, specialized brain cells, are activated both when we perform an action and when we observe someone else performing that same action. These neurons play a critical role in empathy and social connection. According to a study published in the journal *Cognitive Brain Research*, mirror neurons are fundamental in human social interactions, as they help us understand and empathize with others' actions and emotions. By mirroring your client's body language, you engage their mirror neurons, fostering a subconscious sense of alignment and understanding.

Imagine a sales meeting as a flow of energies, where your goal is to harmonize and guide these energies towards a successful outcome. Mimicking is like tuning into the same frequency as your client, creating a resonance that facilitates smoother communication and deeper connection. This esoteric dance of energy allows you to subtly influence the emotional and psychological dynamics of the meeting. Begin by keenly observing your client's body language, posture, and gestures. Notice how they sit, move their hands, and even the rhythm of their breathing. The goal is to absorb their physical cues without making it obvious. Then, start mirroring their movements subtly. If they lean forward, you lean forward slightly. If they cross their legs, you do the same. The key is to be subtle enough that it goes unnoticed, yet significant enough to create a subconscious connection. Extend your mirroring to their vocal patterns. Match their speaking pace, tone, and volume. If they speak softly and slowly, adjust your voice to mirror theirs. This auditory mirroring reinforces the sense of rapport and alignment. Reflect their facial expressions to show empathy and understanding. If they smile, smile back. If they show concern or curiosity, mirror those emotions with your expressions. This creates an emotional synchronicity that deepens the connection. Synchronize your breathing with theirs. This subtle alignment can create a powerful sense of harmony, helping to calm nerves and establish a more relaxed and open atmosphere.

Trust is the cornerstone of any successful sales relationship. Mimicking / mirroring creates a subconscious sense of similarity and understanding, which fosters trust. According to a study by the Journal of Experimental Social Psychology, mimicking behavior increases trust and rapport in social interactions, making clients more likely to trust someone who seems to be in tune with their own behavior and energy. Mirroring facilitates smoother communication by creating a comfortable and familiar interaction. Clients are more likely to open up and share their needs and concerns when they feel understood and aligned with you. The ability to guide and control the energy in the room is crucial in a sales meeting. By mirroring, you can subtly steer the emotional tone of the conversation. If a client is anxious, matching and then gradually calming your movements can help soothe their nerves. Conversely, if they are disengaged, matching their energy and then increasing your enthusiasm can reignite their interest. Emotional alignment is a powerful tool in sales. When clients feel that you are on the same emotional wavelength, they are more likely to resonate with your message and feel a deeper connection to your product or service.

When the time is right you can test your synchronicity by making a subtle movement and seeing if your dance partner reciprocates. If so, they have just unconsciously given you full control of the conversation. Imagine a scenario where a client is hesitant and reserved. By subtly mirroring their closed posture and then gradually opening up your own body language, you can lead them towards a more open and engaged state. This technique was used by a seasoned realtor, a mentor to me, Phil Hapke, who, by mirroring the client's cautious body language and slowly adopting a more open posture, encouraged the client to relax and eventually express their concerns more freely. This led to a successful resolution and a sale. Conversely, if a client is energetic and enthusiastic, mirroring their high energy can create a dynamic and exciting interaction. A recruiter, for instance, might mirror the animated gestures of a passionate candidate, creating a lively and engaging conversation that highlights the mutual excitement for the opportunity.

While mirroring is a powerful technique, it must be used ethically and authentically. The goal is to foster genuine connection and understanding, not to manipulate. Authenticity is key—clients will sense if your mirroring is forced or insincere. Always approach mirroring with the intention of creating a positive and empathetic interaction. Start practicing mirroring in casual conversations with friends and family. Observe their body language and subtly mirror it. This will help you develop the skill in a low-stakes environment. Being present and mindful in interactions is crucial for effective mirroring. Focus on truly listening and observing your client without distractions. After sales meetings, reflect on your use of mirroring. What worked well? What could be improved? Seek feedback from colleagues to refine your technique.

The art of mirroring is a subtle yet profoundly powerful technique in the sales professional's toolkit. By tuning into the energy of your clients and reflecting their body language, you create a harmonious and engaging interaction that fosters trust, enhances communication, and guides the energy in the room. This esoteric mastery of mirroring, when practiced with authenticity and ethical intent, can elevate your sales approach and transform your client relationships. Remember, sales is not just about transactions; it's about connections. By mastering the art of mimicking and mirroring, you become not just a salesperson, but a trusted partner in your client's journey. Believe in the power of this technique, harness its subtle influence, and watch as your sales interactions transform into meaningful, successful engagements.

Energy Dynamics: Invisible Forces

Every sales meeting can be viewed as a battlefield of unseen forces—a dynamic interplay of energies between the salesperson and the client. Understanding and mastering this battle can significantly impact the outcome of your interactions. This chapter explores the concept of the battle of energies, providing insights into how to harness and balance these forces to achieve success. Energy in a sales meeting is not just a metaphor; it's a tangible phenomenon that influences emotions, perceptions, and decisions. Both the salesperson and the client bring their own energies into the room, shaped by their mood, expectations, and underlying motivations. These energies interact, clash, and harmonize, creating an ever-shifting landscape that can either drive the conversation forward or create friction.

The first step in mastering the battle of energies is recognizing the different states of energy that both you and your client may exhibit. These states can broadly be categorized as high energy, low energy, positive energy, and negative energy. High energy is characterized by enthusiasm, excitement, and engagement. High energy can be infectious and motivating but can also be overwhelming if not managed properly. Low energy is marked by lethargy, disinterest, or fatigue. Low energy can slow down the interaction and make it difficult to engage the client. Positive energy is exhibited through optimism, openness, and a collaborative spirit. Positive energy fosters trust and a willingness to explore possibilities. Negative energy is manifested as skepticism, defensiveness, or hostility. Negative energy can create barriers and hinder the flow of communication.

To effectively navigate the battle of energies, it's crucial to tune into your client's energy state. Pay close attention to their body language, tone of voice, and overall demeanor. Are they leaning forward, showing interest, or sitting back, displaying disinterest? Is their tone warm and open, or cold and guarded? These cues will help you gauge their energy and adjust your approach accordingly. Once you've identified the energy state of your client, the next step is to balance and harmonize your energies. This involves a delicate dance of matching and leading, where you initially align with your client's energy and then guide it towards a more productive state. Start by mirroring your client's energy. If they are high energy, meet them with enthusiasm. If they are low energy, adopt a calmer demeanor. This creates a sense of alignment and rapport. After establishing alignment, gradually guide your client's energy towards a more positive and engaged state. If they are low energy, subtly increase your own energy to lift the conversation. If they are negative, introduce positivity through your tone, language, and body language. Something like, "don't worry, we're going to fix this for you" with a sincere expression and air of positivity can work wonders for someone who is reaching out for a proverbial lifeline to mend his ailments.

Managing energy in a sales meeting requires a combination of self-awareness, empathy, and strategic techniques. Before the meeting, take a moment to ground yourself. Practice deep breathing, visualize a successful interaction, and set a positive intention. Grounding helps you remain centered and resilient to energy fluctuations. Periodically check in with your own energy levels and adjust as needed. If you feel your energy dipping, take a deep breath, and refocus. If you sense rising tension, consciously relax your body and soften your tone. Engage in active, empathetic listening. This means truly hearing your client's concerns and responding with understanding. Empathy can diffuse negative energy and build a connection. Use positive language and framing to shift the energy. Instead of focusing on problems, highlight solutions. Instead of emphasizing challenges, underscore opportunities. Introduce energy anchors into the conversation—positive stories, success anecdotes, or inspiring examples. These anchors can uplift the mood and redirect the energy towards a more favorable direction.

Imagine a scenario where a client enters the meeting with palpable skepticism and guarded body language. You recognize their negative energy and initially match it with a calm, composed demeanor. Through empathetic listening, you acknowledge their concerns without resistance. As the conversation progresses, you gradually introduce positive framing, highlighting past successes and potential benefits. You share a relevant success story that resonates with them, subtly lifting the energy. By the end of the meeting, the client's posture relaxes, their tone warms, and the energy has shifted towards a more open and collaborative state. While mastering the battle of energies is a powerful skill, it must be wielded ethically. The goal is to foster genuine connections and mutual benefit, not to manipulate or deceive. Authenticity is key—clients will respond positively when they feel your intentions are sincere and aligned with their best interests.

Like any skill, mastering the battle of energies requires practice and continuous improvement. Develop a keen awareness of your own energy states and triggers. Regular self-reflection and mindfulness practices can enhance your self-awareness. Strengthen your ability to empathize with others. Practice active listening and put yourself in your client's shoes to better understand their energy states. Stop. Reread that last sentence please. Put yourself in their shoes to better understand their energy and more importantly their wants and needs. Incorporate energy management exercises into your routine. This can include visualization, deep breathing, and energy grounding techniques. Seek feedback from colleagues and clients to understand how your energy management is perceived. Use this feedback to refine your approach.

The battle of energies in a sales meeting is a profound and esoteric art. By recognizing, tuning into, and harmonizing these energies, you can transform your sales interactions into powerful and positive experiences. Remember, sales is not just about closing deals; it's about creating connections, fostering trust, and guiding the flow of energy towards mutual success. Embrace the dynamic dance of energies, believe in your ability to master this skill, and watch as your sales meetings become harmonious, engaging, and ultimately successful. In the end, it's not just about winning the battle; it's about creating a symphony of energies that resonate with your clients and lead to lasting relationships.

Decision Maker's Role

In the intricate dance of sales, one of the most crucial steps is identifying the decision maker. This person wields the power to say "yes" or "no" to your proposal, making their recognition and engagement essential. However, the decision maker isn't always the most obvious person in the room. This chapter delves into how to accurately identify the decision maker and understand their pivotal role in the sales process. The decision maker is the gatekeeper of success in any sales endeavor. They possess the authority to approve budgets, sign contracts, and give the final nod. Engaging with them effectively can mean the difference between a closed deal and a missed opportunity. Misidentifying this key person can lead to wasted efforts, extended sales cycles, and frustration. Therefore, knowing how to pinpoint the decision maker is a skill that every salesperson must master.

Decision makers come in various forms and titles, often influenced by the size and structure of the organization. Begin with thorough research. Understand the company's hierarchy, key roles, and recent projects. Websites, LinkedIn profiles, and press releases can offer valuable insights into who holds the decision-making power. During your initial interactions, ask strategic questions to uncover the decision maker's identity. Examples include asking about the decision-making process for the project, who needs to approve the budget, and who should be addressed when discussing final approvals. Pay close attention during meetings. The decision maker often guides the conversation, asks probing questions, and seeks detailed information. They may not always be the most vocal, but their comments will carry weight. Don't rely solely on job titles. The true decision maker might not have the highest rank but could hold significant influence. For instance, a project manager might be the key decision maker for specific technical solutions. Sometimes, decisions are made collectively. Engage with multiple stakeholders to understand their influence and contributions to the decision-making process.

Assumptions about decision makers can be misleading. Senior executives often delegate decision-making authority to trusted subordinates. While a CEO might sign off on the final agreement, a department head or project manager may have the real decision-making power. Influencers within an organization can sway decisions significantly. These individuals may not have official decision-making power but can impact the final decision through their opinions and advice. Identifying and winning over these hidden influencers is crucial. In larger organizations, decisions can involve multiple layers of approval. A procurement officer, financial analyst, and department head might all play roles in the decision. Understanding the full decision chain ensures you address all concerns and requirements.

Let's take a look at this from a different sales perspective as well. If you are selling real estate and believe you have identified the husband as the decision maker as he is the primary breadwinner and the one doing all the speaking, you may want to think again because the National Association of Realtors claims that up to 91% of home buying decisions are made by the wife in the transaction. If you happen to work for a college in recruiting and you have scouted a young person with exceptional talent who says they're all in, they may still need to run it by their parents first. You ask or wonder why because they are technically an adult but the decision maker, the person they trust and refuse to disappoint is at home hoping they make the right decisions in life.

Once you've identified the decision maker, engaging them effectively is paramount. Tailor your pitch to address the specific needs, challenges, and goals of the decision maker. Demonstrate that you understand their unique situation and have crafted a solution that meets their requirements. Establish a strong relationship with the decision maker. Be transparent, reliable, and attentive to their concerns. Trust is a critical factor in their willingness to commit to your proposal. Highlight the tangible benefits of your product or service. Use data, case studies, and testimonials to back up your claims. Decision makers need clear, compelling reasons to choose your offering over others. Proactively address potential objections and concerns. Understanding the decision maker's priorities and pain points allows you to preemptively mitigate any doubts. Engage and win over influencers within the organization who can advocate for your solution. Their support can tip the scales in your favor during the decision-making process.

Consider the case of a software company selling an innovative project management tool to a mid-sized manufacturing firm. Initially, the sales team focused on the VP of Operations, assuming he was the decision maker. However, after several meetings, they noticed that a particular project manager consistently asked detailed questions and provided critical feedback. By shifting their focus to the project manager, they discovered she had been given the authority to choose the new tool due to her hands-on experience with the existing systems. Engaging her directly, the sales team addressed her specific concerns, provided targeted demonstrations, and showcased how the tool would streamline her daily operations. Her endorsement led to a swift decision and a successful sale.

The power of the decision maker in the sales process cannot be overstated. Accurately identifying and effectively engaging this key individual—or group of individuals—requires insight, research, and strategic communication. By understanding the dynamics at play and honing your approach, you can navigate the complexities of organizational or familial decision-making and secure more successful outcomes. Remember, the decision maker is not always who you initially think. Keep an open mind, stay observant, and be prepared to adapt your strategy. Mastering the art of engaging the true decision maker will elevate your sales game, driving you closer to achieving your goals and manifesting your success. And speaking of identifying the right person, a supervisor came up to his salesman and asked, "did you get an order today?" The salesman responded, "yes sir!" so the supervisor says, "great, for what?" and the salesman responds, "you ordered me to go out and make a sale...." So, always remember, appearances can be deceiving, people may not be who you think they are, and it's crucial to dig deeper to find the right person and the true decision maker.

Ego Needs - Secrets of Flattery

Why would it be important to cater to someone's ego? In sales, understanding and catering to the ego of your clients can be a powerful tool. The ego, a central aspect of the human psyche, drives much of our behavior and decision-making processes. By leveraging psychological principles, understanding the role of the ego, and applying this knowledge in sales interactions, you can create stronger connections, build trust, and ultimately close more deals. This chapter will explore the ego, the psychology behind it, relevant studies, and practical strategies for catering to it effectively.

The ego, as defined by psychoanalytic theory, is the part of the human psyche that mediates between the conscious mind and the unconscious mind, balancing our innate desires with societal norms and expectations. Sigmund Freud, the father of psychoanalysis, introduced the concept of the ego as one of the three components of the mind, alongside the id (instinctual desires) and the superego (moral standards). The ego is responsible for our sense of self, our self-esteem, and our self-importance. In everyday interactions, the ego influences how we perceive ourselves and how we want others to perceive us. It drives our need for recognition, respect, and validation. Understanding this can help salespeople craft their approach to align with the client's self-perception and desires.

Several psychological principles underpin the importance of catering to the ego in sales. Self-enhancement is one such principle. People have a natural tendency to seek positive reinforcement and avoid negative feedback. They want to feel good about themselves and their decisions. When a salesperson affirms the client's self-image and makes them feel competent and important, it enhances the client's self-esteem and fosters a positive interaction. Social validation is another critical principle. The desire for social validation is closely tied to the ego. People seek approval and recognition from others. By acknowledging the client's expertise, experience, and status, a salesperson can provide this validation, making the client more receptive and open to the sales pitch. The principle of reciprocity suggests that people are more likely to respond positively when they feel valued and respected. When a salesperson caters to the client's ego, showing genuine interest and admiration, the client is more likely to reciprocate with interest in the product or service.

Numerous studies have explored the impact of ego and self-perception on decision-making and behavior. The Dunning-Kruger Effect, identified by psychologists David Dunning and Justin Kruger, describes how individuals with limited knowledge or competence in a domain often overestimate their abilities. Salespeople can use this knowledge to flatter clients by acknowledging their perceived expertise, making them more confident and receptive to the sales pitch. Self-Affirmation Theory, proposed by Claude Steele, suggests that people are motivated to maintain their self-integrity. When individuals feel their self-worth is validated, they are more open to information that might otherwise be perceived as threatening. By affirming the client's positive qualities, salespeople can reduce resistance and increase openness to their message. Social Comparison Theory, introduced by Leon Festinger, posits that individuals determine their own social and personal worth based on how they compare to others. Salespeople can leverage this by positioning their product or service as a means for the client to achieve a higher status or to outperform peers.

Personalization is a powerful strategy for catering to the ego. Tailor your approach to the client's specific needs, preferences, and self-perception. Address them by name, reference their achievements, and acknowledge their expertise. Personalized interactions make clients feel valued and respected. Genuine compliments and positive reinforcement can go a long way. Highlight the client's successes and strengths, making them feel good about themselves. However, ensure that the flattery is sincere and relevant to avoid coming across as disingenuous. Demonstrate genuine interest in the client's opinions, concerns, and aspirations. By actively listening and responding thoughtfully, you show that you value their perspective, which boosts their ego and builds trust. Position your product or service as a tool that empowers the client, enhancing their capabilities and status. Emphasize how it can help them achieve their goals, improve their performance, or gain recognition. Use testimonials, case studies, and endorsements from respected figures or organizations. Social proof validates the client's choice and reinforces their self-perception as a discerning and competent decision-maker.

Establish yourself as an expert in your field. When clients perceive you as knowledgeable and competent, they are more likely to trust your recommendations and feel validated in their choice to engage with you.

Consider a scenario where a salesperson is selling a new software solution to a potential client who is a mid-level manager at a large corporation. The salesperson has done their research and knows that the client recently led a successful project that received internal recognition. During the meeting, the salesperson begins by congratulating the client on their recent achievement, acknowledging their leadership and expertise. This flattery boosts the client's ego and creates a positive atmosphere. The salesperson then positions the software as a tool that will enhance the client's ability to lead future projects even more effectively, empowering them to achieve greater success and recognition within the company. By catering to the client's ego through flattery and empowerment, the salesperson establishes a strong rapport and increases the likelihood of a successful sale.

Understanding and catering to the ego is a powerful strategy in sales. By leveraging psychological principles, recognizing the importance of the client's self-perception, and applying targeted strategies, salespeople can create stronger connections, build trust, and close more deals. Remember, the ego drives much of human behavior, and by acknowledging and affirming your client's sense of self, you can navigate the sales process with greater success and finesse. And here's a fun fact to keep in mind: When you make a client feel good about themselves, you're not just boosting their ego; you're also boosting your chances of making the sale.

Here's a hilarious joke I found online.

A young salesperson peeped into the office of someone who looked like a sales manager, muttered something, then started walking away. After retreating a little, he seemed to change his mind and headed back to the door—where after some hesitation, he started to back away again. The sales manager, feeling sorry for the young man and surprised that he was so badly trained, called him in.

"You're a salesperson, aren't you? What are you selling?"

"Sir, uh, yes, I'm a salesman. I'm sorry to bother you. I was selling insurance, but I'm sure you don't want any. Sorry to have wasted your time."

Feeling sorry for the young bungler, the sales manager bought two policies to give the young salesman some confidence and then started teaching him about selling. He said: "You should have different pre-planned approaches for different kinds of—"

"But I do, sir," the young salesman interrupted, "the one I just used is my planned approach for sales managers. It always works. Thank you!"

Haha, don't forget you can learn from anyone! Onto the next topic, the smell of desperation.

Overcoming Desperation in Sales

The energy you bring to each interaction can make all the difference between success and failure. Desperation, a common pitfall for many salespeople, can severely hinder your ability to close deals. Conversely, projecting confidence and positive energy can attract success almost effortlessly. This chapter explores why desperation is detrimental, the psychology behind it, and how positive energy can transform your sales approach. Desperation in sales manifests as an anxious and needy energy that undermines trust and credibility. When you're desperate to close a deal, it shows in your voice, body language, and overall demeanor. Clients can sense this unease, which raises immediate red flags. It suggests that your focus is on your needs rather than genuinely helping the client. Desperation often leads to over-pushing, inconsistency, and neglecting client needs. Desperate salespeople tend to push too hard, overwhelming clients with aggressive tactics and persistent follow-ups. This approach can make clients feel pressured and uncomfortable, pushing them away instead of drawing them in. In a bid to secure a sale, desperation might lead to making promises you can't keep or offering unrealistic discounts. This inconsistency not only damages potential deals but also harms your reputation in the long run. Desperation narrows your focus to closing the immediate sale, potentially overlooking the client's actual needs and concerns. This shortsighted approach undermines the trust-building necessary for sustained success.

Desperation is rooted in fear and scarcity. When driven by fear—fear of missing targets, financial instability, or failure—you emit negative energy that repels clients. This fear-based mindset triggers a fight-or-flight response, impairing your ability to engage effectively and think strategically. Psychological research underscores that emotions are contagious. Clients pick up on your emotions and mirror them unconsciously. If you project desperation, clients will feel uneasy and skeptical, making them less likely to trust you and your product. On the other hand, positive and confident energy can be remarkably attractive. When you believe in yourself, your product, and your ability to help clients, this confidence shines through, creating a sense of trust and assurance. Clients are naturally drawn to positive energy because it makes them feel safe, valued, and optimistic about their decision. Positive energy leads to authenticity, patience and understanding, and effective communication. Confidence allows you to be authentic in your interactions. You focus on genuinely understanding and addressing the client's needs rather than closing a sale at all costs. This authenticity builds trust and rapport over time. Confidence fosters patience and respect for the client's decision-making process. You create a comfortable environment where clients feel empowered to make decisions without undue pressure. When you exude calmness and positivity, your communication becomes clear, concise, and persuasive. Active listening and thoughtful responses demonstrate your commitment to helping clients, which enhances their confidence in you.

Transforming your energy from desperation to confidence requires a mindset shift and intentional practice. Recognize when desperation creeps in and identify the underlying fears triggering it. Awareness is the first step toward changing your approach. Shift your focus from closing deals to providing genuine value. When you prioritize solving clients' problems and meeting their needs, sales naturally follow as a result of trust and relationship-building. Confidence stems from thorough preparation and practice. Know your product inside out, anticipate objections, and refine your sales pitch until it feels natural and effortless. Use affirmations and reminders of your past successes to reinforce your confidence and self-belief. Positive self-talk and visualization of successful interactions can program your mind for success.

Imagine a seasoned salesperson known for their calm confidence and genuine interest in clients' success. Unlike desperate peers, this salesperson approaches each interaction with a focus on understanding and addressing client needs. During a critical meeting with a skeptical client, they listened attentively, asked insightful questions, and shared relevant success stories without pressure. As the meeting progressed, the client's skepticism dissolved. They saw the salesperson not as someone pushing a sale, but as a trusted advisor genuinely invested in their success. This positive energy and authentic approach ultimately led the client to choose their product, citing the salesperson's confidence and empathy as decisive factors.

Desperation in sales creates a self-defeating cycle that undermines trust and inhibits success. By cultivating confidence, authenticity, and positive energy, you can transform your sales interactions. Clients are drawn to confident, genuine professionals who prioritize their needs and provide value. Remember, success in sales is about building relationships and solving problems, not just closing deals. Embrace confidence, believe in your ability to help clients, and let positive energy guide you toward sustainable sales success.

Embracing a mindset of positive energy and confidence not only enhances your sales outcomes but also enriches your professional journey. By consistently practicing these principles, you position yourself as their guide and a beacon of positive influence in the world of sales. This transformation begins within, by cultivating a deep sense of self-belief and an unwavering commitment to genuinely serving your clients. As you embody these qualities, you will find that success follows naturally, driven by the authentic connections you build and the lasting impact you make in your clients' lives.

Ambitious Goals - Shooting for the Stars

In the world of sales, setting ambitious goals can be a powerful motivator that drives performance and exceeds expectations. This chapter explores the concept of shooting for the stars by setting high sales projections, drawing parallels to historical achievements, and demonstrating the impact of aiming beyond what seems achievable. Imagine setting your sales projections not just to meet your monthly quota, but to exceed it by a significant margin. By aiming high, you challenge yourself to stretch beyond perceived limitations and tap into untapped potential. This mindset shift from aiming for average results to reaching for extraordinary success can transform your approach to sales and elevate your performance.

Consider the story of Roger Bannister, the first person to break the 4-minute mile barrier in 1954. For years, experts believed it was physiologically impossible for a human to run a mile in under 4 minutes. However, Bannister had a different perspective—he set his sights on achieving what others deemed unattainable. His unwavering belief and determination led him to accomplish this feat, running the mile in 3 minutes and 59.4 seconds. What happened after Bannister's breakthrough is equally remarkable. Within a year, several other runners also broke the 4-minute mile barrier. Once the perceived limitation was shattered, others were inspired and motivated to achieve the same feat. This phenomenon illustrates the power of expectation and how setting high goals can not only push individuals to surpass their own limits but also inspire collective achievement within a community or industry.

When you set high projections and firmly believe in their achievability, you activate a powerful mechanism in your mind. Just as buying a new car suddenly makes you notice all the same cars on the road, focusing on success subconsciously directs your attention and actions towards opportunities that align with your goals. This manifestation effect isn't just wishful thinking—it's a cognitive process where your mind filters information and pathways to success become more apparent. It's called the reticular activating system and it is the psychology behind manifestation. When a group prays for something, they align their subconscious to point in the direction of being open to help facilitate that dream. When you say if someone comes into your office you are closing a sale and you truly believe it then the only people you'll invite subconsciously will be ones that have given you the subtle cues or microexpressions that they are ready to close. Digging into the subconscious is a fun and intriguing way to increase your understanding and success in your personal and professional endeavors.

Similarly, in sales, when you set high projections and believe in their achievability, you create a mindset of possibility and determination. Your expectations influence your actions and decisions, leading to more proactive prospecting, effective client engagement, and strategic closing techniques. Even if you don't reach the exact lofty goal, aiming high ensures that you exceed what might have been considered achievable under normal circumstances.

Imagine a sales team that traditionally meets its monthly quota with consistent performance. By adopting the shooting for the stars mentality, the team leader encourages each member to set projections that are 20% above their usual targets. Initially, some team members are skeptical, but with coaching and support, they begin to embrace the challenge. As they focus on exceeding their personal best rather than just meeting expectations, their efforts result in a collective increase in sales performance. Within months, the team not only meets but surpasses their ambitious projections, achieving record-breaking results and earning recognition within their organization.

Shooting for the stars in sales involves setting high projections that challenge your limits and inspire extraordinary performance. By believing in the possibility of surpassing traditional expectations and drawing motivation from historical achievements like Roger Bannister's 4-minute mile, you can elevate your sales strategy and achieve remarkable success. Embrace the mindset of aiming beyond what seems achievable and watch as your determination and belief propel you towards exceeding your goals. Remember, in sales and in life, what you expect often becomes what you achieve. So aim high, believe in your potential, and let your aspirations drive you to unprecedented success.

"Shoot for the moon. Even if you miss, you'll land among the stars." - Norman Vincent Peale

Genuine Enthusiasm - Infectious Positivity

Enthusiasm is often seen as a natural expression of genuine passion and excitement. However, there are times in sales—and in life—where faking enthusiasm can be a strategic advantage, leading to improved performance and outcomes. This chapter explores the concept of leveraging enthusiasm, even when it doesn't come naturally, to enhance both your work experience and your success in sales. Enthusiasm is contagious. When you exude energy and positivity, it influences not only your own mood but also those around you, including colleagues and customers. In sales, maintaining a high level of enthusiasm can create a positive atmosphere that enhances client interactions and fosters trust. However, there are moments when maintaining genuine enthusiasm becomes challenging, especially during periods of stress or when facing rejection.

Faking enthusiasm doesn't mean being insincere or deceptive. Instead, it involves consciously adopting a positive mindset and outward demeanor, even when you might not feel it internally. This strategic approach allows you to manage your emotions effectively, particularly in situations where maintaining professionalism and optimism is crucial. By focusing on the benefits of your product or service and the value it brings to your customers, you can authentically convey enthusiasm, regardless of your initial emotional state. In the workplace, cultivating an environment of positivity through enthusiastic behavior can lead to a more enjoyable and productive atmosphere. When team members see you embodying enthusiasm, it can inspire them to approach challenges with a similar mindset. This positivity can improve team dynamics, boost morale, and encourage collaboration, ultimately contributing to a more cohesive and successful work environment.

In sales, enthusiasm plays a pivotal role in building rapport and trust with potential clients. Customers are more likely to engage with sales professionals who display genuine enthusiasm for their products or services. When you convey excitement about how your offering can solve their problems or enhance their lives, it resonates with them on a deeper level. Even if you initially need to summon enthusiasm, your genuine belief in the benefits you offer can sustain and reinforce this positive energy throughout the sales process. There will inevitably be moments when maintaining enthusiasm feels challenging. Rejections, setbacks, or personal issues can dampen your spirits. However, by consciously choosing to focus on the positive aspects of your work and the impact it has on others, you can navigate these challenges more effectively. Techniques such as visualization, setting small achievable goals, and seeking support from peers can help you recharge and regain enthusiasm when it wanes.

Faking enthusiasm doesn't mean masking your true feelings; it's about channeling your energy in a way that authentically connects with others. By aligning your enthusiasm with genuine care for your customers' needs and aspirations, you create meaningful relationships that extend beyond transactional interactions. These authentic connections are essential for long-term customer loyalty and referrals, as clients appreciate your sincere commitment to their success. Faking enthusiasm strategically in sales and work environments can lead to improved outcomes, enhanced customer relationships, and a more positive work experience overall. By embracing the role of enthusiasm, even in challenging moments, you can harness its contagious nature to inspire others, overcome obstacles, and achieve greater success. Remember, enthusiasm is not just an emotion—it's a powerful tool that can shape your attitude, actions, and ultimately, your success in sales.

Embrace the power of enthusiasm, whether it comes naturally or requires a bit of effort, and watch as it transforms your interactions, strengthens your relationships, and propels you towards your sales goals. Your ability to project enthusiasm can be the key to unlocking new opportunities and achieving exceptional results in your sales career.

Reading Posture and Micro-Expressions

Effective communication extends far beyond words. Understanding and interpreting nonverbal cues such as posture, facial expressions, and microexpressions can provide invaluable insights into the thoughts, emotions, and intentions of your clients. This chapter explores deep into the art of reading nonverbal communication in sales meetings, offering practical strategies to enhance your understanding and influence positive outcomes. Nonverbal communication accounts for up to 93% of human interaction, often conveying emotions and attitudes more powerfully than words alone. In sales, where building trust and rapport are paramount, mastering the ability to read and respond to nonverbal cues can make the difference between a successful deal and a missed opportunity.

Mastering body language is a powerful tool in the arsenal of any successful salesperson. By understanding and interpreting non-verbal cues, you can significantly enhance your ability to connect with clients, build trust, and close deals. This chapter examines the various aspects of body language, offering insights on how to use these subtle signals to your advantage in sales interactions. Your posture speaks volumes about your confidence, engagement, and receptiveness. An upright, open posture typically signals attentiveness and positivity, which can make a significant impact during sales meetings. When you exude confidence through your posture, you not only project an image of competence but also invite your clients to feel more comfortable and engaged. On the other hand, if you notice a client slouching or crossing their arms, it could indicate defensiveness or disengagement. Recognizing these signs allows you to adjust your approach, ensuring you address any concerns and foster a more welcoming environment.

Facial expressions are powerful indicators of emotions. Recognizing and responding to these expressions can help you gauge your client's reactions and adapt your pitch accordingly. A genuine smile, for example, often indicates agreement and positive reception, which you can reflect with your own smile to build rapport. Conversely, a furrowed brow may suggest confusion or concern, prompting you to clarify points and reassure your client. By staying attuned to these subtle cues, you can create a more empathetic and responsive interaction, leading to stronger connections and successful outcomes.

Maintaining appropriate eye contact is essential in establishing trust and demonstrating sincerity. Consistent eye contact shows confidence and honesty, helping to build a connection and trust with your client. It signals that you are engaged and interested in their needs and concerns. However, be mindful not to overdo it, as too much eye contact can be intimidating, while too little can suggest disinterest or insecurity. Striking the right balance in eye contact ensures a comfortable and trustworthy interaction, paving the way for a more productive conversation.

Understanding facial expressions can give you significant insights into what people are thinking or feeling, particularly when they are making things up or trying to remember something. Recognizing these signals can enhance your interpersonal skills, allowing you to respond more effectively in conversations and negotiations. When people fabricate stories, their facial expressions often betray their true intentions. One of the most telling signs of fabrication is irregular eye movement. When someone is making something up, their eyes often dart around as they search for details to support their story. They might avoid direct eye contact, as maintaining it can be uncomfortable while lying. According to Bandler and Grinder's (founders of NLP) research, people tend to look to the right when they are constructing a story, as this activates the creative side of the brain. Microexpressions are brief, involuntary facial expressions that reveal true emotions. When someone is lying, microexpressions of fear, guilt, or anxiety may flash across their face for a fraction of a second. These microexpressions can be difficult to spot but are reliable indicators of deceit. A fabricated story often leads to inconsistent facial expressions.

For instance, if someone is pretending to be happy or amused, their smile may not engage the muscles around their eyes (the Duchenne smile), resulting in a fake or insincere expression. People who are lying often touch their face, especially their nose and mouth. This behavior is thought to be a subconscious attempt to cover up their deceit or to comfort themselves. When fabricating, people might exhibit delayed emotional reactions. For example, if they are pretending to be surprised, there may be a noticeable delay before they express that surprise. Genuine emotions tend to be immediate and spontaneous.

In contrast, genuine memory recall tends to produce different facial and behavioral cues. When recalling a genuine memory, people often look to the left. This activates the part of the brain associated with accessing stored information. Unlike fabricators, their eye movements are typically steadier and more focused. Genuine memory recall usually comes with relaxed and natural facial expressions. There are no signs of stress or discomfort, as the person is simply accessing stored information rather than creating new details. When someone recalls a genuine memory, their facial expressions are consistent with the emotion associated with that memory. For example, if they are recalling a happy event, their smile will be genuine and involve the muscles around their eyes. People trying to remember something often exhibit focused attention. They might stare off into the distance or close their eyes momentarily as they concentrate on retrieving the memory. This focused look is a good indicator that they are engaging with their memory rather than fabricating details. Gestures that accompany genuine memory recall are natural and fluid. Unlike the self-soothing gestures of someone fabricating a story, these gestures are more likely to support the narrative and reflect the content of the memory.

Recognizing these facial cues can greatly improve your ability to read people in various situations, whether in sales, negotiations, or everyday conversations. By identifying when someone is genuinely recalling a memory, you can build trust and rapport. Responding positively to their true emotions can strengthen your connection and facilitate more honest communication. In negotiations, recognizing fabrication can give you an edge. If you suspect someone is not being truthful, you can probe further, ask more detailed questions, or steer the conversation to test their consistency. In conflict resolution, understanding whether someone is recalling events truthfully can help you navigate the situation more effectively. Addressing any signs of fabrication with care and tact can lead to a more honest and constructive dialogue. In personal relationships, being able to discern between genuine recall and fabrication can improve your interactions. It can help you understand your loved ones better and respond to their needs more appropriately.

Mastering the ability to read facial expressions for signs of fabrication and genuine memory recall is a valuable skill. It enhances your emotional intelligence and equips you with the tools to navigate social interactions with greater insight and effectiveness. By paying attention to eye movements, microexpressions, and other subtle cues, you can become more adept at understanding the true intentions and emotions of those around you.

Gestures can reinforce your message and help engage your audience. Open palm gestures suggest honesty and openness, making you appear more trustworthy and inviting. These gestures can emphasize your points and keep your clients engaged. Be cautious with gestures like pointing, which can be perceived as aggressive or rude. Instead, use whole-hand gestures to direct attention or emphasize a point. By using gestures thoughtfully, you can enhance your communication and leave a positive impression on your clients.

The physical distance between you and your client can impact the interaction. Respecting personal space is crucial, as it can influence how comfortable your client feels. Close proximity can create a sense of intimacy and trust but may also be perceived as invasive if too close. Distant proximity may suggest disinterest or formality. By gauging your client's comfort level and adjusting your distance accordingly, you can foster a more personal connection and enhance the overall interaction. Mirroring the client's body language can build rapport and make them feel more understood. Subtle imitation of their posture, gestures, and expressions can create a sense of alignment and empathy. When done naturally and appropriately, mirroring shows empathy and understanding, helping to create a bond and making the client feel comfortable. This technique can significantly enhance your ability to connect with clients on a deeper level, leading to more successful sales interactions. Mastering body language in sales is a game-changer that can elevate your sales skills to new heights. By paying attention to posture, facial expressions, eye contact, gestures, proximity, and mirroring, you can better understand your clients and adapt your approach to meet their needs. This not only improves communication but also helps in building trust and closing more deals. Embrace these techniques, and watch as your ability to connect and succeed in sales transforms, leading to greater personal and professional fulfillment.

Here is a brief rundown on identifying microexpressions. Microexpressions are the fleeting facial expressions that occur unconsciously and reveal true emotions that clients or anyone you interact with may try to conceal. These split-second cues—like a brief flash of surprise, contempt, or frustration—can be crucial indicators of your client's true feelings, offering valuable clues to their thoughts and concerns. Recognizing and interpreting these fleeting cues can provide valuable insights into your client's true feelings and intentions, enabling you to adjust your approach and enhance communication effectively.

- **Happiness:** A brief, genuine smile. Indicates pleasure and agreement. Use this cue to build on positive aspects of your presentation.
- **Sadness:** Downward movement of the eyebrows or a slight frown. Suggests disappointment or concern. Address these feelings to remove obstacles in the client's decision-making process.
- **Surprise:** Widened eyes, raised eyebrows, and an open mouth. Reflects astonishment or unexpected reactions. Use this moment to highlight key benefits or address new concerns.
- **Fear:** Widened eyes, raised eyebrows, and tense facial muscles. Indicates apprehension or uncertainty. Reassure the client and provide additional information to build confidence.
- **Disgust:** A slight curl of the upper lip or nose wrinkling. Suggests aversion or disagreement. Adjust your approach, clarify misunderstandings, or pivot to alternative solutions.
- **Anger:** Narrowed eyes, furrowed brows, and tense facial muscles. Reflects frustration or dissatisfaction. Detect and resolve potential objections to prevent escalation.
- **Contempt:** A slight smirk or one-sided mouth raise. Indicates superiority or disdain. Address credibility concerns and provide evidence of value.
- **Neutrality:** A relaxed face without specific emotional cues. Indicates indifference or neutrality. Gauge client engagement and adjust your presentation to re-engage or clarify points.

Practical Strategies for Reading Nonverbal Cues

1. **Observe Consistently:** Pay close attention to your client's body language throughout the meeting. Look for patterns and changes that can provide insights into their feelings and attitudes.
2. **Context Matters:** Interpret nonverbal cues within the context of the conversation. A crossed arm might be a defensive gesture, or it could simply be a comfortable resting position.
3. **Mirror and Match:** Subtly mirror your client's body language to build rapport. This creates a sense of connection and can make the client feel more comfortable.
4. **Ask Clarifying Questions:** If you notice a negative nonverbal cue, ask questions to address potential concerns. For example, "I noticed you frowned when we discussed this point. Do you have any concerns about this aspect?"

Advanced Techniques for Enhancing Communication

1. **Empathetic Listening:** Show empathy by nodding and using affirmative gestures. This signals to the client that you are engaged and understand their perspective.
2. **Adapt Your Presentation:** Be flexible in your approach. If you notice negative cues, adapt your presentation to address concerns and highlight benefits that resonate with the client.
3. **Follow-Up on Subtle Cues:** If you see a fleeting microexpression, follow up with a statement or question to explore the client's underlying feelings. For example, "It seems like this aspect might be particularly interesting to you. Could you tell me more about what you think?"

By honing your ability to read and respond to nonverbal cues effectively, you can establish stronger connections, influence decisions, and cultivate enduring client relationships. Remember, nonverbal communication is not just about what you say—it's about how you convey authenticity, understanding, and professionalism in every interaction, making it a cornerstone of successful salesmanship.

Imagine entering a sales meeting with a new client. As you begin your presentation, you notice the client's posture is relaxed but their arms are crossed. Their facial expressions shift between interest and slight concern. By staying attuned to these cues, you adjust your presentation, addressing the client's concerns directly and emphasizing the benefits most relevant to them. Your attentiveness and responsiveness to their nonverbal signals help build trust and rapport, ultimately leading to a successful deal. Mastering nonverbal communication requires practice and keen observation, but the rewards are immense. By understanding the unspoken messages your clients convey, you can navigate sales interactions with greater insight and effectiveness, leading to stronger relationships and more successful outcomes.

Just like Dr. Cal Lightman, the main character of the TV show "Lie to Me" used to say, "The truth is written all over our faces."

NOTE - *a simple Google search for facial expression or microexpression tests will give you plenty of resources to practice this fun and beneficial skill set.*

Leading Clients to YOUR Desired Outcome

In the dynamic world of sales, mastering the art of subtle influence is akin to orchestrating a symphony where prospects feel empowered to make decisions while being subtly guided toward the optimal outcome. Let's dive into the psychology and techniques behind this approach, highlighting the importance of rapport, trust, and strategic communication in achieving sales success.

Effective influence in sales often hinges on tapping into psychological triggers that drive decision-making processes. Understanding these triggers, deeply rooted in human behavior, can significantly enhance your ability to guide prospects subtly and effectively. Humans naturally seek autonomy and the feeling of control over their choices. By presenting options and allowing prospects to choose, sales professionals empower them in the decision-making process, subtly guiding them toward mutually beneficial outcomes. This technique taps into the psychological need for control, making the prospect feel more involved and invested in the decision.

Leveraging social proof through testimonials, case studies, and success stories can significantly influence prospects. Demonstrating how others in similar situations have successfully used your product or service builds credibility and subtly encourages prospects to follow suit. This is rooted in the psychological principle that people tend to follow the actions of others, especially when they are uncertain. Creating a sense of scarcity or urgency can prompt prospects to take action. Limited-time offers, exclusive deals, or highlighting diminishing availability can subtly push prospects toward making a decision without overt pressure. This approach plays on the fear of missing out (FOMO), a powerful motivator that can drive quicker decision-making.

Establishing genuine rapport and trust forms the bedrock of effective subtle influence in sales. Without trust, attempts to guide or influence prospects can come across as manipulative. Therefore, building a solid foundation of trust is crucial. Listening attentively to prospects' needs, challenges, and aspirations demonstrates empathy and understanding. This fosters trust and allows sales professionals to align their solutions with the prospect's specific goals seamlessly. Active listening involves not just hearing words but understanding emotions and underlying concerns. Tailoring your approach to each prospect's unique preferences and circumstances helps create a personalized experience. This personal touch builds rapport and enhances the prospect's receptiveness to your guidance. Personalization shows that you value the prospect as an individual, not just a potential sale.

Successfully guiding prospects toward a solution requires employing subtle yet powerful techniques. These techniques should be implemented with finesse to ensure that the prospect feels in control while being gently guided toward a beneficial decision. Framing questions to uncover the prospect's pain points and desired outcomes is crucial. Thoughtful questioning not only demonstrates understanding but also subtly guides the conversation toward solutions that address the prospect's needs effectively. Questions should be open-ended, encouraging the prospect to share more about their needs and concerns. Sharing compelling stories that illustrate how your product or service has positively impacted others can evoke emotions and influence the prospect's perceptions. Stories create a narrative that resonates with the prospect, subtly steering them toward seeing your solution as the answer to their challenges. Emotional engagement through storytelling can be more persuasive than mere facts and figures.

Emphasizing the benefits of your offering over its features helps prospects visualize how your solution can solve their problems or fulfill their aspirations. This approach makes the solution feel tailor-made to their needs, enhancing their willingness to move forward. Benefits-oriented communication focuses on the value and impact your product can have on the prospect's life or business. The essence of subtle influence lies in creating a win-win scenario where both the sales professional and the prospect benefit. Building a shared understanding of the prospect's goals and challenges enables sales professionals to position their solution as the ideal fit. This collaborative approach fosters trust and encourages prospects to see the sales professional as a partner in achieving their objectives. A partnership mentality shifts the focus from selling to solving. Demonstrating how your solution aligns with the prospect's overarching goals and aspirations reinforces its value proposition. By highlighting shared objectives and mutual benefits, sales professionals subtly guide prospects toward a decision that benefits both parties. Aligning goals ensures that the prospect sees the long-term value in the relationship.

Empathy and authenticity are at the core of subtle influence. Without these elements, attempts to guide prospects can feel insincere or manipulative. Empathy involves understanding and sharing the feelings of another, while authenticity means being genuine and transparent in your interactions. By truly understanding the prospect's needs and concerns, you can tailor your approach to address their specific situation. Authenticity builds trust, as prospects can sense when you are genuinely interested in helping them. This combination of empathy and authenticity creates a strong foundation for subtle influence.

Consider the case of a software company looking to sell its new project management tool to a large corporation. The sales professional begins by understanding the client's current challenges with their existing tools through strategic questioning. They then share a compelling story about a similar company that saw significant improvements after adopting the new tool. Throughout the conversation, the salesperson emphasizes the benefits of the tool, such as increased efficiency and better team collaboration, rather than just its features. By highlighting these benefits and aligning them with the client's goals, the salesperson subtly guides the client toward seeing the tool as the perfect solution. As the conversation progresses, the salesperson builds rapport by actively listening and personalizing their approach. They present the software as a way to achieve the client's objectives more effectively, creating a win-win scenario. By the end of the meeting, the client feels understood, valued, and confident in the decision to move forward with the new tool.

Imagine sitting in your office with a client, setting the stage for a transformative conversation. You start with open-ended questions, discovering that your product can make a parent extremely proud—something your client has longed for as long as they can remember. You already know your product is the answer, but instead of selling it outright, you ask your client what they believe the solution to their problem might be. If their answer isn't your product yet, encourage them to dive deeper. Suggest conducting a root cause analysis, much like major corporations do, to unearth the best solution.

Together, you and your client begin with the problem they're trying to overcome. By now, you've built a good rapport, and they're open to discussing their issues with you. Ask why this problem exists, then dig deeper with open-ended questions: why is that a problem? Note their responses and continue this process until you reach at least three layers deep, aiming for five or more. You'll know you've hit the real root cause when the true raw feeling is there. Beware though these conversations can become emotional. Rather than telling them your product is the fix, let them arrive at that conclusion themselves. Ask them for potential solutions and gently guide them toward your product. By the end of this discussion, they should be telling you that your product is the solution to their issue. If you can make the client, feel that you're the key to obtaining your product and solving their problems, you've won this interaction. Closing the deal should be effortless, and you'll have gained an advocate who will enthusiastically promote your product to everyone they meet and know.

Mastering subtle influence in sales demands finesse, empathy, and a deep understanding of human behavior. By empowering prospects to make informed decisions while subtly guiding them toward solutions that meet their needs, sales professionals can build enduring relationships based on trust and mutual success. This comprehensive exploration of subtle influence in sales underscores the significance of authenticity, empathy, and strategic communication. By mastering these techniques, sales professionals can navigate complex sales environments with confidence, ultimately achieving greater success and fostering long-term client relationships.

Be the Inspiration, Be the Wizard

Being the wizard means embodying confidence, expertise, and enthusiasm that inspire prospects to see you as someone who has what they want and as a catalyst for their success. This chapter explores how to harness these qualities positively, demonstrating your capability while inviting prospects to envision themselves achieving similar feats with your product or service. Confidence is contagious in sales. When you exude assurance in your knowledge and abilities, prospects are more likely to trust your recommendations and view you as a reliable source of solutions. Comprehensive knowledge of your product or service instills confidence not only in yourself but also in your prospects. Be prepared to answer any question, address concerns, and highlight the unique value your offering brings to the table. Share compelling success stories and case studies that demonstrate how your product has empowered others to achieve remarkable results. By showcasing real-world examples of success, you bolster your credibility and inspire confidence in your prospects.

Let's look at the wizardry of Merlin or Gandalf or Harry Potter and Dumbledore. Wizards in popular culture exude a unique blend of qualities that make them both admirable and majestic. Their profound wisdom and vast knowledge, as seen in characters like Gandalf and Dumbledore, command respect and admiration. The extraordinary magical abilities of wizards such as Doctor Strange and Merlin showcase their power and skill, setting them apart as awe-inspiring figures. The strong moral integrity, exemplified by Harry Potter, stands for justice, courage, and selflessness, often driving them to protect others and fight against evil. An air of mystery surrounds many wizards, adding intrigue and captivating audiences with their complex personalities and hidden motives. Natural leaders like Dumbledore and Gandalf provide guidance and support in times of need, earning them the love and respect of those they lead. Charismatic wizards like the Wicked Witch of the West leave a strong impression with their unique and often flamboyant personalities. Remarkable resilience is demonstrated by wizards like Harry Potter, whose ability to overcome challenges and grow stronger in the face of adversity inspires audiences. These qualities combine to create wizards who are not only powerful and mystical but also relatable and human in their struggles and virtues.

Just as wizards captivate audiences with their unique qualities, salespeople and business professionals can emulate these traits to create a powerful and compelling presence with their clients. Imagine harnessing the profound knowledge and expertise of Gandalf and Dumbledore to earn the respect and trust of your clients. Picture yourself demonstrating exceptional skill and competence, much like the magical prowess of Doctor Strange and Merlin, showcasing your capability and reliability. Upholding strong moral integrity, as Harry Potter and Gandalf do, builds a foundation of trust and loyalty, reassuring clients that they are in the best hands. Embrace an air of mystery and sophistication to intrigue and keep clients engaged. Lead with confidence and provide clear guidance, just like Dumbledore and Gandalf, positioning yourself as a reliable mentor and advisor. Let your charisma and strong presence, inspired by the Wicked Witch of the West, leave a lasting impression and make every interaction memorable. Demonstrate resilience and perseverance, like Mr. Potter, showing clients that you are committed and capable of overcoming any challenges that arise. Finally, embrace complexity and depth in your approach, adding a fascinating dimension to your professional persona. By embodying these qualities, you can make your clients feel as though they are working with someone who holds the power of wizards, creating a magical and impactful experience.

Excitement is key to captivating prospects and igniting their imagination about what they can accomplish with your solution. Use vivid language and storytelling to paint a picture of how your product can transform the prospect's challenges into opportunities for success. Help them envision a future where they achieve their goals with your support. Showcase the capabilities of your product through live demonstrations, interactive presentations, or visual aids. Allow prospects to see firsthand how your solution can enhance their efficiency, productivity, or quality of life. Instead of manipulating prospects, invite them to join you on a journey toward mutual success. Engage prospects in meaningful discussions about their challenges and goals. Position yourself as a partner who listens actively, understands deeply, and collaborates on finding solutions that align with their objectives. Empower them with knowledge that enables informed decision-making and reinforces their confidence in choosing your product.

Being the wizard in sales isn't just about closing deals; it's about building enduring relationships based on trust, respect, and mutual benefit. Provide exceptional post-sale support and follow-up to ensure that your customers derive maximum value from your product or service. Address any concerns promptly and continue to demonstrate your commitment to their success. Actively solicit feedback from customers to understand their evolving needs and challenges. Use this feedback to continuously improve your offerings and enhance customer satisfaction. Embracing the role of the wizard in sales involves embodying confidence, inspiring excitement, and guiding prospects toward envisioning their success with your solution. By fostering a positive and empowering sales environment, you not only enhance your credibility and influence but also build lasting partnerships based on shared goals and mutual growth. This chapter underscores the importance of authenticity, empathy, and a positive mindset in sales. By approaching sales as an opportunity to empower prospects and make a meaningful impact on their journey to success, you can cultivate trust, inspire confidence, and achieve sustainable growth in your sales endeavors. Remember, being the wizard in sales is about creating a bit of magic in every interaction, making even the most unlikely sales possible with the right touch of confidence, expertise, and enthusiasm.

Storytelling - Captivating Narratives

Storytelling is a powerful tool in sales, enabling you to engage prospects, convey your message effectively, and build a compelling narrative that resonates with your audience. Here's what it means to be a great storyteller in sales, broken down into key components with examples. Great storytellers in sales are authentic and genuine, creating a connection with their audience through personal anecdotes or relatable experiences. They share stories that illustrate their values, challenges overcome, or insights gained. Imagine a salesperson sharing how their own experience struggling with a particular problem led them to discover and eventually champion the solution they are offering. This personal connection builds trust and empathy with the prospect, making the interaction feel more like a shared journey than a sales pitch. According to a study by Nielsen, 92% of consumers trust recommendations from individuals over brands, emphasizing the power of personal connection in storytelling.

Effective storytelling in sales is about understanding the prospect's needs and framing your story in a way that resonates with their challenges or aspirations. It's about making the story relevant to their situation. For example, a salesperson might tell a story about a client who faced similar business challenges and how they successfully implemented the solution, achieving remarkable results. By aligning the story with the prospect's current concerns, they demonstrate empathy and understanding, showing that they truly grasp the unique hurdles the prospect faces. Harvard Business Review highlights that emotionally connected customers are more than twice as valuable as highly satisfied customers, showcasing the importance of relevance and empathy in storytelling.

A well-crafted story in sales follows a clear structure: introduction, development of conflict or challenge, climax or turning point, and resolution. This structure maintains engagement and guides the prospect towards the desired outcome. Begin with a compelling introduction that captures the prospect's attention, such as an intriguing statistic or a thought-provoking question. Develop the story by outlining the specific challenge faced, how it was addressed using your product or service, and the positive outcomes achieved. This narrative flow ensures that the prospect stays engaged and follows the logical progression of how your solution can benefit them. Research by the Stanford Graduate School of Business found that stories are up to 22 times more memorable than facts alone.

Great storytellers in sales use vivid language and imagery to paint a picture in the prospect's mind, evoking emotions and making the story memorable. They appeal to both the rational and emotional aspects of decision-making. Describe the tangible benefits of your product or service through a story that creates a visual image of success. Use descriptive language to illustrate how using your solution transforms the prospect's operations, making it easier for them to envision the impact. For instance, instead of simply stating that your software increases efficiency, describe a scenario where a client's chaotic workflow was transformed into a streamlined, productive process, allowing them to focus on growth rather than daily firefighting. A study by the Journal of Marketing Theory and Practice suggests that emotional engagement in stories can increase the perceived value of a product by over 20%.

Every story in sales should have a purpose—a call to action that encourages the prospect to take the next step towards a mutually beneficial outcome. The resolution should reinforce the value proposition and leave a lasting impression. Conclude the story by inviting the prospect to explore how your solution can similarly benefit their organization or personal goals. Emphasize the transformative effects highlighted in the story and align them with the prospect's desired outcomes. A well-placed call to action might be as simple as inviting them to a demo or suggesting a follow-up meeting to discuss implementation strategies tailored to their needs. The Corporate Executive Board found that providing customers with a compelling reason to act immediately can increase their likelihood of following through by 25%.

To be a great storyteller in sales, combine authenticity with relevance, structure with emotional appeal, and a clear call to action. Craft stories that resonate with your audience's needs, demonstrate the value of your solution, and inspire action. By mastering the art of storytelling, you can effectively engage prospects, differentiate yourself from competitors, and drive meaningful connections that lead to successful sales outcomes.

Owning the Sale: They Came to YOU

When a prospect steps into your office or engages in a conversation with you, they've already shown a significant level of interest. Imagine in today's day and age what it takes to get you to leave your comfort zone, leave your home and go out to seek a solution to a problem. This initial step indicates that they are open to exploring solutions or products that could potentially address their needs or challenges. It's crucial to recognize and appreciate this readiness, as it sets the stage for a productive interaction where you can effectively showcase the value you can offer. Understanding the intent behind a prospect's visit or inquiry is key to guiding the conversation towards a successful outcome. Whether they've scheduled a meeting, visited your website, or reached out through a referral, these actions signify a proactive interest in what you have to offer. This initial engagement serves as an opportunity to study more intently their motivations and expectations, laying the foundation for a tailored approach to addressing their specific requirements.

Building upon the initial interest demonstrated by the prospect requires a strategic approach that goes beyond a simple sales pitch. It involves actively listening to their concerns, asking insightful questions to uncover their pain points, and demonstrating how your product or service can effectively meet their needs. By focusing on their unique challenges and offering personalized solutions, you enhance the likelihood of cultivating a meaningful connection that resonates with their goals. Central to converting interest into a committed sale is the creation of tangible value and establishing trust. This involves showcasing your expertise, industry knowledge, and a genuine commitment to helping the prospect achieve their objectives. By highlighting past successes, case studies, or testimonials relevant to their situation, you reinforce credibility and build confidence in your ability to deliver results. Transparency and authenticity in your interactions further solidify the foundation of trust necessary for a mutually beneficial relationship.

Perception plays a pivotal role in shaping the prospect's decision-making process. How they perceive your professionalism, sincerity, and alignment with their needs significantly influences their willingness to move forward. Therefore, maintaining a polished demeanor, actively listening to their concerns, and demonstrating empathy are crucial in shaping a positive impression. Your ability to articulate how your offering addresses their pain points and provides unique benefits reinforces their confidence in choosing your solution. A study by McKinsey & Company reveals that 70% of buying experiences are based on how the customer feels they are being treated, highlighting the importance of perception in sales.

While the sale may seem within reach, it's essential to navigate potential pitfalls that could derail the process. Avoiding overly aggressive sales tactics, failing to address critical objections, or not adequately understanding their specific requirements can jeopardize the opportunity. By actively listening and adapting your approach based on their feedback, you mitigate the risk of misunderstandings and ensure that every interaction contributes positively to their decision-making journey. According to Salesforce, 75% of buyers expect companies to anticipate their needs and make relevant suggestions, emphasizing the importance of responsiveness and adaptability.

Recognizing that not every prospect converts into an immediate sale underscores the importance of nurturing relationships over time. Lant's Rule of 7 suggests that prospects need to see marketing about seven times before being willing to take action. Even if they don't commit immediately, maintaining regular communication, providing additional resources or insights, and staying accessible demonstrates your ongoing commitment to their success. This proactive approach fosters a supportive environment where prospects feel valued and supported, enhancing the likelihood of future opportunities. Research by Bain & Company indicates that increasing customer retention rates by 5% increases profits by 25% to 95%, underscoring the long-term value of nurturing relationships.

In conclusion, when a prospect engages with you, whether face-to-face or virtually, they've signaled a genuine interest in what you offer. The sale is indeed yours to lose at this pivotal moment. By taking a thorough and personalized approach that emphasizes value creation, trust-building, and proactive relationship management, you maximize the potential for converting their interest into a successful, long-term partnership. Embrace the opportunity presented when a prospect shows interest, focusing on building a relationship founded on trust, understanding, and mutual benefit. The future of your sales success hinges on your ability to turn that initial interest into enduring loyalty and satisfaction. And to end on a personal anecdote; I've had clients approach me, and I'm sure you have too, saying it was just time. They saw your ad on a billboard, heard it on the radio, and when you emailed them, it felt like fate was steering them to you. That level of psychodynamic marketing feels like a sign from the heavens that you have the answer they've been seeking. How could that be viewed as anything but yours to lose? Remember, the ball is in your court. It's a home game, and they've already done their homework and stepped out of their comfort zone for you. All you have to do now is not mess it up.

Wants and Needs Stacking

In the exhilarating world of sales, mastering the art of balancing wants and needs is what transforms a good pitch into an extraordinary one. Picture yourself not just as a salesperson but as a maestro, orchestrating a symphony that resonates perfectly with your prospect's deepest desires and most pressing necessities. Ready to dive into the excitement? This chapter will reinvigorate your approach and reignite your passion for crafting the perfect pitch! Always remember this; people may pursue your solution to fill their needs but they take action because of their wants.

First, let's lay the groundwork. Needs are the essentials – the fundamental requirements that your prospects cannot live without. Think of these as the bread and butter of their existence. Wants, on the other hand, are the cherry on top – the desires and aspirations that make life more enjoyable and fulfilling. They might not be essential, but they sure make everything a lot sweeter. Now, imagine if you could masterfully blend these two elements in your sales pitch. The result? A persuasive masterpiece that not only meets the basic needs but also ignites a fervent desire for your product or service. To captivate your audience, you must take them on a journey. Begin by addressing their needs. Paint a vivid picture of how your product or service can solve their most pressing problems. Use concrete examples, powerful statistics, and compelling stories to highlight how their life or business will improve by meeting these needs. Once you've firmly established that your offering is the solution to their problems, it's time to add some flair.

Here's where the magic happens – transitioning from needs to wants. Imagine your product as a multi-layered cake. The base layer (needs) is already making your prospect's mouth water, but it's the frosting and decorations (wants) that will make them crave that first bite. By appealing to their desires, you tap into their emotions, making your pitch not just compelling but irresistible. For example, if you're selling a software solution, start by demonstrating how it solves the critical issue of data security (need). Once that foundation is laid, pivot to show how it also boosts productivity and offers a sleek, user-friendly interface that will make their daily operations smoother and more enjoyable (want). This dual approach ensures that you're covering all bases and making your pitch as enticing as possible.

Now, let's turn up the excitement a notch by creating a sense of urgency. Your prospects should feel that by not acting now, they might miss out on something truly valuable. Scarcity and urgency are powerful psychological triggers. Highlight limited-time offers, exclusive deals, or upcoming deadlines to encourage immediate action. "This offer is available for a limited time," or "Only a few units left at this price," can create a fear of missing out that compels prospects to make a decision quickly. Consider the example of a fitness program. Address the need by emphasizing the importance of health and fitness in combating lifestyle diseases. Then, appeal to the want by showcasing testimonials of people who not only became healthier but also more confident and happier after joining the program. Finally, inject urgency by offering a limited-time discount or exclusive access to a special class. This strategy not only meets the prospect's immediate needs but also taps into their desires and motivates swift action.

The next ingredient in crafting the perfect pitch is building rapport and trust. Authenticity and transparency are key. Prospects are more likely to engage with you if they believe you genuinely care about their success. Share your passion for the product, demonstrate your expertise, and most importantly, listen to their concerns and feedback. A study by the Harvard Business Review found that 58% of buyers report that salespeople who "listen to their needs and understand them" are the most valuable in closing deals. Engage your prospects in meaningful conversations. Ask questions that show you're interested in their specific situation. "What are the biggest challenges you're facing right now?" or "How do you envision the perfect solution for your needs?" These questions not only provide valuable insights but also show that you're focused on their unique needs and desires.

Don't underestimate the power of social proof. Testimonials, case studies, and endorsements from satisfied customers can significantly boost your credibility. Prospects are more likely to trust your offering if they see that others have had positive experiences with it. According to Nielsen, 92% of consumers trust recommendations from individuals over brands, emphasizing the importance of leveraging social proof in your pitch. Share stories of clients who faced similar challenges and how your product helped them overcome these obstacles. Highlight specific results and benefits they experienced. This not only builds trust but also helps prospects visualize the positive impact your product can have on their lives. Finally, wrap up your pitch by tying everything together in a cohesive and compelling narrative. Reinforce how your product addresses both the needs and wants of your prospect. Reiterate the urgency of acting now and leave them with a clear and confident call to action. Your goal is to make them feel that choosing your product is not just a smart decision but an exciting opportunity they can't afford to miss.

When a prospect engages with you, whether face-to-face or virtually, they've signaled a genuine interest in what you offer. The sale is indeed yours to lose at this pivotal moment. By taking a thorough and personalized approach that emphasizes wants stacked on needs, value creation, trust-building, and proactive relationship management, you maximize the potential for converting their interest into a successful, long-term partnership. Embrace the opportunity presented when a prospect shows interest, focusing on building a relationship founded on trust, understanding, and mutual benefit. The future of your sales success hinges on your ability to turn that initial interest into enduring loyalty and satisfaction.

Buyer's Remorse: Ensuring Satisfaction

Imagine a customer making a purchase and walking away, only to be struck by a wave of doubt and regret. This feeling, known as buyer's remorse, is a common experience that can significantly impact customer satisfaction and trust. As a sales professional, mastering the art of addressing buyer's remorse is crucial for ensuring long-term success and customer loyalty. Buyer's remorse often surfaces when customers start questioning their decision and the value of the product they've just bought. They might worry about the financial commitment or whether the product will meet their expectations and deliver the promised benefits. These doubts can create a ripple effect, leading to dissatisfaction and potential returns. So, how can you, as a salesperson, effectively address and mitigate these concerns?

Start by recognizing the importance of thorough education during the sales process. It's not enough to highlight the positives of your product; you need to manage expectations by providing clear, detailed information about its features and benefits. Transparency is key here. Don't shy away from discussing any potential limitations or challenges. This honesty builds trust and helps customers feel more prepared and confident about their purchase. When a customer expresses remorse, the first step is to listen empathetically. Avoid getting defensive; instead, acknowledge their concerns and validate their feelings. A decision that seems minimally invasive to you, could be perceived as a mountain to a client. This approach shows that you understand their perspective and are genuinely committed to their satisfaction. For instance, if a customer is worried about the financial aspect, discuss the return on investment and long-term benefits. If they're unsure about the product's suitability, offer customization options, additional support, or even alternative products that might better meet their needs.

Consider this scenario: A customer purchases a high-end camera but later feels it might be too complex for their needs. By listening to their concerns, you can offer a personalized tutorial, additional resources, or suggest a simpler model if necessary. This proactive approach not only addresses their immediate worries but also reinforces your commitment to their satisfaction. Moreover, buyer's remorse provides a valuable opportunity for feedback. When customers share their doubts, they're giving you insights into how you can refine your sales approach and improve your product offerings. Embrace this feedback as a chance to enhance the overall customer experience. By addressing their concerns promptly and professionally, you demonstrate the value of your product and build stronger trust in your brand.

A great way to counter buyer's remorse is by emphasizing the benefits that initially attracted the customer. Highlight success stories and testimonials that showcase how others have benefited from the product. These real-world examples can reassure customers about their decision, reminding them of the positive impact your offering can have on their lives. Encourage them to focus on the reasons they chose your product in the first place and the goals it helps them achieve. For instance, if a customer regrets purchasing a gym membership, remind them of their fitness goals and share success stories of others who have achieved significant health improvements. This not only reaffirms the value of their purchase but also motivates them to stay committed to their goals.

In handling buyer's remorse, your goal is to transform potential regrets into opportunities for strengthening customer loyalty and satisfaction. By addressing concerns with empathy and offering proactive solutions, you can turn a moment of doubt into a reaffirmation of the customer's decision. This approach not only resolves immediate issues but also enhances the overall perception of your brand, leading to repeat business and positive referrals. You should view buyer's remorse as a valuable opportunity to reinforce the value of your product and build stronger relationships with your customers. By addressing their concerns empathetically and proactively, you can turn potential regrets into lasting satisfaction and loyalty. This strategy not only ensures customer happiness but also bolsters your brand's reputation, paving the way for continued success in the competitive world of sales.

Staying Humble: Learning from Everyone

In the world of sales, confidence is essential, but there is a delicate balance between confidence and arrogance. The most successful salespeople understand that no matter how much they know or how skilled they are, there is always something to learn. This mindset of humility is not only a key to personal growth but also a powerful tool in building genuine connections with clients. Imagine a successful businessman, John, who has climbed the corporate ladder with sheer determination and skill. He has closed million-dollar deals, spoken at conferences, and is revered in his industry. One day, John is on his way to a crucial meeting when he encounters a young boy selling lemonade on the street. Initially, John walks past without a second thought. But something about the boy's enthusiastic pitch and genuine smile makes him turn back.

John watches as the boy confidently engages with each passerby, not deterred by those who ignore him. Intrigued, John decides to buy a cup of lemonade. As he sips the drink, he strikes up a conversation with the boy. The boy, named Alex, shares his story of saving money for a new bike and how he learned to make the best lemonade by experimenting with different recipes. John realizes that Alex, despite his age, embodies many qualities of a successful entrepreneur: resilience, creativity, and a willingness to learn from trial and error. John is reminded of the fundamental principles of sales and customer engagement that he might have overlooked in his busy, high-stakes world. Inspired by Alex's story, John reflects on his own approach to business. He decides to adopt a fresh perspective, embracing curiosity and open-mindedness in his interactions.

A Japanese parable tells the story of a Zen master who invited a scholar to tea. The master began to pour tea into the scholar's cup, but didn't stop when the cup was full, causing it to overflow. The scholar exclaimed that the cup was already full and couldn't hold any more tea. The master replied, "Like this cup, you are full of your own opinions and speculations. How can I show you Zen unless you first empty your cup?" This parable beautifully illustrates the essence of humility in sales. To truly grasp new knowledge and insights, one must first empty their cup—acknowledging that there is always more to learn. Humility in sales is about recognizing that knowledge and wisdom can come from the most unexpected places. It's understanding that every interaction is an opportunity to learn and grow.

Here are some key components of practicing humility in sales:

Active listening truly reveals insights that you might miss if you're too focused on your own perspective. It shows respect and genuine interest, which builds stronger relationships. Admitting mistakes and acknowledging when you don't know something or when you've made a mistake can be powerful. It demonstrates integrity and builds trust. Regularly asking for feedback from clients and peers helps you identify areas for improvement. It also shows that you value their opinions and are committed to providing the best service. Embracing the mindset that learning never stops keeps you adaptable and innovative. This can involve formal education, reading industry blogs, or learning from everyday experiences, like John's interaction with Alex. Valuing all perspectives means every person you interact with, regardless of their position or background, has unique experiences and insights. Recognizing this can lead to valuable lessons and unexpected opportunities.

Humility isn't just about learning from those who are more experienced or knowledgeable; it's also about recognizing that everyone has something to teach. Your clients can provide the most direct feedback on your product or service. They can highlight pain points, suggest improvements, and even inspire new ideas. Analyzing your competitors can provide insights into what works and what doesn't in your industry. It can also help you identify gaps in the market that you can fill. Your colleagues, both superiors and subordinates, have different strengths and perspectives. Collaborating and sharing knowledge can lead to better strategies and solutions. Everyday experiences, like John's encounter with Alex, can offer profound lessons. Being open to these moments ensures you are always growing and evolving.

Practicing humility doesn't just make you a better salesperson; it makes you a better person. It fosters a culture of respect and continuous improvement. When you approach sales with humility, you build stronger, more authentic relationships with your clients. They feel valued and understood, which leads to greater loyalty and trust. In the end, humility is about understanding that no matter how much success you achieve, there is always room for growth. It's about being open to new ideas, willing to learn from anyone, and committed to constantly improving. By embodying humility, you not only enhance your skills but also enrich your life and the lives of those around you. So, take a page from John's book and always be ready to learn from the world around you. Whether it's a seasoned mentor, a new client, or a young boy selling lemonade, there's a lesson waiting to be discovered. Embrace humility, and you'll find that the journey of growth and learning is both rewarding and endless.

Strategic Dismissal: Commanding Respect

In the intricate dance of sales, one of the most underestimated yet powerful moves you can make is the act of dismissal. At first glance, the idea of dismissing a potential client might seem counterintuitive. After all, isn't the goal to secure as many sales as possible? However, understanding and harnessing the power of dismissal can transform your approach, your energy, and ultimately, your success. The foundation of the power of dismissal lies in a deep understanding and appreciation of your own value. You bring a unique proposition to the table, built on your skills, knowledge, experience, and the quality of your product or service. Recognizing this value instills a sense of confidence that is palpable to your prospects. It's not about arrogance; it's about a quiet, unshakeable belief in what you offer.

Consider a scenario where a top-performing salesman, Alex, is pitching a high-end software solution to a prospective client. Throughout the meeting, the client seems disinterested and makes derogatory comments about the product's pricing and features. Instead of scrambling to appease the client, Alex calmly addresses the concerns and highlights the unique benefits of the software. When the client continues to show disrespect, Alex decides to end the meeting early, politely suggesting that perhaps their product isn't the right fit. This action isn't about dismissing the client as unworthy; it's about recognizing that the partnership wouldn't be mutually beneficial. Alex's confidence and decisiveness reinforce the value of the product and his own expertise.

The energy you project when you're willing to dismiss an applicant is profoundly different from the energy of desperation. Desperation is repellent; it signals to the prospect that you are uncertain, that you need them more than they need you. This imbalance can undermine your position and diminish the perceived value of your offering. On the other hand, the willingness to dismiss an applicant exudes strength and self-assurance. It communicates that you are not desperate for the sale because you are confident in the value of your proposition. Imagine a situation where two salespeople are vying for the same client. The first salesperson, Sarah, is eager to close the deal at any cost. She offers excessive discounts and makes numerous follow-ups, almost pleading for the client's business. The second salesperson, David, presents his offer confidently, addresses the client's needs, and sets clear boundaries. When the client tries to haggle aggressively, David remains firm, explaining the rationale behind the pricing and subtly indicating that if the client isn't interested, that's perfectly fine. In the end, the client gravitates towards David because his demeanor and approach suggest that his product is worth the investment.

Dismissal doesn't only serve to protect your energy and value; it also empowers your client. By showing that you are willing to walk away, you create a space for the client to reflect on the true worth of your offering. It shifts the dynamic, encouraging them to consider why they should work with you rather than why you should work with them. This psychological shift can lead to a more balanced and respectful negotiation. Consider the case of a real estate agent, Lisa, who is showing a luxury home to a potential buyer. The buyer continually makes lowball offers and disparaging remarks about the property. Lisa remains professional but firm, highlighting the home's unique features and the fair market value. When the buyer refuses to budge, Lisa thanks them for their time and suggests they might be happier with a different property. A few days later, the buyer returns, having reconsidered their approach, and makes a reasonable offer. Lisa's willingness to walk away had given the buyer the time and space to recognize the home's value on their own terms.

To illustrate the power of dismissal further, let's look at a case study involving a freelance graphic designer named Emily and a start-up company looking for a rebrand. Emily was highly sought after for her innovative designs and had a portfolio that showcased her talent and expertise. The start-up, impressed by her work, scheduled a meeting to discuss their vision. During the meeting, the start-up's CEO repeatedly questioned Emily's rates and suggested she should lower her prices since they were a new company. Instead of caving to the pressure, Emily stood her ground. She explained the value she brought to the table, the quality of her work, and how her designs could significantly enhance their brand image. When the CEO continued to push for a discount, Emily politely ended the meeting, stating that if they couldn't see the value in her work, it might be best for them to find another designer. A week later, the start-up CEO contacted Emily again, this time with a newfound respect. They agreed to her terms and even recommended her to other businesses. Emily's willingness to dismiss the client initially had reinforced her value, and ultimately led to a stronger, more respectful working relationship.

The power of dismissal is not about arrogance or turning away business without cause. It is about recognizing and asserting your value, projecting confidence, and creating a dynamic where the client is encouraged to see the worth in what you offer. This approach not only protects your energy and self-respect but also often leads to more meaningful and mutually beneficial client relationships. Remember, in the world of sales, it's not always about the quantity of deals you close but the quality of those engagements. By understanding and utilizing the power of dismissal, you position yourself as a professional who knows their worth and isn't afraid to stand by it. This confidence is contagious and often results in better outcomes for both you and your clients.

Leveraging Cialdini's Six Principles

Robert Cialdini's book "Influence: The Psychology of Persuasion" outlines six key principles that are invaluable in sales and personal interactions. This book probably changed my entire perspective on sales and marketing and is my overall #1 recommendation for those that would like to explore the psychology behind influence. Personally, it ignited a burning desire to understand the human psyche and social sciences. Understanding and applying these principles can enhance your ability to influence others ethically and effectively, transforming your approach and driving success. The foundation of these principles lies in recognizing and leveraging psychological triggers that drive human behavior. These principles are not just theoretical concepts but practical tools that can be seamlessly integrated into your sales strategy to create meaningful and lasting relationships with your clients.

Reciprocity is the principle that people feel obligated to return favors and acts of kindness. This deeply ingrained social norm can be leveraged in sales to create a sense of obligation. An example of this principle in action is the story of monks who give flowers or small gifts to people on the street. After receiving the gift, many people feel a social obligation to give a donation, even if they didn't initially plan to. In sales, offering something valuable to potential customers without expecting immediate returns can trigger the reciprocity principle. This could be a free trial, an informative eBook, or exceptional customer service. While something of great value is ideal, a gesture as simple as offering a bottle of water at the beginning of the meeting, even if they decline, will subconsciously trigger this reciprocity principle. When customers receive something of value first, they are more inclined to reciprocate by making a purchase or showing loyalty. A software company offering a free month of their premium service demonstrates this principle well. Users who experience the benefits firsthand are more likely to subscribe after the trial period ends, feeling they have already received significant value.

The next principle of commitment and consistency highlight that people have a desire to be consistent with what they have previously said or done. Once individuals commit to something, they are more likely to follow through with consistent actions. The Foot-in-the-Door Technique exemplifies this principle, where researchers found that people who agreed to place a small sign in their yard promoting safe driving were significantly more likely to agree to a larger, more obtrusive sign later on. In sales, starting with small commitments can be highly effective. For instance, getting a customer to sign up for your newsletter or take a brief survey increases the likelihood that they will make larger commitments, such as purchasing a product or service. A charity asking potential donors to sign a petition supporting their cause is a practical application of this principle. Once the petition is signed, the donors are more likely to contribute financially because they want to be consistent with their initial support.

Social proof is the phenomenon where people look to the actions of others to determine their own, especially in uncertain or unfamiliar situations. The Elevator Experiment is a striking example, where individuals in an elevator conformed to the actions of others, such as facing the wrong direction, simply because everyone else was doing it. In sales, displaying reviews, testimonials, and case studies prominently can build social proof. Highlighting how many people are using and benefiting from your product reassures potential customers that they are making a good decision. An online retailer that prominently displays customer reviews and ratings on their product pages sees significantly higher conversion rates, demonstrating the power of social proof. I've seen this as a wall of pictures of happy customers, but the most intriguing study that I can recall is the one where the researchers just stood looking up in awe at the sky. Slowly but surely others began to look up at the sky until everyone in the vicinity looked up at the sky to see what was going on. There was nothing there, though the onlookers began to believe there was, there was just an experiment that demonstrated social proof and how people tend to act.

Authority explains that people are more likely to be influenced by individuals they perceive as authorities or experts. The Milgram Experiment, where participants were willing to administer what they believed were painful electric shocks to others because an authoritative figure in a lab coat instructed them to do so, is a stark example of this principle. In sales, positioning yourself or your brand as an authority in your industry can be achieved through professional certifications, endorsements from experts, and publishing insightful content that demonstrates expertise. A health supplement brand partnering with well-known doctors and nutritionists who endorse their products significantly boosts consumer trust and sales. Surprisingly, this is why companies pay millions of dollars to celebrities to tell you to drink their drink or eat their snack. If they are willing to pay millions per year for this endorsement based almost solely on this principle, it must be worth trying to incorporate into your sales strategy.

Liking shows that people are more likely to comply with requests from individuals they like. Factors that increase likability include physical attractiveness, similarities, compliments, and cooperation. Tupperware Parties exemplify this principle, as products are sold through social gatherings where the host, often a friend or acquaintance, presents the products. People are more likely to buy from someone they know and like. In sales, building genuine relationships with your customers by showing empathy, finding common interests, and being personable can significantly influence purchasing decisions. A car salesperson who takes time to get to know their customers, asking about their needs and preferences, creates a comfortable environment that encourages sales.

Scarcity is the principle that people assign more value to opportunities that are less available. Limited availability can create a sense of urgency and desirability. Retail stores often use phrases like "Only 2 left in stock!" or "Sale ends tomorrow!" to create urgency and prompt immediate purchases. In sales, highlighting the limited availability of your products or promotions can be very effective. Using time-sensitive offers and emphasizing unique features that are hard to find elsewhere can drive urgency. An e-commerce site that advertises a flash sale with a countdown timer often sees a spike in purchases as customers rush to take advantage of the deal.

Combining these six principles creates a powerful, cohesive strategy for mastering influence and sales. Begin by offering a valuable freebie or service to invoke the principle of reciprocity. Once the customer accepts, encourage them to make a small commitment, such as subscribing to a newsletter or joining a loyalty program. This initial engagement makes them more likely to continue interacting with your brand. Use testimonials, reviews, and case studies to build social proof, and showcase endorsements from experts and highlight your credentials to establish authority. This dual approach reassures potential customers of your credibility and the value of your product. Build rapport with customers by being personable and finding common ground to leverage the principle of liking. Create a sense of urgency by emphasizing the limited availability of your offer, whether through time-sensitive promotions or exclusive deals.

Imagine you are selling a premium fitness program. You start by offering a free one-week trial, tapping into the principle of reciprocity. During the trial, you encourage users to complete daily check-ins and share their progress, fostering a sense of commitment and consistency. On your website and in follow-up emails, you display testimonials and before-and-after photos of satisfied clients to build social proof, and highlight endorsements from fitness experts and certifications to establish authority. During interactions, you engage with users on social media, offering personalized advice and building a community, thereby increasing your likability. You also promote a limited-time discount for those who sign up within the next 48 hours, creating a sense of scarcity.

By weaving these principles together, you create a powerful, ethical influence strategy that not only drives sales but also fosters trust and long-term customer relationships. Mastering the six virtues of influence—reciprocity, commitment and consistency, social proof, authority, liking, and scarcity—allows you to ethically and effectively influence others. By understanding and applying these principles, you can enhance your sales techniques, build stronger relationships, and create lasting value for your customers. The key is to integrate these principles seamlessly, ensuring that each interaction is authentic, respectful, and focused on genuinely helping your customers achieve their goals. By doing so, you not only achieve sales success but also build a reputation for integrity and excellence in your field.

Power of Testimonials: Social Proof

Testimonials are the gold standard in the world of sales. They are powerful tools that can transform a hesitant prospect into a confident customer. Testimonials leverage the power of social proof, demonstrating that others have benefited from your product or service. When used effectively, testimonials can be one of the most compelling elements in your sales arsenal. Let's delve into the power of testimonials, how they can close sales, and how to obtain valuable ones. The impact of testimonials cannot be overstated. Studies have shown that testimonials can significantly impact consumer behavior. According to a survey by BrightLocal, 88% of consumers trust online reviews as much as personal recommendations. Furthermore, a study by Spiegel Research Center found that displaying reviews can increase conversion rates by 270%. These statistics highlight the critical role that testimonials play in influencing purchasing decisions.

There is a marked difference between good and bad testimonials. For instance, a good testimonial might say: "Working with Joey's team was a game-changer for our business. We saw a 40% increase in sales within the first three months. The professionalism, dedication, and results-driven approach were unparalleled. I highly recommend Joey's services to any business looking to grow." This testimonial is effective because it is specific, mentions measurable outcomes, and reflects positively on the service and the provider's attributes. On the other hand, a bad testimonial might read: "Joey's service was good. We were satisfied with the results." This testimonial is vague and lacks specifics. It doesn't provide any measurable outcomes or highlight particular strengths, making it far less compelling.

Obtaining valuable testimonials requires asking at the right time. Timing is crucial when requesting testimonials. Ask for feedback when your customer has just experienced a positive outcome or completed a successful project. This is when their satisfaction is highest, and they're most likely to provide a glowing review. Make it easy for your customers to provide testimonials by simplifying the process. Provide them with a template or a few guiding questions to help them structure their testimonial. This could include asking about the specific problem they faced, how your product or service helped solve it, and the tangible results they experienced.

Being specific is another critical aspect of collecting testimonials. Encourage your customers to include specific details in their testimonials. Ask them to mention any measurable outcomes, such as increased sales, time saved, or improved efficiency. Specifics add credibility and make the testimonial more relatable to potential customers. Highlight different aspects of your service or product by collecting testimonials that address various facets. This could include customer service, ease of use, results achieved, and overall experience. A well-rounded collection of testimonials can address different concerns and interests of your prospects. Video testimonials can be even more persuasive than written ones. They allow potential customers to see and hear from real people, adding an extra layer of authenticity and trust. If possible, ask your customers to provide a short video testimonial. The energy of testimonials is undeniable. When you confidently present testimonials, you exude an energy of certainty and reliability. Prospects can sense this confidence, and it reassures them about the decision they are making. Knowing that others have had positive experiences with your product or service makes prospects more comfortable and excited to move forward.

Crafting your testimonial strategy involves identifying your best customers who have had particularly positive experiences with your product or service. These individuals are likely to provide the most enthusiastic and detailed testimonials. Always ask for permission before using a customer's testimonial. This is not only respectful but also ensures that you comply with any legal or privacy requirements. Showcase testimonials strategically by placing them prominently on your website, in marketing materials, and during sales presentations. Highlight the ones that address common concerns or showcase impressive results. Keep testimonials updated to maintain their relevance and freshness. As your business grows and evolves, ensure that your testimonials reflect your latest successes and offerings.

Personally, I kept a blue binder of about 25-35 testimonials when I was still selling, these went back over two decades and I really just kept the ones that I loved, the lives that I really changed and every time I looked through the book it put a smile on my face. One time I had an older woman named Lucille follow up with me once a week for over a year just because she was grateful of the job I did for her and told me I saved her life. When clients came to the office, I would ask them to have a seat and hand them my testimonial binder prior to heading into my office to clean up and finish up a couple key tasks. Either that or my admin would seat them and offer water and hand them the book depending on what stage of my career we are talking about. I'll never forget the time I spoke with the owner of a well water company who said he mails hundreds of testimonials to anyone who asks for them. While that is one way to do it and an impressive way, I would probably just scan them and upload to the cloud and offer a QR code to any and all of my clients if I kept hundreds or thousands of testimonials.

  In conclusion, the power of testimonials cannot be overstated. They are a testament to the value and effectiveness of your product or service, offering potential customers the reassurance they need to take the leap and make a purchase. Beyond that, they reflect on your character and trustworthiness, showcasing your dedication to delivering results. Testimonials also provide invaluable feedback, highlighting any blind spots that may need your attention. By mastering the art of obtaining and utilizing testimonials, you can significantly enhance your sales process and close more deals. Embrace the power of social proof, and let the voices of your satisfied customers pave the way to your success. Testimonials are, without a doubt, one of the greatest and easiest tools to procure, helping you become the best salesman and unravel the complexities of the salesman's paradox.

Delivery of Exceptional Customer Service

In the competitive world of sales and business, great customer service is the linchpin that can set you apart from your competitors. It is the key to building strong, lasting relationships with your customers and ensuring their loyalty. The value of exceptional customer service cannot be overstated—it can lead to repeat business, positive word-of-mouth referrals, and a stellar reputation. Exceptional customer service goes beyond addressing customer inquiries or complaints; it involves anticipating their needs, exceeding their expectations, and creating a positive experience at every touchpoint. Acquiring new customers is essential, but retaining existing ones is even more crucial. Studies show that it costs five times more to attract a new customer than to keep an existing one. Great customer service fosters loyalty and encourages repeat business. Positive customer experiences translate into positive reviews, testimonials, and word-of-mouth referrals. A strong reputation for exceptional customer service can be your most powerful marketing tool. In a crowded market, outstanding customer service can be your unique selling proposition. Happy customers are more likely to make additional purchases and recommend your business to others. According to research, improving customer retention rates by just 5% can increase profits by 25% to 95%.

To truly understand the value of great customer service, it's essential to break down its core components and see how they contribute to the overall customer experience. Empathy is the ability to understand and share the feelings of others. In customer service, it involves putting yourself in the customer's shoes and viewing their concerns from their perspective. Empathy helps in building a connection with the customer and shows that you genuinely care about their experience. Imagine a customer who is frustrated because their order was delayed. An empathetic response would be, "I understand how frustrating this must be for you. I'm really sorry for the inconvenience. Let me see what I can do to resolve this issue as quickly as possible." Being responsive means addressing customer inquiries, complaints, and feedback promptly. Customers appreciate timely responses, as it shows that their concerns are a priority. Quick resolution of issues can turn a negative experience into a positive one. If a customer emails about a malfunctioning product, a prompt reply acknowledging the issue and providing steps for a solution can significantly improve their perception of your business.

Clear and effective communication is vital in customer service. It involves actively listening to customers, providing clear information, and keeping them informed about any updates or changes. Good communication helps in managing customer expectations and preventing misunderstandings. Keeping a customer informed about the status of their order, including any delays or shipping updates, helps manage their expectations and reduces anxiety. Personalization involves tailoring your interactions to meet the specific needs and preferences of each customer. It makes customers feel valued and appreciated. Personalization can be as simple as using the customer's name or as complex as offering customized solutions based on their previous interactions. A customer service representative who remembers a customer's previous purchases and suggests complementary products is providing a personalized experience that can enhance customer satisfaction. Effective problem-solving skills are crucial for great customer service. It involves identifying the root cause of an issue, finding a suitable solution, and ensuring the customer is satisfied with the outcome. A proactive approach to problem-solving can turn a negative experience into a positive one. If a customer receives a damaged product, promptly offering a replacement or refund, along with a sincere apology, demonstrates effective problem-solving and can restore the customer's trust.

Creating great customer service starts with your attitude and approach towards each customer interaction. Here are some strategies to ensure your customers have an exceptional experience every time they engage with you or your business. First, always greet your customers with a genuine smile and a warm welcome. This sets a positive tone for the interaction and makes the customer feel valued right from the start. One of the silliest but effective recommendations I have is to place a small mirror at your desk and take a look at yourself prior to making or receiving a call. Think, would I want to work with this person, and then let the call commence. Your smile and positivity can be heard/ felt through the call or through whichever medium is used for communication. When addressing their needs, actively listen without interrupting. This not only shows respect but also helps you understand their concerns fully, allowing you to provide a more accurate and helpful response.

Secondly, personalize your interactions. Use the customer's name and refer to their previous interactions or purchases to make them feel special. You can use sir or ma'am or a preferred honorific regardless if the customer is younger or less established than you are. You'd be surprised at how often the ego can get in the way of salesmen I have trained. This small effort goes a long way in building a strong rapport and demonstrating that you care about them as an individual, not just a transaction. Next, be proactive in solving problems. Don't wait for the customer to express their frustration. If you notice a potential issue, address it before it escalates. This proactive approach can prevent dissatisfaction and show the customer that you are committed to their satisfaction. Follow up with your customers after resolving an issue or completing a sale. A simple call or email to check if they are satisfied with their purchase or if there is anything else you can assist them with can leave a lasting positive impression. Always seek feedback from your customers. Encourage them to share their thoughts on their experience with your service. Use this feedback to continually improve and adapt your approach. By showing that you value their opinions and are willing to make changes based on their input, you reinforce their importance to your business.

To illustrate the transformative power of great customer service, let's consider a hypothetical scenario involving a company called "TechSolutions." Sarah, a small business owner, purchases a software package from TechSolutions to streamline her operations. After installing the software, she encounters several technical issues that disrupt her business processes. Frustrated and on the verge of returning the product, she contacts TechSolutions' customer service. Sarah is greeted by a friendly and empathetic customer service representative named Alex. Alex listens attentively to Sarah's concerns and apologizes for the inconvenience. He immediately schedules a remote session to diagnose and resolve the technical issues. During the session, Alex patiently guides Sarah through the troubleshooting process and ensures that the software is working perfectly. He also provides Sarah with additional resources and tips to maximize the software's benefits. Sarah is not only satisfied with the resolution but is also impressed by the level of support she received. She decides to keep the software and even recommends TechSolutions to other business owners in her network. TechSolutions gains a loyal customer and positive word-of-mouth referrals, all thanks to exceptional customer service.

Great customer service is a powerful driver of business success. It builds customer loyalty, enhances your brand reputation, and sets you apart from the competition. By understanding the components of great customer service and implementing strategies to cultivate it, you can create a positive and lasting impact on your customers. Every interaction with a customer is an opportunity to demonstrate your commitment to their satisfaction. By prioritizing empathy, responsiveness, communication, personalization, and problem-solving, you can deliver exceptional service that keeps customers coming back and singing your praises. In the end, the value of great customer service lies in its ability to turn customers into advocates and ensure the long-term success of your business.

Handling Objections with Grace

Handling objections is a vital skill for any salesperson, but it's more than just about closing the sale. It's about understanding, empathy, and truly caring for the customer's needs and concerns. Let's delve into how to handle objections with finesse, compassion, and a proactive approach. Firstly, it's essential to understand that objections are a natural part of the sales process. They are not personal attacks but rather opportunities to address concerns and provide clarity. Objections often stem from uncertainty, misinformation, or previous negative experiences. By addressing these head-on, you demonstrate your commitment to helping the client make an informed decision. When a prospect raises an objection, the most important thing you can do is listen—really listen. Hear them out without interrupting. This shows respect and gives you a full understanding of their concern. For instance, if a customer says, "I'm not sure this is within my budget," don't jump straight into explaining the cost benefits. Instead, say, "I understand that budget is a concern. Can you tell me more about your financial priorities right now?" We'll talk more about this during the extraction phase of the sale, but being able to create a situation where your customer believes in you and you trust in them is paramount to the success of you as a salesman.

By going deeper, you show empathy and gain valuable insights into their situation, which will help you address the objection more effectively. Once you've listened, it's crucial to validate their concerns. Acknowledge that their feelings are legitimate. This doesn't mean you agree with the objection but rather that you understand why they feel that way. For example, "I can see why you might be concerned about the cost. Many of our clients initially felt the same way." This approach not only builds trust but also opens the door for you to provide reassurance and solutions. Now, you can gently guide the conversation towards reassurance. Share stories or examples of other clients who had similar concerns but found value in your product or service. Use testimonials or case studies to illustrate your points. For example, "One of our clients, John, also hesitated because of budget constraints. However, after using our product, he realized the return on investment far exceeded the initial cost."

This technique not only addresses the objection but also reinforces the benefits of your offering. Arm yourself with information and be ready to counter objections with facts and benefits. If a client is worried about the reliability of your product, provide data or third-party reviews that highlight its dependability. If they are concerned about integration with their current systems, offer a demonstration or a trial period. For instance, if a client says, "I'm not sure this will work with our existing software," you could respond with, "I understand your concern. In fact, we offer a seamless integration process and have a dedicated support team to assist you every step of the way. Let me show you how it works."

One of the best ways to handle objections is to anticipate them before they arise. This requires a deep understanding of your product and the common concerns prospects may have. During your pitch, address potential objections proactively. For example, "You might be wondering if this product fits within your budget. Let me explain how the cost is justified by the benefits you'll receive." One caveat here is that you never want to enter a potential concern if it does not exist with the customer. If a prospect has been referencing a concern like saying, "I have enough money for this" or "it's not outside of my budget" then you may pick up on the subtle cues and use this method. If there has been no reference to the issue then do not create a potential issue for the prospect to consider.

Using this method, you demonstrate foresight and confidence, reducing the likelihood of objections derailing the conversation later on. Sometimes, objections can be vague or rooted in deeper, unspoken concerns. Don't hesitate to seek clarification. Ask open-ended questions to uncover the real issue. For example, "Can you tell me more about why you feel this product might not be a good fit?" This not only shows your willingness to understand but also helps you address the true objection effectively. Even after addressing objections, some prospects may still need time to process the information. Follow up with them compassionately. Send a thoughtful email or make a call to see if they have any further questions. Reinforce your availability and willingness to assist them.

Patience is crucial in handling objections. Rushing to close the sale can backfire. Give your prospects the space to voice their concerns and the time to consider your responses. Sometimes, a little patience can turn a hesitant client into a loyal one. Handling objections is not just about countering resistance; it's about building trust, showing empathy, and demonstrating genuine care for your client's needs. It's an opportunity to prove your commitment to their success. Remember, every objection is a chance to strengthen your relationship with your prospect and to showcase the value you bring.

In your journey as a salesperson, you'll encounter many objections. Embrace them as opportunities to learn, to grow, and to connect more deeply with your clients. By handling objections with compassion and confidence, you transform potential roadblocks into stepping stones for a successful, trust-filled relationship. Keep your focus on the client's needs, and you'll find that objections become less of a hurdle and more of a pathway to mutual success. As we tie this chapter up, I'd like to look at objections from the position of being on their side. Approach an objection not like it is you and your product versus the customer rather you and your customer using your product versus their problem. If you can truly work that out then overcoming objections will be a simple path to ensuring great success for both you and the client.

Transparency Builds Trust

Transparency is a cornerstone of trust, and trust is the foundation of any successful sales relationship. Being open and honest with your clients can significantly enhance your credibility, foster stronger connections, and ultimately lead to more successful sales outcomes. Transparency in sales means being open about your product or service, your processes, and your intentions. When you are transparent, you build trust, and trust leads to stronger, longer-lasting relationships. When clients feel you are honest and forthcoming, they are more likely to trust you and your recommendations. By being transparent, you set clear and realistic expectations, which reduces the chances of dissatisfaction and increases their confidence in your product or service. Honesty and transparency enhance your credibility. When clients know that you are open about both the strengths and limitations of your product, they see you as a credible and reliable source of information. Transparency ensures that clients have all the necessary information to make informed decisions, helping them feel more confident in their choice and reducing the likelihood of buyer's remorse.

In today's market, consumers are more informed and discerning than ever before. They have access to a wealth of information at their fingertips and can easily research and compare products. With the internet, consumers can quickly discover discrepancies between what you've told them and what they find online, which can damage your credibility and trust. Transparency can be a significant competitive advantage. Many companies are still hesitant to be fully transparent, fearing it will expose their weaknesses and I've seen this firsthand as I'm sure you have as well. By being open and honest, you differentiate yourself from competitors and position yourself as a trustworthy and reliable partner. Sales is not just about making a single transaction; it's about building long-term relationships. This potentially minor interaction to you may be an opportunity to make a lifelong impact on your client. Transparency fosters trust and loyalty, which are crucial for long-term success and repeat business.

While transparency is essential, it's also important to strike the right balance.

Always be honest, but be strategic about how much information you share at once. Focus on the information that is most relevant to the client's needs and concerns. When a client raises a concern or objection, address it directly and honestly. Don't try to evade or downplay the issue. Instead, provide clear and concise information that addresses their concern. Be open about both the strengths and limitations of your product. Clients appreciate honesty, and being upfront about limitations can actually increase your credibility. My meetings typically include the phrase - there are downsides too, but the benefits way outweigh the negative.

Transparency can be enhanced through the use of testimonials and case studies. These provide real-world examples of how your product has helped other clients and offer a balanced view of the benefits and potential challenges. While transparency is crucial, there is such a thing as too much information. Too much information can be overwhelming and counterproductive. Focus on the most relevant information and avoid bombarding clients with excessive details. Different clients have different needs and concerns. Tailor your level of transparency to each client's specific situation. Some clients may appreciate a deep dive into technical details, while others may prefer a high-level overview. Refer back to our section on different personality types and how to determine them to help you with what information may be the most appropriate.

While it's important to be honest about limitations, always frame them in a positive light. Focus on how your product can still meet the client's needs and how any limitations can be managed or mitigated. Too little transparency can create suspicion and mistrust. Don't wait for clients to ask questions or raise concerns. Proactively provide information that you know will be important to them. This demonstrates that you are knowledgeable and trustworthy. Ensure that your communication is clear and concise. Avoid jargon or overly technical language that can confuse clients. For those of us that used to serve in the military, regular people don't know the hundreds of military acronyms we used. Use straightforward language that is easy to understand. After providing information, follow up with the client to ensure they understood everything and to address any additional questions or concerns. This shows that you care about their understanding and satisfaction.

Also don't downplay or put potential issues in the minds of your clients. I was training a young man one time in recruiting who stated that he doesn't fall into the traditional stereotypes of recruiters. He doesn't lie, can't pressure people, etc. While I appreciated the effort of thinking outside of the box, you never want to put reasons to doubt you or your product in the mind of the client or customer. By making those statements, the client who probably wasn't thinking of those potential issues now has them in his mind. While the salesman was trying to overcome potential barriers before they became an issue, it was clear that his bias against the stereotypical salesman was affecting his approach. There's transparency, and then there's unnecessary divulging of information. This example was the latter.

Transparency is a powerful tool in sales. It builds trust, creates realistic expectations, and enhances your credibility. By finding the right balance and being honest and strategic, you can foster stronger relationships and achieve greater success. Clients value honesty and integrity. By being transparent, you not only meet their needs but also demonstrate your commitment to their success. Embrace transparency, don't say more than what should be said and you'll find that it paves the way for lasting relationships and sustained success.

Obnoxious Optimism: Creating Silver Lining

Optimism is a powerful force. It can transform a mundane day into an extraordinary one, turn challenges into opportunities, and infuse life with a sense of hope and possibility. When it comes to sales, optimism isn't just a nice-to-have trait; it's a vital tool that can shape outcomes and build lasting relationships. I like to call this approach "obnoxious optimism," where we bring an overwhelming wave of positivity into every sales situation and every moment in life, pushing away negativity and setting the stage for success.

Optimism begins with a mindset. It's about choosing to see the potential in every situation, believing in positive outcomes, and focusing on the good even when faced with challenges. In sales, this mindset is crucial. When you approach each interaction with optimism, you create a positive energy that is contagious. Clients and prospects can sense your enthusiasm and positivity, and it often influences their own attitudes and decisions. Optimism breeds confidence. When you believe in a positive outcome, you exude confidence that reassures your clients. They are more likely to trust your recommendations and feel good about their decisions. It's about resilience. Sales can be tough, and setbacks are inevitable. It's that optimistic mindset that helps you bounce back from rejections and keep moving forward with renewed energy and determination.

Optimism doesn't just transform sales; it transforms life. When you carry a positive attitude into every aspect of your life, you create a ripple effect that touches everything and everyone around you. You become a beacon of light in a world that often feels heavy with negativity. Optimism attracts positive experiences and people. When you focus on the good, you naturally draw more good into your life. It's a self-fulfilling prophecy that leads to a happier, more fulfilling life. Challenges become opportunities for growth. With an optimistic mindset, you see obstacles as chances to learn, grow, and become stronger. This resilience is key to personal and professional success. Optimism fosters better relationships. When you approach interactions with positivity, you create deeper, more meaningful connections. People are drawn to your positive energy and are more likely to respond in kind.

In sales, optimism is a game-changer. It can turn a hesitant prospect into an enthusiastic client and transform a challenging situation into a successful outcome. Here's how to infuse your sales process with optimism: Start each day with a positive intention. Set the tone for your day by focusing on what you're grateful for and what you hope to achieve. This mindset will carry through to your interactions with clients. When discussing your product or service, highlight the positive impact it can have on your client's life or business. Focus on the benefits and the value it brings. When faced with objections or challenges, maintain a positive attitude. See these moments as opportunities to better understand your client's needs and find creative solutions. Celebrate every win, no matter how small. Recognize and appreciate your successes, and use them as fuel to keep moving forward with optimism.

Optimism is powerful in life. It can change your perspective, influence your experiences, and improve your overall well-being. Here's how to embrace optimism in every aspect of your life: Surround yourself with positive influences. Spend time with people who uplift and inspire you, and limit your exposure to negativity. Focus on solutions, not problems. When faced with a challenge, shift your focus to finding a solution rather than dwelling on the problem. Practice gratitude. Take time each day to reflect on what you're grateful for. This simple practice can shift your mindset and help you see the good in every situation. Be kind and compassionate. Approach every interaction with kindness and empathy. Even when someone is rude or disrespectful, choose to respond with positivity. Kill them with kindness, as I'm sure you've heard. Your optimism can diffuse negativity and create a more positive environment.

Let's face it: not everyone will respond to your optimism with open arms. Some people are set in their negative ways, and others might even see your positivity as naive or annoying. But this is where the real power of obnoxious optimism shines. When someone is rude or disrespectful, choose to respond with kindness and positivity. This doesn't mean being a pushover; it means maintaining your positive attitude regardless of their negativity. By doing so, you take control of the situation and refuse to let their negativity affect you. People often mirror the behavior they see. When you respond to negativity with positivity, you set an example for others to follow. Over time, your optimism can influence those around you and create a more positive environment. Staying positive doesn't mean ignoring problems or challenges. It means addressing them with a hopeful attitude and a focus on solutions. This approach can lead to more creative and effective outcomes. You want to be known as the type of person who can spin any situation into a positive and create an opportunity of any scenario.

Here's a story that illustrates the power of obnoxious optimism. I once worked with a client who was notoriously difficult. He was skeptical, critical, and often downright rude. But I decided to approach every interaction with unwavering optimism. No matter how negative he was, I responded with positivity. During one particularly tough meeting, he was tearing apart my proposal, pointing out every flaw he could find, actually fabricate. Instead of getting defensive, I acknowledged his concerns and responded with enthusiasm about the solutions I could offer. By the end of the meeting, something shifted. He started to soften, and eventually, he agreed to move forward with the project. Later, he admitted that my positive attitude had won him over. He said, "I was ready to walk away, but your optimism made me believe that we could make this work." That experience reinforced the power of optimism in sales and life. It's not about ignoring challenges or being unrealistically positive. It's about choosing to focus on the good, finding solutions, and maintaining a hopeful attitude, even in the face of negativity.

Optimism is a powerful tool that can transform your sales approach and your life. By embracing obnoxious optimism, you create a positive energy that influences those around you, builds trust, and fosters stronger relationships. Remember, your attitude is contagious. When you choose to be optimistic, you not only improve your own life but also positively impact the lives of others. So, bring that wave of positivity into every interaction, and watch as it transforms your world.

"Can Do" Mentality: Unwavering Belief

Perseverance is the cornerstone of success in any endeavor. The "If it can be done, I can do it" mentality embodies the spirit of relentless determination, a refusal to give up in the face of adversity, and a commitment to continuous improvement. This chapter delves into the power of perseverance, drawing inspiration from historical figures and timeless examples that showcase the indomitable human spirit.

Henry Ford famously captured the essence of perseverance in his speech, "The Man in the Arena," where he said: "It is not the critic who counts; not the man who points out how the strong man stumbles, or where the doer of deeds could have done them better. The credit belongs to the man who is actually in the arena, whose face is marred by dust and sweat and blood; who strives valiantly; who errs, who comes short again and again, because there is no effort without error and shortcoming; but who does actually strive to do the deeds; who knows great enthusiasms, the great devotions; who spends himself in a worthy cause; who at the best knows in the end the triumph of high achievement, and who at the worst, if he fails, at least fails while daring greatly, so that his place shall never be with those cold and timid souls who neither know victory nor defeat."

This quote encapsulates the spirit of perseverance—embracing failure as a part of the journey, learning from it, and continuing to push forward despite the challenges. Take, for instance, Colonel Harland Sanders. At the age of 65, after being turned down 1,009 times while trying to sell his fried chicken recipe, he finally found a partner who believed in him. His recipe became Kentucky Fried Chicken, a global brand known and loved by millions. Sanders' story teaches us that age is just a number and that persistence, even in the face of repeated rejection, can eventually lead to monumental success.

Thomas Edison, the inventor of the lightbulb, famously failed thousands of times before he succeeded. Edison didn't view these attempts as failures but as necessary steps to finding the right solution. When asked about his many failures, Edison responded, "I have not failed. I've just found 10,000 ways that won't work."

This perspective on failure is crucial—each setback is an opportunity to learn and improve, bringing you one step closer to success. Similarly, sliced bread, which we now take for granted as a staple in households, didn't catch on immediately. Invented by Otto Frederick Rohwedder in 1928, it faced initial skepticism and resistance. It wasn't until the 1930s, when the Wonder Bread brand started marketing it aggressively, that sliced bread gained widespread acceptance. This example illustrates that even great ideas may take time to be recognized and appreciated, and perseverance in promoting and refining them is essential.

Embracing a "fail forward" mindset means viewing failure not as a dead-end but as a learning experience. Each failure provides valuable insights and lessons that can be applied to future endeavors. This mindset encourages continuous growth and development, fostering resilience and adaptability. Consider the story of J.K. Rowling, who faced numerous rejections before finding a publisher for her first Harry Potter book. Despite being a single mother on welfare, she persevered, believing in her story and its potential. Her determination paid off, and today, Harry Potter is one of the best-selling book series of all time, inspiring millions worldwide. Another example is the journey of Walt Disney, who was fired from a newspaper for "lacking imagination" and faced multiple business failures before creating the iconic Disneyland and Disney brand. Disney's vision and perseverance transformed the entertainment industry, leaving a lasting legacy of creativity and innovation.

In sales, this mentality translates to not being discouraged by rejections or setbacks. Each "no" brings you closer to a "yes," and each challenge is an opportunity to refine your approach. Building resilience, staying motivated, and continuously improving your skills are crucial for long-term success.

Practical Ways to Build Perseverance:

1. **Utilize Online Resources**: The internet is a treasure trove of information and inspiration. Platforms like YouTube offer countless tutorials, motivational talks, and success stories. Watching videos of successful individuals in your field can provide practical advice and the motivation to keep going. For example, if you're in sales, look for videos by top salespeople who share their techniques and strategies. I particularly enjoy

the motivational mash-ups and when I find one I like, I'll save it to play any time I am struggling to find the obnoxious optimism I am known for.
2. **Research and Learn from Others**: Seek out articles, books, and online courses related to your endeavor. Websites like Coursera, Udemy, and LinkedIn Learning offer courses taught by experts in various fields. Learning from those who have succeeded before you can provide valuable insights and shortcuts to success.
3. **Network with Successful Individuals**: Attend industry conferences, webinars, and networking events to meet successful individuals in your field. Connecting with mentors and peers can provide support, guidance, and new perspectives. Online forums and social media groups related to your industry are also great places to network and learn from others.
4. **Set Small, Achievable Goals**: Break down your larger goals into smaller, manageable tasks. This not only makes the process less daunting but also provides a sense of accomplishment as you complete each step. Celebrate these small victories to keep your motivation high.
5. **Embrace a Growth Mindset**: Adopting a growth mindset means believing that your abilities can be developed through dedication and hard work. This perspective encourages learning and resilience in the face of challenges. Remind yourself that each failure is an opportunity to grow and improve.
6. **Reflect and Adapt**: Regularly take time to reflect on your progress and learn from your experiences. Adjust your strategies based on what you have learned and keep moving forward. Keeping a journal to document your journey can help you track your progress and stay focused on your goals.
7. **Stay Positive**: Maintain a positive attitude and focus on your strengths. Surround yourself with supportive people who encourage and uplift you. Positive thinking can significantly impact your perseverance and overall success.

To cultivate this mentality, set clear goals, maintain a positive attitude, and surround yourself with supportive and like-minded individuals. Celebrate small victories along the way, and don't be afraid to take calculated risks. Remember, perseverance is not just about enduring hardship but about pushing through it with a purpose, knowing that every step forward, no matter how small, is progress. In conclusion, the "If it can be done, I can do it" mentality is about embracing challenges, learning from failures, and relentlessly pursuing your goals. Whether it's Colonel Sanders' relentless pursuit of sharing his chicken recipe, Edison's determination to create the lightbulb, or the eventual success of sliced bread, these stories remind us that perseverance, resilience, and an unwavering belief in oneself are the keys to achieving greatness. By leveraging practical tools and resources, continuously learning from others, and maintaining a positive and growth-oriented mindset, you can overcome any obstacle and achieve your dreams.

Believing in Yourself: Confidence is Key

Faith in yourself is a vital component of success in any endeavor. Believing in your abilities and potential gives you the courage to take risks, the strength to persevere, and the resilience to bounce back from failures. This chapter explores the importance of self-belief, offers practical strategies for cultivating and maintaining it, and includes introspective talks and mantras to help you through adversity.

Self-belief is the foundation of confidence. It allows you to face challenges head-on, venture into the unknown, and persist even when the going gets tough. Having faith in yourself means trusting your judgment, capabilities, and potential to succeed. It is this inner confidence that propels you forward, even in the face of setbacks. Think of Michael Jordan, widely regarded as one of the greatest basketball players of all time. Jordan was cut from his high school basketball team, an experience that could have easily discouraged him. Instead, he used it as motivation to work harder and improve his game. His unwavering belief in his abilities played a crucial role in his journey to becoming a legend in the sport. Similarly, Oprah Winfrey, a global media mogul, faced numerous challenges and rejections in her early career. Despite these obstacles, she remained steadfast in her belief that she could succeed. Her faith in herself, coupled with hard work and determination, ultimately led her to achieve unparalleled success.

Building and maintaining faith in yourself requires deliberate effort and introspection. One way to strengthen your self-belief is through positive self-talk and mantras. Your inner dialogue profoundly impacts your self-belief. Replace negative thoughts with positive affirmations and mantras that reinforce your confidence. Some powerful mantras include "I am capable of achieving my goals," "I trust in my abilities and strengths," and "Every challenge I face is an opportunity for growth." Repeating these affirmations daily can help shift your mindset and strengthen your belief in yourself. Engage in introspective practices like journaling, meditation, and mindfulness to connect with your inner self. Reflect on your achievements, strengths, and areas for improvement. Acknowledge your progress and celebrate your successes, no matter how small. This practice helps you develop a deeper understanding of yourself and fosters self-belief.

Setting realistic goals is another crucial aspect of building self-belief. Breaking down your larger goals into smaller, achievable milestones boosts your confidence and reinforces your belief in your ability to succeed. Each step forward, no matter how small, is a testament to your capabilities. Surrounding yourself with supportive and positive individuals who believe in you and your potential can also bolster your self-confidence. Seek out mentors, friends, and colleagues who encourage and uplift you. Their belief in you can reinforce your own self-confidence.

Viewing failures as opportunities to learn and grow rather than as reflections of your worth is essential for maintaining self-belief. Understand that setbacks are a natural part of the journey to success. Embrace the "fail forward" mentality, where each failure provides valuable lessons that contribute to your growth. Visualization is a powerful tool for building self-belief. Spend time each day visualizing yourself achieving your goals. Picture the steps you need to take, the obstacles you might face, and the feeling of accomplishment when you succeed. Visualization reinforces your belief in your ability to achieve your dreams.

In a fascinating study published in 2004 in the *Journal of Neurophysiology* by Guang Yue, an exercise psychologist at the Cleveland Clinic Foundation, researchers explored the power of the mind by comparing the effects of actual physical exercise with simply thinking about exercising. Participants were divided into three groups: one group engaged in regular physical exercise, another group was instructed to mentally visualize specific muscle contractions without physically moving, and a control group did neither. Remarkably, the results showed that the group who only imagined exercising experienced a significant increase in muscle strength, about 13.5%, compared to the 30% increase in the physical exercise group, while the control group saw no improvement. This phenomenon is believed to stem from the brain's ability to activate neural pathways involved in muscle contraction, even without physical movement. The study highlights the powerful connection between the mind and body, suggesting that mental training alone can produce tangible physical benefits.

Maintaining faith in yourself during challenging times requires resilience and a strong support system. Practice self-compassion by being kind to yourself during difficult times. Acknowledge your efforts and remind yourself that it's okay to make mistakes. Treat yourself with the same compassion and understanding that you would offer a friend. Focus on the aspects of your situation that you can influence. Taking proactive steps, no matter how small, can help you regain a sense of control and confidence. Let go of what is beyond your control and focus on your actions and responses.

Challenging and reframing negative thoughts that undermine your self-belief is also important. Ask yourself if these thoughts are based on facts or assumptions. Replace them with positive and empowering thoughts that support your confidence. Look for inspiration in the stories of others who have overcome adversity. Reading about their journeys and how they maintained faith in themselves can provide motivation and reassurance during tough times. Perseverance is key to maintaining self-belief. Keep pushing forward, even when progress seems slow. Remember that every step, no matter how small, brings you closer to your goals. Trust in the process and stay committed to your vision.

Believing in yourself is not a one-time achievement but an ongoing journey. It requires continuous effort, reflection, and adaptation. Embrace the highs and lows of your journey, knowing that each experience contributes to your growth and self-belief. Consider the KFC story of Colonel Sanders again, who at the age of 65 faced 1,009 rejections before finding a partner to sell his fried chicken recipe. His unwavering belief in his product and himself eventually led to the global success of the company. This story exemplifies the power of persistence and self-belief. Similarly, Thomas Edison's journey to invent the lightbulb involved thousands of failed attempts. Yet, his belief in his vision and his ability to achieve it never wavered. Edison's resilience and self-belief are powerful reminders that success often comes after numerous failures.

In the digital age, there are numerous resources available to help you strengthen your self-belief. Utilize platforms like YouTube to find motivational talks, personal development seminars, and success stories from individuals who have overcome challenges similar to yours. The internet is a treasure trove of information and inspiration, offering countless articles, podcasts, and videos designed to boost your confidence and provide practical strategies for self-improvement. Search out people who have been successful in your field of interest. Reach out to them for advice, mentorship, or simply to learn from their experiences. Networking with successful individuals can provide valuable insights and encouragement, reinforcing your belief in your potential.

Faith in yourself is a powerful force that can propel you toward your goals, even in the face of adversity. By cultivating self-belief through positive self-talk, introspection, setting realistic goals, and surrounding yourself with positivity, you can build a strong foundation of confidence. During challenging times, maintaining self-belief requires resilience, self-compassion, and a focus on what you can control. Remember, believing in yourself is an ongoing journey that requires continuous effort and reflection. Embrace the journey, learn from your experiences, and stay committed to your vision. As you cultivate and maintain faith in yourself, you will find the strength to overcome obstacles, achieve your goals, and realize your full potential.

Strong Support System = Success Network

Having a strong support system is crucial to personal and professional success. It provides emotional encouragement, practical assistance, and a sense of belonging, all of which are essential for overcoming challenges and achieving your goals. Understanding the value of a support system is the first step towards leveraging its benefits. A support system is a network of individuals who provide various forms of assistance, including emotional support, advice, mentorship, and tangible help. These individuals believe in your potential, celebrate your successes, and stand by you during tough times. They can be family members, friends, colleagues, mentors, or even members of a community group.

The "crabs in a bucket" analogy perfectly illustrates the importance of a positive support system. When one crab tries to escape the bucket, the others pull it back down, preventing it from climbing out. Similarly, negative influences in your life can drag you down, undermining your confidence and progress. A strong support system, on the other hand, lifts you up and helps you reach new heights.

Creating a supportive home environment begins with open communication and mutual respect. Share your goals and aspirations with your family members, and encourage them to do the same. This fosters a sense of unity and shared purpose. Identify the strengths and interests of each family member and find ways to support and encourage one another. This could involve helping with tasks, offering emotional support, or simply being present during important moments. Celebrate each other's achievements, no matter how small, to reinforce the importance of mutual support. Set boundaries and expectations within the household to ensure a harmonious environment. Respect each other's space and time, and address conflicts openly and constructively. A home that values communication and respect creates a solid foundation for a supportive environment. Encourage a positive mindset within the family. Practice gratitude together, acknowledging the good things in your lives. This helps to build a culture of positivity and resilience, which is essential for a strong support system.

In the workplace, a supportive environment is equally important. Start by building strong relationships with your colleagues. Take the time to get to know them, understand their strengths and challenges, and offer your support. This creates a sense of camaraderie and mutual respect. Seek out mentors and role models within your organization. These individuals can provide valuable advice, guidance, and encouragement. Don't be afraid to ask for help or advice; most people are willing to share their knowledge and experience. Be a positive influence yourself. Support your colleagues in their endeavors, offer constructive feedback, and celebrate their successes. By fostering a culture of support and collaboration, you contribute to a positive work environment. Participate in team-building activities and professional development opportunities. These not only enhance your skills but also strengthen your relationships with your colleagues, creating a more supportive and cohesive work environment.

Negativity can be a significant barrier to building and maintaining a strong support system. It is essential to recognize and address negative influences in your life, both at home and at work. The "crabs in a bucket" mentality can manifest in various ways, such as criticism, jealousy, or lack of support. Identify individuals or behaviors that consistently bring you down or undermine your confidence. Distance yourself from these influences or address the behavior directly, tell them to kick bricks as I like to say. Surround yourself with positive, uplifting individuals who encourage and support you. Seek out friends and colleagues who share your goals and values, and who genuinely want to see you succeed. They say,"hang around with 4 broke fools and you'll be the 5th. Hang around 4 geniuses and you'll be the 5th, so care about who you share your circle with." Practice self-care and set boundaries to protect your mental and emotional well-being. This might involve saying no to certain requests, limiting time spent with negative individuals, or seeking support from a therapist or counselor. Cultivate a positive mindset by focusing on your strengths and achievements. Practice gratitude and mindfulness to stay grounded and resilient in the face of negativity.

A great support system is invaluable for personal and professional growth. It provides the encouragement, advice, and practical assistance needed to overcome challenges and achieve your goals. By building a supportive environment at home and at work, and by eliminating negativity, you can create a network of individuals who lift you up and help you reach your full potential. Remember, just as the crabs in a bucket can drag each other down, negative influences can hinder your progress. Surround yourself with positive, supportive individuals who believe in you and your potential. You can typically read a person's energy to tell what type of person they are. Sometimes within the first few seconds of meeting someone, you already know the type of person you are dealing with. Trust your instincts and be friends with the people that will make you grow and succeed. By fostering this culture of support and positivity, you not only enhance your own success but also contribute to the success and well-being of those around you as well.

Your network is also one of the most valuable intangibles in sales. It's more than just a list of contacts—it's the foundation of your professional success and a vital tool for long-term growth. By adding past clients and prospective clients to your network, you not only maintain relationships that could lead to repeat business, but you also create opportunities for new connections that can expand your influence and open doors to new possibilities. When you stay connected with past clients, you reinforce the trust and rapport you've already built. This connection often leads to referrals, testimonials, and even new business opportunities. People are more likely to do business with someone they know and trust, and keeping these relationships alive ensures that you remain top of mind when they—or someone they know—needs the products or services you offer.

Incorporating prospective clients into your network is equally important. It allows you to build relationships before the sales process even begins, establishing a foundation of trust and value. By engaging with prospects early, you position yourself as a resource, someone who is knowledgeable and helpful rather than just another salesperson. This approach is crucial for initiating the reciprocity principle, where the value you provide encourages others to reciprocate with their business or referrals. Having a strong network also empowers you to leverage the reciprocity principle effectively. When you can reach out to someone in your network to accomplish something—whether it's a favor, an introduction, or valuable advice—you demonstrate your value and create a sense of being "their guy".

In essence, a robust network is the backbone of your success in sales. It's not just about who you know, but how well you maintain and leverage those relationships. By consistently adding past clients and prospective clients to your network, you're not just securing potential sales—you're building a community of supporters who can help you achieve your professional goals. Remember, your network is an ever-growing, ever-evolving asset, and nurturing it is key to sustaining long-term success in sales.

Couple that with creating a network of positivity and people that like working with you and others like you and you are building something of greatness. You lock the negativity out because you have someone that can check the box that person checked but with the right progressive and successful mindset. You then take that positivity home and impact your kids, your spouse, even your neighbors and all the sudden it becomes cyclic. The next time negativity creeps in, you are known as the guy with the positive and great network and anyone in your big or small circle can help to knock you out of your funk and get you back on the road to success.

Rest and Recuperation: Recharge to Excel

In our fast-paced, always-on world, the importance of disconnecting, resting, and recuperating cannot be overstated. Constant work without adequate rest leads to burnout, decreased productivity, and even serious health issues. This chapter explores the necessity of taking breaks, how often you should disconnect, the signs of burnout, and both lavish and inexpensive ways to recharge. Additionally, it emphasizes the importance of self-care, including regular exercise and a healthy diet. In the relentless pursuit of success, it is easy to fall into the trap of constant work. However, disconnecting from work and daily stressors is crucial for maintaining mental and physical health. Regular breaks help to rejuvenate the mind, reduce stress, and improve overall well-being. Just as a muscle needs rest after intense exercise to grow stronger, our minds and bodies need downtime to function optimally. Steve Jobs, the co-founder of Apple, was known for taking regular breaks to disconnect and recharge. He often retreated to his Zen Garden or took long walks, which he found to be essential for his creativity and problem-solving abilities. By disconnecting from his hectic schedule, Jobs was able to return to his work with renewed energy and fresh perspectives.

Burnout is a state of chronic physical and emotional exhaustion, often accompanied by feelings of cynicism and detachment from work. Recognizing the signs of burnout early is crucial for taking proactive steps to avoid it. Common signs include constant fatigue, irritability, difficulty concentrating, decreased productivity, and a lack of satisfaction or sense of accomplishment. If you notice these symptoms in yourself or others, it is essential to take immediate action to prevent further deterioration. Ignoring burnout can lead to serious health issues, including anxiety, depression, and cardiovascular problems. I was burning myself out one year and started to suffer from alopecia. I was in my mid-thirties and too young to be suffering from such an embarrassing ordeal. When I went to the dermatologist (a woman who looked and sounded exactly like Nicole Kidman) told me that this was my body telling me to rest and slow down. She said the next step would be ulcers then a heart attack. That resonated with me and is why I focus so much on ensuring my teams are getting enough rest and recuperation.

To avoid burnout, it is important to implement regular breaks and vacations into your schedule. Taking short breaks throughout the day, such as a few minutes to stretch, walk, or meditate, can help refresh your mind and prevent fatigue. Additionally, scheduling longer breaks, such as weekends off and annual vacations, is crucial for maintaining long-term well-being. Taking time off doesn't necessarily mean expensive vacations, although they can be a wonderful way to recharge. Lavish vacations might include a week at a luxury resort, a spa retreat, or an exotic travel destination. These experiences provide complete disconnection from daily stressors and allow for total relaxation and indulgence. However, there are many inexpensive ways to disconnect and recharge as well. A weekend camping trip, a day at the beach, or even a staycation where you explore your own city can be incredibly rejuvenating. The key is to engage in activities that you enjoy and that take you away from your regular routine. Taking care of yourself is not just about taking breaks; it also involves maintaining a healthy lifestyle. Regular exercise, a balanced diet, and adequate sleep are fundamental components of self-care. Exercise helps to reduce stress, boost mood, and improve overall health. A healthy diet provides the necessary nutrients for optimal brain and body function. Adequate sleep is essential for physical and mental recovery.

Famous entrepreneur Richard Branson attributes much of his success to his commitment to physical fitness. He starts each day with exercise, whether it's swimming, running, or playing tennis. Branson believes that staying active is key to maintaining his energy levels and mental clarity, enabling him to tackle the demands of his businesses effectively. Incorporate physical activity into your daily routine by finding exercises you enjoy, such as jogging, yoga, or cycling. Regular exercise helps to reduce stress hormones and increase endorphins, leading to improved mood and energy levels. Prioritize a balanced diet rich in fruits, vegetables, whole grains, and lean proteins. Avoid excessive consumption of processed foods, sugar, and caffeine, which can negatively impact your energy levels and overall health.

Establish a regular sleep routine by going to bed and waking up at the same time each day. Aim for 7-9 hours of quality sleep per night to ensure your body and mind have enough time to rest and recover. Disconnecting, resting, and recuperating are essential practices for maintaining mental and physical health.

Recognizing the signs of burnout and taking proactive steps to avoid it can prevent serious health issues and improve overall well-being. Whether through lavish vacations or inexpensive getaways, taking time to recharge is crucial for sustaining long-term success.

In addition to taking breaks, self-care practices such as regular exercise, a healthy diet, and adequate sleep play a vital role in maintaining overall health and productivity. By prioritizing your well-being and creating a balanced lifestyle, you can ensure that you are always performing at your best, both personally and professionally. And remember, as the joke goes:

"Why did the supermom cross the road? To get to the spa on the other side—but she had to drop off the kids, finish that work report, clean the house, cook dinner, and somehow still look fabulous for date night before she even got there! Sometimes it feels like being a superhero without the cape, right? But remember, even Wonder Woman took breaks on Themyscira to rejuvenate. So, give yourself some credit, take a breath, and know you're doing amazing—even if you can't fit it all in one day."

Positive Thinking: Mind Over Matter

Positive thinking is a transformative mindset that goes beyond mere optimism—it is a powerful force that shapes our experiences, influences our actions, and ultimately determines our success and happiness in life. This chapter delves into the profound impact of positive thinking, how it aids in achieving goals, fosters resilience during challenges, and cultivates a deeply fulfilling life. Positive thinking is not about denying reality or glossing over difficulties; rather, it involves approaching life with a constructive and hopeful mindset. Research consistently shows that individuals who maintain a positive outlook tend to experience lower levels of stress, stronger immune systems, and overall better health. This mindset isn't just about feeling good; it's about actively seeking opportunities for growth and learning from setbacks. Psychologist Martin Seligman, known for his work in positive psychology, suggests that our mental attitudes profoundly influence our ability to thrive. By focusing on positive outcomes and opportunities, we not only enhance our mood but also open ourselves up to greater possibilities in life.

One of the most significant benefits of positive thinking is its impact on goal achievement. When we approach our aspirations with optimism and belief in our capabilities, we are more likely to persevere through challenges and setbacks. Positive thinkers view obstacles as temporary hurdles rather than insurmountable barriers, which allows them to stay motivated and proactive in pursuing their goals. Remember the story of Thomas Edison, whose relentless pursuit of inventing the light bulb involved numerous failed attempts. Edison famously remarked, "I have not failed. I've just found 10,000 ways that won't work." His positive mindset and unwavering determination eventually led to one of the most transformative inventions in history. Edison's example illustrates how resilience and a positive outlook can turn setbacks into stepping stones toward success.

Happiness and positive thinking are intricately linked. When we consciously focus on the positive aspects of our lives and practice gratitude for what we have, we enhance our overall sense of well-being. Studies in positive psychology have shown that individuals who regularly engage in gratitude exercises, such as keeping a gratitude journal or expressing thanks to others, experience higher levels of happiness and life satisfaction. Psychologist Shawn Achor argues that happiness precedes success, not the other way around, in his book "The Happiness Advantage." By cultivating a positive mindset, individuals can improve their performance, creativity, and resilience—key ingredients for achieving both personal and professional goals. The way I look at this is that the happier you are the more resilient you can be. Take a scale of 1-10 on resilience. If you are at a 10, you can take L's, losses or learning opportunities, until you get down to 1 or 0, but if you start at a 3, you'll give up long before the Mr. Happy who starts at a 10. While not a scientific answer, it does make sense. If you are at a happy 10, then you are at a high resilience, if your resilience is high then you can take more L's, take more L's eventually you have more success.

    Life presents us with inevitable challenges, but it's how we respond to them that shapes our outcomes. Positive thinking equips us with the resilience and mental fortitude needed to navigate difficult situations effectively. Instead of succumbing to despair or self-doubt when faced with setbacks, positive thinkers maintain an optimistic outlook and actively seek solutions. Consider the journey of Oprah Winfrey, who faced numerous hardships and setbacks on her path to becoming a media mogul and philanthropist. Oprah credits her success to her ability to maintain a positive mindset even in the face of adversity. She views challenges as opportunities for growth and learning, which has fueled her determination to create meaningful impact in the world.

    To cultivate and maintain a positive mindset, practice mindfulness by cultivating awareness of your thoughts and emotions, and consciously choose to focus on positive aspects of your life. Use visualization techniques to imagine yourself achieving your goals, enhancing motivation, and reinforcing your belief in your capabilities. This works, visualization as we have discussed earlier can be the make-or-break technique that gets you over the hump of failure to success. Surround yourself with positivity by building a supportive network of friends, mentors, and colleagues who uplift and encourage you, while avoiding negative influences that drain your energy and optimism. Challenge negative thoughts when they arise with positive affirmations or alternative perspectives, replacing self-doubt with self-compassion and belief in your abilities. Finally, celebrate your progress and achievements, no matter how small, as recognizing your progress reinforces a positive mindset and boosts confidence. Set minor targets so that when you achieve them you treat yourself to something. It could be small and then when you hit a landmark you do something grand or maybe you just do nothing and recharge and dream because you are one step closer to watching that dream come true.

Positive thinking is a mindset that empowers us to embrace life's challenges with resilience, pursue our goals with determination, and cultivate lasting happiness and fulfillment. By fostering optimism, practicing gratitude, and maintaining a supportive network, anyone can harness the transformative power of positive thinking to lead a more successful and meaningful life. Remember, our thoughts shape our reality through our RAS (Reticular Activating System) — choose positivity and watch how it transforms your journey towards success and happiness.

Self-Sabotage: Your Worst Enemy

Self-sabotage is like driving with one foot on the gas and the other on the brake—it's when our actions contradict our goals, often without us realizing it. This behavior stems from deep-seated beliefs and fears that hold us back from achieving our true potential. It can show up as procrastination, self-doubt, or even perfectionism, all of which lead us away from our desired outcomes. Recognizing self-sabotage requires introspection and self-awareness. Pay attention to patterns in how you approach challenges. Do you consistently procrastinate on important tasks? Do you often feel unworthy of success or downplay your abilities? These behaviors might indicate self-sabotage. It's essential to identify the triggers, whether they stem from a fear of failure, low self-esteem, or past experiences. These triggers fuel self-sabotaging behaviors, keeping you from reaching your goals.

To overcome self-sabotage, start with awareness and self-compassion. Challenge the negative beliefs that fuel your self-doubt and replace them with empowering thoughts. Setting realistic and achievable goals helps build confidence. If you think you are setting small enough mini goals but failing to achieve them, scale back a bit. Mini goals aren't to make significant impact, they are to keep you motivated and watch your progression in the overall scheme of things. How do you eat an elephant? One bite at a time. But the only elephant you should be eating is an elephant ear from the local fair. Boom Zinger, you didn't see that one coming I bet. Celebrate small victories to maintain momentum. Developing healthy coping mechanisms, such as mindfulness and seeking support, is essential. Mindfulness helps you stay present and reduces anxiety, while support from friends or mentors provides encouragement and accountability.

Imposter syndrome, on the other hand, is that nagging feeling of being a fraud despite evidence of your competence. It's when you attribute your successes to luck or external factors rather than acknowledging your skills and efforts. This syndrome thrives on self-doubt and a constant fear of being exposed as inadequate. Imposter syndrome is real and we all fall prey to it. Recognizing imposter syndrome involves noticing how you think and feel about your achievements. Do you dismiss praise or minimize your accomplishments? These behaviors are common signs. Imposter syndrome often sets unrealistic standards for yourself, leading to stress and perfectionism. It's a cycle of feeling like you're not good enough, even when you've achieved success.

To overcome imposter syndrome, change your perspective. Acknowledge your achievements and give yourself credit for your hard work. Keeping a journal of your successes and positive feedback can help combat feelings of inadequacy. Keep a gratitude list, every time you do something that can be considered successful, write it down and look at it when you feel imposter syndrome sneaking in. Seeking support from friends, mentors, or colleagues who can provide perspective and encouragement is also beneficial. Ultimately, managing imposter syndrome involves cultivating a growth mindset—seeing challenges as opportunities for learning and growth rather than threats to your competence. Embracing this mindset helps you break free from self-limiting beliefs and empowers you to pursue your goals with confidence and resilience.

Both self-sabotage and imposter syndrome are internal barriers that can hinder personal and professional growth. By fostering self-awareness, practicing self-compassion, and seeking support when needed, you can overcome these challenges and realize your full potential. Remember, your thoughts shape your reality—choosing to believe in yourself and your abilities is the first step towards achieving success and happiness. Here's a practical way to break free from self-sabotage: utilize online resources and seek inspiration. Platforms like YouTube offer countless tutorials, motivational talks, and success stories from individuals who have overcome challenges similar to yours. I have included one of my favorite motivational speeches as well as some other motivational resources in the additional resources list at the end of the book. The internet is a treasure trove of information and inspiration, offering countless articles, podcasts, and videos designed to boost your confidence and provide practical strategies for self-improvement.

Building a strong network of support is crucial. Seek out people who have been successful in your field of interest. Reach out to them for advice, mentorship, or simply to learn from their experiences. Networking with successful individuals can provide valuable insights and encouragement, reinforcing your belief in your potential. This approach can help you recognize self-sabotage in others, offering a compassionate perspective and practical solutions to help them overcome their barriers. Intervening when you notice self-sabotage in others involves offering support and guidance without being intrusive. Start by having a conversation about their goals and challenges. Listen actively and empathize with their feelings. Encourage them to set realistic goals and celebrate their progress. Suggest healthy coping mechanisms, such as mindfulness or seeking professional help if needed. Your support can make a significant difference in helping them overcome self-sabotage.

In conclusion, self-sabotage and imposter syndrome are significant barriers to personal and professional growth. Recognizing these behaviors in yourself and others is the first step toward overcoming them. By fostering self-awareness, practicing self-compassion, and seeking support when needed, you can break free from these limiting beliefs. Cultivating a growth mindset and positive thinking empowers you to face challenges with resilience and confidence. Remember, your thoughts shape your reality—choosing to believe in yourself and your abilities is the first step towards achieving success and happiness. And, as a lighthearted reminder: Why did the scarecrow become a successful salesperson? Because he was outstanding in his field! Keep cultivating your positive mindset, and watch your success grow.

"It is what it is": Acceptance and Growth

In the world of sales, the wisdom of Buddhist teachings offers profound insights that can transform our approach and mindset, guiding us towards greater effectiveness and peace in our professional journey. Highly similar to many Buddhist principles, "it is what it is" teaches us lessons in acceptance, resilience, and inner peace. It invites us to release the need for control and surrender to the wisdom of the present moment. By aligning ourselves with the natural rhythms of life, we cultivate a deeper understanding of ourselves and our place in the universe. The phrase "it is what it is" is not a formal Buddhist principle, but it does reflect a concept that can be found in Buddhist teachings. The idea behind the phrase is one of acceptance of reality as it is, without attachment or aversion, which aligns with the Buddhist practice of mindfulness and equanimity. In Buddhism, the concept of *equanimity* (in Pali, *upekkhā*) is a mental state of balance and composure, particularly in the face of pleasure and pain. This state is cultivated through meditation and mindfulness practices, helping individuals to accept things as they are without getting caught up in emotional reactions. I'd be remiss if I didn't mention the correlation with stoicism as well.

Imagine a tranquil mountain stream flowing gently through a lush forest. Along its banks, a traveler encounters this stream and decides to swim against its current. Despite their best efforts and determination, the traveler finds themselves struggling against the relentless force of the water. Each stroke becomes a battle against the stream's unyielding flow, leaving them exhausted and frustrated. After struggling for some time, the traveler pauses, realizing the futility of fighting against the stream. They decide to surrender to the current, letting go of resistance and allowing themselves to float effortlessly downstream. As they relax into the flow, a remarkable shift occurs—their journey transforms from a struggle into a serene and peaceful experience. They notice the beauty of their surroundings, the gentle murmur of the water, and a sense of harmony with nature.

Stoicism and Buddhism, though emerging from different cultural and historical backgrounds—Stoicism from ancient Greece and Buddhism from ancient

India—share several philosophical similarities, particularly in their approaches to dealing with suffering, impermanence, and acceptance of reality. The phrase "it is what it is" embodies a concept that overlaps with both traditions: the acceptance of things beyond our control.

In Stoicism, there is a strong emphasis on distinguishing between what we can control and what we cannot. Stoics advocate for accepting the things we cannot change, known as externals, while focusing our efforts on our internal responses, which we can control. This idea is encapsulated in the Stoic notion of *amor fati*, or love of fate, where one embraces whatever happens as necessary and part of the whole. Similarly, Buddhism teaches that suffering arises from attachment to things being a certain way. Through the practice of non-attachment and mindfulness, Buddhists aim to accept the transient nature of reality, understanding that everything is impermanent. This acceptance is key to achieving peace of mind.

Both Stoicism and Buddhism recognize that everything in life is temporary, and they encourage a practice of detachment from outcomes to maintain tranquility. In Stoicism, this recognition leads to an effort to remain unaffected by external circumstances, knowing that they are beyond one's control. For Buddhists, the concept of impermanence, or *anicca*, is central. By understanding and accepting impermanence, Buddhists seek liberation from suffering, knowing that attachment to impermanent things leads to distress.

Emotional resilience is another area where Stoicism and Buddhism converge. Stoicism teaches that we should not be disturbed by emotions like fear, anger, or grief but should instead cultivate inner strength and resilience through rational thought and self-discipline. The Stoic goal is to maintain a state of *apatheia*, or freedom from destructive emotions. In Buddhism, mindfulness and meditation practices help individuals observe their emotions without being swept away by them, leading to a state of equanimity where one remains balanced and calm in the face of life's challenges.

The phrase "it is what it is" reflects the Stoic and Buddhist acceptance of reality without unnecessary judgment or emotional turmoil. In both traditions, this mindset helps practitioners remain calm and centered, regardless of external circumstances. In Stoicism, the phrase aligns with the practice of accepting the world as it is, focusing on our response rather than the event itself, to maintain peace of mind. For Buddhists, "it is what it is" could be seen as an expression of accepting the present moment, a key aspect of mindfulness. By fully accepting the present without craving or aversion, one reduces suffering and finds contentment. While "it is what it is" is not a direct teaching of either Stoicism or Buddhism, it captures a core idea shared by both philosophies: acceptance of reality and the cultivation of inner peace in the face of life's inevitable challenges. Both Stoicism and Buddhism encourage a mindful, detached approach to the world, emphasizing that tranquility and contentment come from within, not from external conditions.

In sales, embracing acceptance means acknowledging the present moment without resistance or frustration. It involves understanding that challenges, rejections, and market fluctuations are part of the journey. By accepting these realities with equanimity, sales professionals can maintain focus on their goals while adapting their strategies with grace and resilience. This parable offers a profound reflection on life's challenges and our responses to them. When we resist the natural flow of events—whether in relationships, work, or personal growth—we often expend unnecessary energy and create inner turmoil. This resistance can manifest as stress, frustration, and a sense of being out of sync with the universe. In contrast, embracing the principle of "it is what it is" invites us to accept the present moment with mindfulness and equanimity. It does not imply passive resignation or ignoring problems but rather a conscious choice to acknowledge reality as it unfolds. This attitude enables us to navigate challenges more gracefully, with a greater sense of clarity and resilience.

Adaptability in sales mirrors the stream flowing around obstacles. Successful salespeople adjust their approach based on customer feedback, market trends, and competitive dynamics. This flexibility allows them to remain responsive and proactive, seizing opportunities that align with their goals and fostering long-term relationships with clients. Mindfulness in sales requires being fully present and attentive during customer interactions. It means listening deeply to understand the customer's needs, concerns, and aspirations. By cultivating this mindful awareness, sales professionals can forge genuine connections, uncover valuable insights, and offer personalized solutions that resonate deeply with their clients.

Attachment to specific outcomes in sales can lead to stress and disappointment. Sales professionals who focus excessively on closing deals may miss opportunities for authentic engagement and relationship-building. By letting go of rigid expectations and focusing instead on delivering value and building trust, they create a more sustainable and fulfilling sales process. Aligning sales efforts with the natural flow of customer needs and market dynamics conserves valuable energy and promotes harmony. Resisting setbacks or rejections drains emotional resources and hinders long-term success. By embracing the principle of "it is what it is," sales professionals preserve their energy for meaningful activities such as nurturing relationships, strategic planning, and continuous improvement.

Applying Buddhist wisdom to sales empowers professionals to navigate challenges with wisdom and resilience. By embracing acceptance, adaptability, mindfulness, and letting go of attachment, sales professionals cultivate a more balanced and effective approach. This mindset not only enhances their ability to achieve sales targets but also fosters deeper connections and sustainable success in their professional endeavors. Remember, in sales as in life, surrendering to the present moment allows for growth, understanding, and fulfillment.

Practicing "it is what it is" in daily life involves several key aspects: acceptance, adaptability, mindfulness, and letting go. Embracing the reality of a situation without judgment or resistance allows us to respond more effectively and authentically. Being flexible and open to change empowers us to adjust our approach as circumstances evolve, fostering growth and learning. Cultivating present-moment awareness helps us stay grounded and responsive rather than reactive, fostering inner peace and clarity. Releasing attachment to specific outcomes frees us from unnecessary worry and anxiety, enabling us to focus on what truly matters. From an energetic perspective, aligning ourselves with the natural flow of life conserves our inner energy and vitality. When we fight against the current, we create inner tension and resistance that disrupts our natural balance. This imbalance can manifest physically, emotionally, and spiritually, affecting our well-being and relationships. By embracing "it is what it is," we harmonize our energy with the universal flow, allowing life to unfold with greater ease and grace. This alignment promotes a sense of interconnectedness with the world around us, fostering harmony and a deeper appreciation for the interconnectedness of all things.

This Buddhist/ Stoic principle of "it is what it is" teaches us profound lessons in acceptance, resilience, and inner peace. It invites us to release the need for control and surrender to the wisdom of the present moment. By aligning ourselves with the natural rhythms of life, we cultivate a deeper understanding of ourselves and our place in the universe. Remember, in the gentle surrender to what is, we discover the profound beauty and tranquility that comes from embracing life's inherent flow.

Here's a giggle -

A Stoic, a Buddhist monk, and a Western salesman walk into a bar. The bartender asks, "What can I get you?"

The Stoic replies, "Nothing, I'm content with what I have."

The Buddhist monk says, "Water is fine, but I'll let go of any attachment to it."

The Western salesman sighs and says, "I'll take a shot of whatever's strongest. I can't control my sales numbers, but at least I can control how much I drink! You know what, let's make it a double!"

Neurolinguistic Programming: Mind Mastery

Neurolinguistic Programming (NLP) is a comprehensive approach to understanding human behavior, communication, and personal development. Developed in the 1970s by Richard Bandler and John Grinder, NLP emerged from their study of successful therapists such as Fritz Perls, Virginia Satir, and Milton H. Erickson. These pioneers sought to model the effective techniques these therapists used to achieve profound results in their practices. Bandler and Grinder's initial aim was to identify the specific language patterns and behaviors that contributed to therapeutic success. Through careful observation and analysis, they distilled these patterns into a structured methodology that forms the basis of NLP. Their approach emphasizes the interconnectedness of neurology (neuro), language (linguistic), and behavioral patterns (programming) in shaping human experience and potential.

NLP operates on several key principles that underpin its approach to personal transformation and communication enhancement. One core principle is subjective experience, which recognizes that each person's perception of reality is shaped by their unique experiences, beliefs, and values. By understanding and respecting individual perspectives, NLP practitioners aim to facilitate more effective communication and personal growth. Sensory awareness is another fundamental aspect, involving the enhancement of sensory awareness across visual, auditory, kinesthetic, olfactory, and gustatory domains. This heightened sensitivity allows individuals to better understand how they perceive and process information, leading to more nuanced communication and behavior. Behavioral flexibility is also crucial, encouraging adaptability in behavior and communication styles to interact more harmoniously with others. By expanding behavioral options, individuals can navigate challenges and achieve desired outcomes more successfully. Outcome orientation, which involves setting clear, achievable goals and aligning thoughts, language, and actions with these objectives, is essential for enhancing motivation, focus, and overall performance.

NLP employs a range of techniques designed to facilitate personal change and improve communication effectiveness. Anchoring, for instance, involves associating a specific stimulus (such as a touch or a word) with a desired emotional or behavioral state. By anchoring positive states, individuals can access and reinforce desired responses in various contexts. Reframing, on the other hand, involves changing the way an individual interprets a situation or experience. By shifting perspectives and focusing on positive aspects or alternative viewpoints, reframing helps individuals overcome challenges and adopt more empowering beliefs. The Meta Model is based on linguistic patterns and is used to clarify and challenge distortions, generalizations, and deletions in communication. By asking precise questions, practitioners can uncover deeper meanings and enhance understanding in interpersonal interactions. The Milton Model, named after Milton H. Erickson, utilizes vague language, metaphors, and storytelling to induce trance states and facilitate therapeutic change. It is particularly effective in promoting relaxation, creativity, and subconscious exploration. Visualization and mental rehearsal involve utilizing guided imagery and mental rehearsal, allowing individuals to visualize desired outcomes and rehearse actions in their minds. This technique enhances performance, builds confidence, and prepares individuals for future challenges. Submodalities involve refining sensory perceptions (e.g., brightness, size, location) to alter the subjective experience of memories or mental representations. By modifying these sensory attributes, individuals can change emotional responses and transform limiting beliefs.

NLP has diverse applications across fields such as therapy, coaching, education, business, and personal development. It is used to improve communication skills, enhance leadership capabilities, manage emotions effectively, and foster personal growth and resilience. Despite its popularity, NLP has faced criticisms regarding its scientific validity and empirical evidence supporting its effectiveness. Critics argue that some NLP practices lack rigorous scientific validation and may rely more on anecdotal evidence and placebo effects. As a result, debates persist within academic and professional communities about the validity and applicability of NLP techniques.

Anchoring involves associating a specific stimulus with a desired emotional or behavioral state to trigger that state at will. For instance, think of a time when you felt incredibly confident, such as after a successful presentation. Recall the sensations, thoughts, and feelings associated with that moment. As you vividly remember that experience, apply a physical touch, like pressing your thumb and forefinger together (the anchor), at the peak of that confident state. Whenever you need to access confidence before a meeting or presentation, repeat the physical touch (pressing thumb and forefinger together). This action should recall the anchored confident state, helping you feel more self-assured and capable.

Reframing involves changing the way an individual interprets a situation to create a more positive or empowering perspective. For example, you receive feedback from a client that initially seems critical: "Your proposal is missing some key details." Instead of feeling defensive or discouraged, reframe the feedback positively: "The client's input highlights areas where I can enhance my proposal to better meet their needs." View the feedback as an opportunity to improve your proposal and strengthen your client relationship. This perspective shift can motivate you to approach revisions with enthusiasm and creativity.

Visualization involves creating mental images of successful outcomes, while mental rehearsal involves mentally practicing actions and scenarios. For example, visualize yourself confidently delivering a sales pitch. Imagine the setting, your gestures, and the positive responses from your audience. Engage all senses: see yourself succeeding, hear the applause, and feel the satisfaction of closing the deal. Before a meeting, mentally rehearse introducing yourself, outlining key points, and addressing potential objections. Practice visualizing smooth interactions and effective communication, reinforcing your preparedness and boosting your confidence.

Submodalities involve refining sensory perceptions to change emotional responses or transform limiting beliefs. For example, you have a belief that "cold calling is intimidating and unproductive." Recall a specific memory of cold calling and notice the sensory details: Is the image bright or dim? Is the sound loud or soft? Change the submodalities: Make the image smaller and less vivid, decrease the volume of the sound associated with cold calling. As you modify these sensory elements, notice how your emotional response changes. The task may feel less daunting, allowing you to approach cold calling with increased confidence and effectiveness.

Here's how you can apply NLP in sales:

1. Anchoring:

- **Concept:** Anchoring involves associating a specific state or emotion with a particular stimulus, like a word, gesture, or tone of voice.
- **Application in Sales:** During a positive interaction with a prospect, use a specific word or gesture. Later, when you repeat that word or gesture, it can trigger the same positive feelings. For example, if a prospect gets excited about a product feature, subtly touch your pen or use a specific phrase. Repeating this action when asking for the sale can help elicit the same positive emotion.

2. Mirroring and Matching:

- **Concept:** People tend to feel more comfortable and connected with those who are similar to them. Mirroring and matching involve subtly mimicking the body language, speech patterns, or tone of voice of the person you're interacting with.
- **Application in Sales:** If your prospect speaks slowly and softly, try to match their pace and tone. If they use certain phrases or terminology, incorporate those into your conversation. This builds rapport and makes the prospect feel more understood and aligned with you.

3. Language Patterns:

- **Concept:** NLP emphasizes the use of specific language patterns to influence thought processes. This includes using embedded commands, presuppositions, and metaphors.
- **Application in Sales:** Use language that presupposes a positive outcome, like, "When you decide to go with our product..." instead of "If you decide to go with our product..." This subtly suggests that choosing your product is the natural and expected choice.

4. Future Pacing:

- **Concept:** Future pacing involves getting the prospect to imagine a future where they have already purchased and are benefiting from your product or service.
- **Application in Sales:** Ask your prospect to visualize how their life or business will improve after using your product. For instance, "Imagine how much more productive your team will be once you've implemented our software."

5. Reframing:

- **Concept:** Reframing involves changing the way a person perceives a situation by altering the context or meaning.
- **Application in Sales:** If a prospect expresses a concern, reframe it as a positive. For example, if they say, "This product seems expensive," you could respond, "Yes, it's an investment, and that's because it's designed to provide long-term value and save you money over time."

6. Pacing and Leading:

- **Concept:** Pacing involves matching the prospect's current state or behavior. Once you've established rapport through pacing, you can then lead the prospect towards the desired outcome.
- **Application in Sales:** Start by matching the prospect's concerns or doubts ("I understand this is a big decision"), then gradually guide them towards a more positive state ("Imagine the impact this decision will have on your business in six months").

7. Utilizing Triggers:

- **Concept:** Similar to Pavlov's conditioning, you can create triggers in your sales process that automatically elicit a positive response.
- **Application in Sales:** If you notice certain words, phrases, or scenarios that consistently lead to a positive response, incorporate them regularly in your pitch. For instance, if mentioning "time-saving" repeatedly gets a good reaction, make it a key part of your sales narrative.

8. Sensory Language:

- **Concept:** People process information differently—some are more visual, some are auditory, and others are kinesthetic (feeling-based).
- **Application in Sales:** Tailor your language to match the prospect's preferred sensory mode. For example, if they are more visual, use phrases like "Can you see how this works?" If they are more auditory, try "How does this sound to you?"

By applying these NLP techniques, you can subtly influence the outcome of your sales interactions, guiding prospects towards making decisions that are beneficial for them and for your business. The key is to practice these techniques ethically, always aiming to build genuine relationships and provide real value to your clients. Neurolinguistic Programming offers a multifaceted framework for understanding and influencing human behavior, communication, and personal transformation. By exploring the intricate connections between neurology, language, and behavioral patterns, NLP provides valuable tools and techniques for individuals seeking to enhance their effectiveness, achieve personal goals, and facilitate positive change in their lives. While NLP continues to evolve and be debated within psychological and coaching circles, its practical applications and insights into human behavior remain influential and relevant in fields focused on personal development and communication enhancement. The principles and techniques of NLP can help individuals cultivate resilience, enhance performance, and achieve desired outcomes in various aspects of their personal and professional lives.

Psychodynamic Marketing: Deep Influence

In the fiercely competitive world of marketing, where every interaction can make or break a brand, Psychodynamic Marketing emerges as a game-changing strategy. This approach taps into the subconscious drivers of consumer decision-making, recognizing that many decisions are emotionally and psychologically driven, rather than purely rational. By understanding these hidden motivators, you can transform your marketing efforts, create lasting impressions, and drive consumer behavior in ways you never thought possible. Imagine harnessing the power of the human mind to connect deeply with your audience and turn them into loyal advocates for your brand.

Psychodynamic Marketing isn't just about selling a product—it's about creating an emotional connection that resonates with consumers on a profound level. Picture this: instead of bombarding potential customers with bland product details, you send them an email that tells a compelling story, a narrative that aligns with their values and aspirations. This isn't just marketing; it's a powerful tool that speaks directly to the heart, encouraging them to see your product as not just another option, but as the perfect choice that fulfills their needs and desires.

Think about the impact of personalized storytelling. A luxury travel agency could craft emails that don't just list destinations and prices but paint vivid pictures of exotic locations. They weave in personal anecdotes from satisfied customers, evoking emotions of wanderlust and adventure. These emails do more than inform—they inspire, nudging recipients to book that dream vacation. You have the power to create this kind of magic with your marketing. Educational seminars and webinars are another goldmine. Imagine a software company hosting webinars on cybersecurity. These sessions don't just aim to educate—they position the company as a trusted advisor. By presenting insightful case studies and practical solutions, the company instills a sense of confidence in their expertise. Over time, attendees start to associate the brand with reliability and innovation, making them more likely to choose their products in the future. You too can establish yourself as an authority in your field, guiding potential customers and earning their trust through valuable, engaging content.

Retargeting and behavioral remarketing are also incredibly effective. Picture browsing online for a new pair of running shoes. Later, as you visit other websites, you notice ads for the exact shoes you viewed earlier. This subtle reminder keeps the brand top-of-mind, increasing the likelihood that you'll return to complete your purchase. It's a gentle nudge that says, "Hey, remember us? We're here when you're ready." You can use this strategy to stay connected with your audience, subtly reminding them of your value without being intrusive. Advocate marketing leverages the power of satisfied customers. These advocates, whether through social media posts, online reviews, or word-of-mouth recommendations, serve as powerful influencers. Their authentic enthusiasm and positive experiences resonate deeply with potential customers, fostering trust and credibility. This strategy capitalizes on the power of social proof, where people are influenced by the actions and opinions of others, especially those they trust. Imagine the impact of having a community of passionate customers who voluntarily promote your brand—it's marketing gold.

To implement Psychodynamic Marketing successfully, you need a deep understanding of consumer psychology and behavior. Start by segmenting your target audience based not only on demographics but also on psychographic factors such as values, interests, and lifestyle choices. Crafting a compelling content strategy is equally crucial. Your content should not only inform but also emotionally engage and align with the subconscious desires of your audience. For instance, a health and wellness brand might publish articles that not only educate readers about nutrition but also inspire them to adopt healthier lifestyles through relatable stories and motivational tips.

Consider a beverage company that launched a campaign focused on sustainability and community engagement. Through a series of emotionally resonant videos and social media posts, they highlighted their commitment to environmental stewardship and support for local communities. By aligning their brand with values that resonate deeply with their target audience, they strengthened customer loyalty and attracted new customers who shared those values. This case study demonstrates the immense power of aligning your brand with the core values of your audience to create a powerful and lasting connection.

Psychodynamic Marketing represents a shift towards more empathetic and nuanced approaches to consumer engagement. By understanding and leveraging subconscious motivations, you can forge deeper connections with your audience, driving loyalty, advocacy, and sustainable growth. This approach not only enhances marketing effectiveness but also cultivates meaningful relationships that endure beyond individual transactions. By focusing on the psychological drivers of consumer behavior, you can create more personalized and impactful marketing campaigns.

Color psychology is another powerful tool. Studies show that colors evoke specific emotions and perceptions. Using warm tones like red and orange in promotional materials can stimulate excitement and urgency, while cool colors like blue and green convey trust and calmness. Integrating these insights into branding and design can enhance emotional appeal and brand perception, making your marketing message more effective. Behavioral conditioning, similar to Pavlovian conditioning, allows marketers to reinforce positive associations with their brand through repeated exposure to favorable stimuli. This might include consistent messaging, positive customer experiences, and personalized interactions that nurture trust and loyalty over time. By creating positive associations, you can influence consumer behavior in subtle but powerful ways.

In a practical example of an email marketing funnel, the process starts with awareness. A welcome email highlights the brand's unique value proposition and establishes a positive first impression. This is followed by educational content that builds interest and deepens engagement, using storytelling techniques to connect with the reader on a personal level. The next stage, desire, presents compelling offers or exclusive promotions tailored to the recipient's preferences and behavior, incorporating social proof such as customer testimonials to reinforce trust and credibility. Finally, the action stage drives conversion with a clear call-to-action and urgency tactics like limited-time offers or countdown timers to motivate immediate response.

By applying Psychodynamic Marketing principles effectively, you can enhance engagement, increase conversions, and foster long-term customer loyalty. This approach goes beyond traditional marketing tactics by addressing deeper psychological needs and aspirations, creating meaningful connections that resonate with consumers on a subconscious level. Through strategic deployment of psychological insights in marketing campaigns, you can optimize ROI and achieve sustainable growth in competitive markets. Psychodynamic Marketing offers a comprehensive and innovative approach to understanding and influencing consumer behavior. By leveraging psychological principles and techniques, you can create more effective and impactful marketing campaigns that resonate deeply with your target audience. This approach not only enhances marketing effectiveness but also fosters deeper connections and long-term loyalty, ultimately driving sustainable growth and success.

You have the power to revolutionize your marketing strategy. By tapping into the subconscious mind of your consumers, you can create emotional connections that drive loyalty and advocacy. Embrace Psychodynamic Marketing, and watch as your brand resonates more deeply with your audience, leading to unparalleled growth and success. Remember, you have the tools and insights to make a profound impact—now go out there and make it happen!

Physical Fitness: Body and Brain

The connection between physical health and mental acuity is profound and scientifically validated. Taking care of your body transcends mere physical fitness; it's about maintaining mental sharpness, emotional balance, and overall resilience. Exercise increases blood flow to the brain, promoting the growth of new brain cells and enhancing brain function. It releases endorphins, the body's natural mood lifters, which can reduce stress, anxiety, and depression. Regular physical exercise improves memory, cognitive function, and mental clarity. People who exercise regularly perform better on cognitive tasks and have a lower risk of cognitive decline as they age. Exercise is a powerful stress reducer, boosting the production of endorphins, which help create a sense of well-being and happiness. It also helps lower levels of cortisol, the body's stress hormone. Physical activity can help you fall asleep faster and enjoy deeper sleep, essential for cognitive function, emotional regulation, and overall health. Moreover, regular exercise enhances your energy levels and productivity. When you feel physically strong and energetic, you approach tasks with enthusiasm and resilience.

Finding time to exercise can be challenging, especially with a busy schedule. However, prioritizing physical activity is crucial for maintaining both physical and mental health. Starting your day with a quick workout, even a 20-minute routine, can energize you and set a positive tone for the day. Using part of your lunch break for a brisk walk or a short workout can refresh your mind and break the monotony of the workday. Breaking your workout into shorter sessions throughout the day, such as ten-minute bursts of activity, can be just as effective as longer workouts. If possible, walk or bike to work. If you use public transportation, get off a stop early and walk the rest of the way. You don't need a gym to get in shape; home workouts using bodyweight exercises can be highly effective and time-efficient.

Calisthenics involves bodyweight exercises that improve strength, flexibility, and endurance. Imagine starting your week with a full-body workout, beginning with a warm-up of jumping jacks or jogging in place. Transition into push-ups, squats, and planks, and conclude with stretching. The next day, focus on the upper body with arm circles, shoulder rolls, dips, pull-ups if you have a bar, and pike push-ups, followed by a cool-down. Midweek, shift to lower body exercises with high knees and butt kicks to warm up, then proceed to lunges, calf raises, and glute bridges, wrapping up with stretches. On the fourth day, a core workout can start with light cardio, followed by sit-ups, leg raises, and bicycle crunches, ending with a cool-down. An active recovery day on the fifth day can feature light yoga or stretching, focusing on deep breathing and relaxation. On the sixth day, revisit a full-body workout, incorporating burpees, step-ups using a sturdy chair or bench, and Russian twists, finishing with stretching. The seventh day is dedicated to rest and recovery, allowing your body to recuperate.

By integrating these exercises into your daily routine, you can achieve significant benefits for both your body and mind. Consistency is key, and with this simple, effective calisthenics plan, you can improve your physical fitness without needing a gym or expensive equipment. Investing time in physical exercise is an investment in your mental and emotional well-being. By understanding the profound connection between body and mind, you can harness the power of fitness to stay sharp, resilient, and ready to tackle life's challenges. The practical strategies outlined here, combined with a straightforward calisthenics plan, will help you achieve better health and mental clarity, ultimately enhancing your overall quality of life and of course your spouse will see you as that sexy beast you once were again, (insert cheesy smile). Embrace the journey of working out the body to better the mind, and witness the transformative impact it has on every aspect of your life.

Here is a week-long calisthenics plan that requires no equipment and can be done anywhere. Start the week with a full-body workout by warming up with five minutes of jumping jacks or jogging in place, then move on to push-ups, squats, and planks, ending with five minutes of stretching. On the second day, focus on the upper body with arm circles, shoulder rolls, dips using a chair, pull-ups if possible, and pike push-ups, followed by a cool-down. The third day emphasizes the lower body with high knees and butt kicks to warm up, then lunges, calf raises, and glute bridges, finishing with stretching. Day four targets the core, beginning with light cardio, then sit-ups, leg raises, and bicycle crunches, ending with a cool-down. On the fifth day, engage in active recovery with light yoga or stretching, focusing on deep breathing and relaxation. The sixth day revisits a full-body workout, incorporating burpees, step-ups using a sturdy chair or bench, and Russian twists, concluding with stretching. Finally, the seventh day is for rest and recovery, allowing your body to recuperate.

Consistency in following this plan will yield significant benefits for both your body, your mind and your love life (wink). You don't need a gym or expensive equipment to stay fit and healthy.

Physical exercise is a cornerstone of mental and emotional well-being. Understanding the profound connection between body and mind, you can harness the power of fitness to stay sharp, resilient, and ready to tackle life's challenges. The practical strategies outlined here, combined with a simple yet effective calisthenics plan, will help you achieve better health and mental clarity. Embrace the journey of working out the body to better the mind, and witness the transformative impact it has on every aspect of your life. The time you invest in your physical health is an investment in your overall quality of life. By making physical activity a priority, you set yourself up for success, not just physically but mentally and emotionally as well.

Week-Long Calisthenics Plan

Here is a week-long calisthenics plan that requires no equipment and can be done anywhere:

Day 1: Full Body Workout

1. Warm-up: 5 minutes of jumping jacks or jogging in place.
2. Push-ups: 3 sets of 10-15 reps.
3. Squats: 3 sets of 15-20 reps.
4. Plank: 3 sets of 30-60 seconds.
5. Cool-down: 5 minutes of stretching.

Day 2: Upper Body Focus

1. Warm-up: 5 minutes of arm circles and shoulder rolls.
2. Dips (using a chair): 3 sets of 10-15 reps.
3. Pull-ups (if possible, using a bar): 3 sets of 5-10 reps.

4. Pike Push-ups: 3 sets of 10-12 reps.
   5. Cool-down: 5 minutes of stretching.

Day 3: Lower Body Focus

   1. Warm-up: 5 minutes of high knees and butt kicks.
   2. Lunges: 3 sets of 10-15 reps per leg.
   3. Calf Raises: 3 sets of 15-20 reps.
   4. Glute Bridges: 3 sets of 15-20 reps.
   5. Cool-down: 5 minutes of stretching.

Day 4: Core Workout

   1. Warm-up: 5 minutes of light cardio.
   2. Sit-ups: 3 sets of 15-20 reps.
   3. Leg Raises: 3 sets of 10-15 reps.
   4. Bicycle Crunches: 3 sets of 15-20 reps.
   5. Cool-down: 5 minutes of stretching.

Day 5: Active Recovery

   1. Light yoga or stretching routine for 20-30 minutes.
   2. Focus on deep breathing and relaxation.

Day 6: Full Body Workout

   1. Warm-up: 5 minutes of jumping jacks or jogging in place.
   2. Burpees: 3 sets of 10-15 reps.
   3. Step-ups (using a sturdy chair or bench): 3 sets of 10-15 reps per leg.
   4. Russian Twists: 3 sets of 15-20 reps.
   5. Cool-down: 5 minutes of stretching.

Day 7: Rest and Recovery

   1. Take a complete rest day to allow your body to recover.

By following this week-long plan, you can improve your physical fitness without needing a gym or expensive equipment.

Creating Urgency - Timely Temptation

Creating a sense of urgency in the sales process is a critical technique that can drive decision-making and accelerate the sales cycle. In today's fast-paced market, buyers often hesitate, pondering over multiple options, which can delay or derail the sales process. Instilling a sense of urgency helps counteract this inertia, compelling prospects to act swiftly and decisively.

Urgency taps into the psychological principle of scarcity. When people perceive a product or offer as limited in availability or time-sensitive, they are more likely to make a prompt decision. This fear of missing out (FOMO) triggers a heightened emotional response, pushing them to prioritize the purchase over other considerations. Urgency also minimizes the risk of losing interest or attention. In a world saturated with information and choices, maintaining a prospect's focus is crucial. By emphasizing the immediacy of an offer, you keep their attention and steer them towards a quicker commitment. I also want to point out that they say that only 2-3% of prospects are ready to purchase at 1st touch. The concept of marketing touches refers to when you, your brand, or your marketing reach out and get in front of the prospect. I always loved when a client said the timing was right because they got an email from me, saw a billboard and heard about us on the radio so they just knew. That means marketing is working.

For a bit more on touches, here you go. The concept of marketing "touches" refers to the number of interactions or engagements a potential customer has with your brand before making a purchase decision. The number of touches required can vary widely depending on factors such as the industry, product, and customer demographics. Around 2-3% of people might be ready to buy at the first touch, typically those who are highly motivated and already have a clear need. As customers become more familiar with your brand through repeated interactions, the likelihood of purchase increases, with about 10-20% ready to buy by the fifth touch. It's often said that 80% of sales are made between the 7th and 12th touches, by which point customers have usually moved through a consideration phase and gathered enough information to feel confident in making a purchase decision.

Beyond 12 touches, if a customer hasn't made a purchase, they might need more nurturing or could be less likely to buy, although some sales cycles, particularly for high-ticket items, may require even more touches. Consider your product cost, not necessarily financial, for your prospects. Consider from the perspective of the consumer as I have had many salesmen tell me it's not a big deal but that's because they have been dealing with the solution for quite some time. How is the 1st look?

The understanding of marketing touches and the idea that multiple interactions are often necessary before a customer decides to purchase is supported by insights from various sources that have examined the sales and marketing process. While there isn't a single definitive study that encapsulates all of these touchpoints, several key findings have contributed to this understanding. The "Rule of 7," a long-standing marketing principle, suggests that a person needs to see or hear a message at least seven times before taking action. This concept originated from studies conducted by movie studios in the 1930s and has been widely adopted in marketing ever since. Further research from SiriusDecisions suggests that, on average, a customer interacts with a company between 7 and 12 times before making a purchase decision, especially in the B2B sector. This highlights the importance of multiple touchpoints across various channels. Forrester Research on customer engagement has also shown that the buyer's journey is no longer linear, with buyers often more than halfway through their decision-making process before even engaging with a sales team. This underscores the importance of multiple touchpoints, from content marketing to social media and beyond. Google's research into the "Zero Moment of Truth" (ZMOT) adds that customers increasingly conduct research, compare options, and read reviews before making a purchase, with customers often engaging with 11-13 pieces of content before deciding.

HubSpot's data further supports this by suggesting that inbound leads typically require 5 to 7 touchpoints before they are ready to be converted into customers. Their research emphasizes that the nurturing process through email marketing, content distribution, and follow-ups is crucial for driving conversions. Across these studies and insights, the common theme is that modern customers rarely make a purchase after just one interaction. A well-executed multi-touchpoint strategy is essential to guide potential customers through their decision-making process, with nurturing over several interactions being critical to closing sales.

However, creating urgency must be done with integrity. It's about emphasizing the value and timeliness of the offer without resorting to falsehoods. For instance, you can highlight that the current offer might not last indefinitely. Even if there's no fixed end date, framing it this way is not deceitful. Markets fluctuate, company policies change, and new promotions arise. By stating that the offer may not be available in the future, you are simply acknowledging these potential changes, encouraging the prospect to act now. Words matter. Instead of saying, "This offer ends tomorrow," you can say, "This offer is subject to change and may not be available later." This approach maintains honesty while still conveying the need for timely action. Similarly, if your product has features or benefits that are particularly valuable, stress their current relevance and how they might be adjusted or removed in future iterations.

Another effective way to create urgency is by introducing incentives for early action. Limited-time discounts, exclusive bonuses, or preferential treatment for quick decisions can significantly motivate buyers. These incentives not only add value to the immediate purchase but also make delaying the decision less attractive. Properly prioritizing leads is also essential in this process. Not all leads are created equal; some will naturally exhibit higher levels of excitement and readiness to buy. Focus on these leads, as their enthusiasm indicates a stronger likelihood of conversion. Tools like lead scoring can help identify and rank prospects based on their engagement levels and buying signals. Engage with these high-priority leads more aggressively, offering them tailored incentives and emphasizing the urgency of your offer. For example, if a lead has repeatedly visited your pricing page or engaged extensively with your content, they are demonstrating clear buying intent. Reaching out with a personalized message that highlights the unique, time-sensitive value they can gain by acting now can be very effective. We'll touch on tracking cookies, split-testing and internet marketing later on in this book.

Case studies and testimonials can also be powerful tools in creating urgency. Sharing stories of other customers who quickly made the decision and are now reaping the benefits can create a sense of urgency by showing tangible outcomes and reinforcing the value of acting promptly. Moreover, leveraging deadlines and limited availability can effectively create urgency without misleading your prospects. If you have a genuine deadline due to inventory limitations, seasonal offers, or upcoming price increases, communicate these clearly. Transparency about these constraints builds trust while encouraging timely decisions. Incorporating urgency into your sales process should always balance persuasive techniques with ethical practices. The goal is to facilitate decision-making by highlighting the immediate value and potential risks of delaying. By doing so, you help your prospects overcome hesitation and move forward confidently, knowing they are making a timely and beneficial choice.

An example email marketing funnel can illustrate these principles in action. Imagine an email sequence that begins with an introduction to your product (sales letter), followed by a series of messages that progressively build urgency. The first email might showcase customer success stories, the second could highlight a special offer, and subsequent emails could emphasize the limited availability of the offer or the upcoming expiration date. For instance, the initial email might read: "Discover how our innovative solution transformed businesses like yours." The next email: "Exclusive offer: Get 20% off for a limited time!" Follow-up emails could then stress: "Only a few days left to take advantage of this offer!" and "Final reminder: Don't miss out on this opportunity!" Each step in the funnel reinforces the urgency, making it clear that acting now is in the prospect's best interest. This approach, can significantly enhance your sales efforts, driving quicker and more decisive actions from your prospects.

Creating a sense of urgency is a powerful strategy in sales. By understanding the psychology behind it and applying techniques ethically, you can effectively motivate prospects to act quickly, enhancing your sales success and fostering stronger customer relationships. Incorporating these principles into your sales strategy will not only drive immediate results but also build a foundation of trust and reliability with your clients. Every interaction becomes an opportunity to demonstrate value, urgency, and integrity, ensuring that your prospects feel confident and motivated to make timely decisions. The blend of urgency and ethical persuasion creates a compelling narrative that aligns with the fast-paced nature of today's market, ultimately leading to sustained growth and success in your sales endeavors.

Compounding Interest - Building Momentum

Before diving into the transformative power of turning leads into advocates, consider the principle of compounding interest in finance. Albert Einstein famously referred to compounding interest as the "eighth wonder of the world." It's a simple yet profoundly powerful concept that exponentially grows investments over time. In finance, compounding interest means that the value of an investment increases as the earnings on both capital gains and interest earn further interest. For example, if you invest $1,000 and double it ten times, the result isn't merely substantial—it's staggering. After the first doubling, you have $2,000. Doubling it again gives you $4,000. Continue this process, and after ten doublings, you have an impressive $1,024,000. This exponential growth showcases the incredible potential of compounding interest. When applied to sales and marketing, the principle of compounding interest can yield similarly extraordinary results.

Imagine applying this principle to your sales strategy. When you convert a lead into an advocate, you essentially plant a seed that grows into a tree, bearing fruit for years to come. These advocates become your brand ambassadors, spreading positive word-of-mouth and creating a compounding effect that can exponentially increase your reach and influence. This powerful strategy hinges on a few key principles. The journey from lead to advocate begins with exceptional customer service. Every interaction with a prospect or customer should aim to exceed expectations. This means being responsive, empathetic, and proactive. When customers feel valued and understood, they are more likely to become loyal advocates. Make every customer touchpoint an opportunity to demonstrate your commitment to their satisfaction.

After ensuring top-notch customer service, the next step is to engage your customers continuously. This can be achieved through regular communication and providing valuable content. Personalized follow-ups, newsletters, and exclusive offers make customers feel appreciated and keep them informed about new products or updates. By keeping the lines of communication open, you remain top of mind, which is essential for fostering advocacy. Creating a community around your brand is another powerful strategy. People love to feel part of something bigger than themselves. You can build this community through social media groups, forums, or exclusive membership programs. These platforms allow customers to connect with each other, share their experiences, and feel a sense of belonging. Encourage discussions, host events, and celebrate milestones to strengthen these bonds. You could even consider throwing quarterly parties for current clients to mix and network. The point is that your sales endeavor doesn't end at the close, the close is just an opportunity to showcase how you're an asset for years to come.

A critical element in turning customers into advocates is recognizing and rewarding their loyalty. Loyalty programs, referral bonuses, and special discounts for repeat customers show your appreciation and incentivize advocacy. Publicly acknowledging their contributions through testimonials or social media shoutouts also reinforces their connection to your brand. To fully utilize your advocates, provide them with the tools and resources they need to share their positive experiences. This could include branded merchandise, pre-written social media posts, or referral links. Make it easy for them to spread the word by offering shareable content and clear incentives for doing so. Advocates are more likely to promote your brand if they feel equipped and rewarded for their efforts.

However, it is essential to strike a balance and not overburden your advocates. Asking too much of them can lead to burnout or resentment. Ensure that any requests for referrals or testimonials are reasonable and respect their time and effort. Your goal is to cultivate a genuine and enthusiastic advocacy, not to exploit it. Social media plays a crucial role in amplifying the efforts of your advocates. Start by creating an engaging and authentic social media presence. Share content that resonates with your audience, including behind-the-scenes looks, customer success stories, and interactive posts. Encourage your advocates to tag your brand and share their experiences online. User-generated content is a powerful tool that adds authenticity and credibility to your marketing efforts.

Building a social media following requires consistency and engagement. Post regularly and respond to comments and messages promptly. Show appreciation for your followers by acknowledging their contributions and encouraging interactions. Contests, giveaways, and exclusive content can also drive engagement and attract new followers. Your goal is to create a vibrant and active community that feels connected to your brand. One example of leveraging social media is the use of Instagram stories or TikTok challenges. Encourage your customers to create content featuring your product, offering a prize for the best post. This not only engages your current advocates but also attracts new potential customers who see the posts. Highlight these user-generated content pieces on your official page, giving recognition to those who participate and creating a sense of community.

Another approach is to use LinkedIn for B2B advocacy. Encourage satisfied clients to write recommendations on your profile or share their positive experiences in posts. This can significantly enhance your professional credibility and attract new business leads. Email marketing also remains a valuable tool in nurturing advocates. Regular newsletters that offer value—such as tips, industry news, and special offers—keep your audience engaged. Feature stories of satisfied customers and case studies that showcase the success your product or service has brought them. This not only reinforces their decision to support your brand but also provides social proof to potential customers.

Consider creating a referral program where advocates earn rewards for bringing in new customers. This could be discounts, freebies, or exclusive access to new products. By providing tangible benefits, you incentivize your advocates to actively promote your brand. Ensure the process is simple and transparent, making it easy for them to participate. Advocates can also be instrumental in providing feedback and insights. Engage them in beta testing new products or services, gathering their input to refine and improve your offerings. This not only makes them feel valued but also ensures that your product development is aligned with customer needs and expectations.

A practical example of an email marketing funnel could look like this: Start with a welcome email thanking the customer for their purchase and offering a discount on their next purchase if they refer a friend. Follow up with a series of emails that provide valuable content related to the product they bought, such as usage tips, success stories, and additional offers. Periodically include calls to action encouraging them to share their positive experiences on social media or refer friends for additional rewards.

In conclusion, converting leads into advocates is a powerful strategy that can drive sustainable growth for your business. By providing exceptional customer service, engaging continuously, building a community, recognizing loyalty, and leveraging social media, you can create a compounding interest effect that significantly amplifies your reach and influence. Advocates are not just repeat customers; they are enthusiastic promoters who can bring in new business and help your brand thrive in the competitive market. By investing in these relationships and providing the tools and incentives for advocacy, you can harness their power to achieve lasting success.

F.I.T. - Fortitude, Integrity and Temperance

In the competitive world of sales, embodying core principles can set you apart and ensure long-term success. My personal mantra, encapsulated in the acronym F.I.T., stands for Fortitude, Integrity, and Temperance. These principles are not just the foundation of a successful sales career but also the pillars of a fulfilling and balanced life. I believe I came up with this years ago and have used it with all of my teams thus far. I haven't come upon a book or program that uses it so I still believe I came up with it. However, if I didn't then please forgive me and still use it because it is extremely valuable.

Fortitude is the strength of mind that enables a person to encounter danger or bear pain or adversity with courage. In sales, fortitude is essential because the journey is often fraught with challenges and setbacks. It's the ability to push through tough times, maintain focus, and continue striving towards your goals despite obstacles. Building fortitude begins with developing a resilient mindset, viewing failures and rejections not as roadblocks but as opportunities to learn and grow. Embrace each setback as a lesson, asking yourself what you can learn from the experience and how you can apply that knowledge to future endeavors. Resilience is like a muscle; the more you exercise it, the stronger it becomes.

Another key aspect of fortitude is setting clear, achievable goals. When you have a clear vision of what you want to achieve, it becomes easier to stay motivated and committed, even when the going gets tough. Break your larger goals into smaller, manageable tasks and celebrate each milestone along the way. This will help you maintain momentum and keep your eyes on the prize. Surrounding yourself with supportive and like-minded individuals can also bolster your fortitude. Having a network of people who encourage you, offer advice, and share their own experiences can provide the emotional and mental support needed to persevere. Remember, fortitude is not about going it alone; it's about having the courage to seek and accept help when needed.

Integrity is the quality of being honest and having strong moral principles. In sales, integrity is paramount because it builds trust and credibility. At one point in my life I was in the Air Force and one of their core values is integrity first. Think about that, the greatest Air Force in the world has one of three core values as integrity first. They attribute 33% of their air superiority over all other nations to integrity. While that's obviously a crude interpretation, one could view it that way. Anyway, customers need to believe that you are acting in their best interests and that your recommendations are sincere. Without integrity, even the most skilled salesperson will struggle to maintain long-term relationships and repeat business. Cultivating integrity begins with self-awareness. Understand your values and ensure that your actions align with them. Reflect on what matters most to you and let those principles guide your decisions and interactions. When you operate from a place of honesty and authenticity, your clients will recognize and appreciate your genuine approach. Also, I am sure you have noticed, this book highly emphasizes the need for truth, integrity, honesty and a willingness to truly help. All attributes of a high level of integrity in the F.I.T. model.

Transparency is another critical component of integrity. Be open and honest about what your product or service can and cannot do. Set realistic expectations and never promise more than you can deliver. If a mistake happens, take responsibility and work to resolve it promptly and fairly. This level of honesty will earn you respect and loyalty from your clients. Consistency in your actions also builds integrity. Ensure that your behavior is consistent, regardless of who you are dealing with or the situation you are in. This means treating everyone with the same level of respect and professionalism, whether they are a potential client, a long-term customer, or a competitor. Consistency reinforces your reputation as a trustworthy and reliable individual.

Temperance is the practice of self-control, moderation, and restraint. In the context of sales, temperance means balancing ambition with patience, enthusiasm with composure, and assertiveness with empathy. It's about maintaining a level-headed approach and avoiding the extremes that can lead to burnout or ethical compromises. To understand temperance, think back to our chapter on - it is what it is - the Stoic/ Buddhist pseudo principle. Developing temperance starts with self-regulation, and self-regulation starts with accepting what you can control and accepting the reality of life and living in the now. You also have to learn to manage your emotions and responses, particularly in high-pressure situations. You should practice mindfulness and stress-relief techniques such as deep breathing, meditation, or exercise to help maintain your composure. By staying calm and focused, you can think more clearly and make better decisions.

Moderation is also key to temperance. While it's important to be driven and ambitious, it's equally crucial to recognize when to step back and recharge. Set boundaries to ensure a healthy work-life balance. This might mean scheduling regular breaks throughout your day, taking time off when needed, or simply allowing yourself to disconnect from work outside of business hours. By pacing yourself, you can maintain your energy and enthusiasm over the long haul. Empathy is another important aspect of temperance. Being able to understand and appreciate your clients' perspectives and needs helps build stronger relationships. Listen actively to what they are saying, show genuine interest in their concerns, and respond thoughtfully. This not only helps in closing sales but also in creating lasting connections. Offer grace to any and everyone. If your subordinate frustrates you over seemingly nonsense, expect that from their perspective there is a legitimate concern and reason for the frustration. If you've done everything you can and used all of the principles in this book and a client still isn't ready to commit then assume you have not uncovered all that needs uncovered. If someone is tailing you on the highway and you want to cuss them out, take a breath and assume that they are on the way to the hospital to deliver a baby and have an absolute need for their actions. Offering grace goes hand in hand with temperance.

When you integrate fortitude, integrity, and temperance into your sales strategy, you create a powerful framework for success. These principles guide your actions, shape your interactions, and ultimately determine your reputation and results. Start by setting a clear example for yourself and others. Demonstrate fortitude by tackling challenges head-on and showing perseverance in the face of adversity. Uphold integrity by being transparent, honest, and consistent in all your dealings. Practice temperance by maintaining self-control, balancing ambition with patience, and showing empathy towards others. Incorporate these values into your daily routines and decision-making processes. For instance, when faced with a difficult client or a tough negotiation, remind yourself of the importance of fortitude and integrity. Use temperance to stay calm and composed, and approach the situation with a balanced perspective.

Additionally, seek opportunities to reinforce these principles within your team or organization. Share your experiences and insights, encourage others to adopt similar values, and recognize and reward those who exemplify fortitude, integrity, and temperance in their work. F.I.T.—Fortitude, Integrity, and Temperance—are not just abstract concepts; they are actionable values that can transform your sales career and your life. By cultivating these principles, you build a foundation of resilience, trustworthiness, and balance that will help you navigate the challenges and opportunities in sales. Whether you are just starting out or are an experienced professional, embracing F.I.T. can lead to greater success, deeper relationships, and a more fulfilling career.

Positivity vs. Misery: Choose Joy

In the complex world of sales, an intriguing paradox often emerges: salespeople frequently engage in comparing their miseries. It's a peculiar dance where one person's struggles are met with another's, each trying to outdo the other's hardships. This strange phenomenon of "misery one-upmanship" stands in stark contrast to the more uplifting practice of sharing positivity and supporting each other's growth. Understanding and navigating this paradox can illuminate a path toward a more constructive and fulfilling approach to both personal and professional life.

"How's it going?" "I lost a major deal today." "Oh, you think that's bad? I got rejected by three clients this week!" This exchange is all too common in sales teams. There's an odd comfort in sharing grievances, as it often fosters a sense of camaraderie and mutual understanding. Misery, like they say, loves company. This tendency can be traced back to our inherent need for social connection and validation. When we share our struggles, we seek empathy and solidarity, hoping to feel less alone in our suffering. However, this constant comparison of woes can create a negative feedback loop, where conversations spiral into a competition of who has it worse. This not only reinforces a negative mindset but also diminishes the possibility of finding solutions or seeing the brighter side of things. Instead of lifting each other up, we end up sinking deeper into the quicksand of despair.

Imagine a different conversation: "How's it going?" "I closed a major deal today!" "That's fantastic! I managed to get a promising lead from a new client." This shift in dialogue fosters an environment of encouragement and growth. Sharing positive experiences and achievements creates a ripple effect, inspiring others to celebrate their victories and strive for more. Positivity is infectious; it breeds hope, motivation, and a sense of community. When we focus on comparing positivity, we open doors to new opportunities and collaborative success. Instead of being mired in a competition of sufferings, we engage in a shared journey towards betterment. This constructive approach can transform workplaces, social circles, and even our internal landscapes.

Shifting from a culture of comparing miseries to one of sharing positivity requires intentional effort and practice. Make a conscious effort to steer conversations towards positive topics. Start by sharing your own achievements, no matter how small, and encourage others to do the same. For example, if someone mentions a failed pitch, you could respond with, "That's tough, but I remember you closed that difficult client last week. How did you manage that?" Create a culture of celebration. Acknowledge and applaud the achievements of those around you. This can be as simple as verbal recognition or more formal acknowledgments like awards or social media shout-outs. In sales meetings, dedicate a segment to sharing wins, big or small. Incorporate gratitude into your daily routine. Reflect on what you are thankful for and share these reflections with others. This practice not only shifts your mindset but also sets a positive tone for interactions. Encourage team members to keep gratitude journals and share their entries. When discussing challenges, steer the conversation towards solutions rather than dwelling on the problem. Encourage brainstorming and collaborative problem-solving. For instance, if a deal fell through, discuss what could be done differently next time or how to turn the setback into an opportunity. Be a beacon of positivity. Your attitude and actions can influence others. Show how positivity can lead to better outcomes and more fulfilling experiences. Share stories of how a positive mindset has helped you overcome challenges and achieve success.

In the realm of sales, the impact of positivity is profound. A positive mindset not only enhances personal performance but also builds stronger relationships with clients and colleagues, they can feel it. Approach every client interaction with enthusiasm and a solution-oriented mindset. Celebrate client successes and highlight how your product or service contributes to their achievements. For instance, when a client shares a positive outcome from using your product, share that success story with your team to boost morale. Foster a supportive team environment. Encourage team members to share their wins and learn from each other's successes. Regularly recognize and reward positive behavior and outcomes. Create a "win wall" where team members can post their achievements for everyone to see. Maintain your own positivity through self-affirmation and visualization techniques. Focus on your goals and visualize your success. This not only keeps you motivated but also sets a positive example for others. Use daily affirmations to reinforce your belief in your abilities and success. Use positive customer feedback to boost morale and reinforce the value of your work. Share success stories and testimonials within your team to highlight the impact of your efforts. Create a feedback loop where positive feedback is celebrated and constructive feedback is used for growth.

Consider the case of a sales team at a software company struggling with declining morale due to a tough market. The manager decided to shift the focus from the challenges they were facing to the successes they were achieving. Each week, team meetings started with sharing wins, big or small. They celebrated new leads, closed deals, and even personal achievements. This change had a dramatic effect. Team members became more motivated, collaborative, and resilient. They began to see challenges as opportunities to learn and grow. The positive energy spread to their client interactions, resulting in improved customer relationships and increased sales. The team transformed from a group bogged down by adversity to one thriving on mutual support and shared success.

The paradox of misery and the power of positivity highlight a fundamental choice in how we interact with the world. By shifting our focus from comparing hardships to sharing triumphs, we can create a more uplifting and productive environment. This transformation not only enhances our personal and professional lives but also builds stronger, more supportive communities. In sales, where relationships and resilience are key, adopting a positive mindset can be particularly transformative. By celebrating successes, fostering a supportive team culture, and approaching challenges with a solution-oriented attitude, we can achieve greater success and satisfaction. Embrace the power of positivity, and watch as it propels you and those around you towards greater heights.

You've Done Your Best, Don't Worry

In the high-stakes world of sales, worry and anxiety often loom large. The pressure to meet targets, satisfy clients, and outshine competitors can be overwhelming. However, there is a powerful principle that can help alleviate these burdens: doing your absolute best. When you know you've given your all, you can rest easy, regardless of the outcome. Committing to your best efforts can eliminate worry and anxiety, ensure you are truly giving your best, and help you celebrate successes while learning from losses.

The essence of this principle is simple yet profound. When you have poured your heart and soul into your work, a sense of peace follows. You can look back and say, "I did everything I could." This self-assurance is a powerful antidote to the nagging doubts and fears that can plague our minds. It's not about being perfect but about striving for excellence within your capabilities. Imagine a scenario where you've prepared meticulously for a sales pitch. You've researched the client, tailored your presentation, and rehearsed until you know it by heart. Even if the client decides not to move forward, you can take solace in the fact that you left nothing on the table. This mindset shift from worrying about the outcome to focusing on the effort can significantly reduce anxiety.

To truly give your best, it's essential to adopt a comprehensive approach that encompasses preparation, execution, and reflection. Begin with thorough preparation. Understand your product inside and out. Know your client's needs, challenges, and preferences. Tailor your pitch to address their specific concerns and highlight how your product can solve their problems. Preparation also involves mental readiness. Visualize your success and mentally rehearse the meeting or presentation. During the execution phase, stay present and focused. Listen actively to your client and be adaptable to their responses. Show genuine enthusiasm and confidence in your product. Ensure that your communication is clear and persuasive, emphasizing the value you bring to the table. After the meeting or presentation, take time to reflect. Assess what went well and identify areas for improvement. Seek feedback from colleagues or mentors to gain different perspectives. This reflection helps you continuously improve and ensures that you are always learning and growing.

Celebrating successes is a crucial part of maintaining motivation and morale. Acknowledging your achievements, no matter how small, reinforces positive behavior and boosts your confidence. Take a moment to appreciate your hard work and the outcome. Reflect on what you did well and how it contributed to your success. This self-recognition is a powerful motivator. Try to get to a point where you are proud of the effort, not the outcome. Also, sharing your success with your team creates a positive environment and encourages others to strive for excellence too. Celebrate together, whether it's through a team meeting, a group email, or a small celebration. Treat yourself to something special as a reward for your hard work. It could be a nice dinner, a day off, or a small gift. Rewards reinforce the connection between effort and positive outcomes.

Not every effort will result in success, and that's okay. What's important is how you handle and learn from losses. Accept that losses are a part of the journey. I like to refer to losses as L's so I can say they really mean learning opportunities but I'm sure you have determined that I am pretty cheesy by now, aye? Reflect on what went wrong and why with your L's. Identify any gaps in your preparation or execution. This reflection is not about self-criticism but about understanding and learning. Reach out to clients or colleagues for feedback. Understanding their perspective can provide valuable insights and help you improve in the future. Use the lessons learned to adjust your approach. Implement changes and improvements in your preparation, execution, and follow-up processes. Each loss is an opportunity to become better. At the end of the day, if you've given your best, you couldn't do anything different or better, you've done what you could so be proud and if you took the L, then learn and reattack. You got this!

Once you've given your best, it's crucial to let go of the outcome. Worrying about results you can't control only drains your energy and focus. Trust in your efforts and embrace the principle of "it is what it is." This mindset not only reduces anxiety but also enhances your overall well-being and productivity. Consider a salesperson who, after giving a stellar presentation, continues to worry about the client's decision. This worry does not change the outcome but only adds to their stress. On the other hand, a salesperson who trusts in their preparation and effort can move forward with confidence and positivity, ready to tackle the next challenge.

Doing your best is a powerful strategy to eliminate worry and anxiety in sales. By focusing on preparation, execution, and reflection, you ensure that you are putting forth your best efforts. Celebrating successes and learning from losses help you grow and maintain a positive mindset. Most importantly, letting go of the outcome and trusting in your efforts provides a sense of peace and confidence. Embrace this principle, and you'll find that not only does your performance improve, but your overall well-being does too. Here's a Buddhist saying that reflects the principle of accepting losses and setbacks with grace:

"In the end, these things matter most: How well did you love? How fully did you live? How deeply did you let go?" This saying emphasizes the importance of letting go, a key teaching in Buddhism. In the context of work, it reminds us that losses and failures are part of life, and our ability to let go of attachment to outcomes can lead to greater peace and resilience.

4-Square Checklist for Success

In the high-stakes world of sales, mastering the art of task management is crucial for success. The 4 Square Checklist, inspired by Stephen Covey's Time Management Matrix from "The 7 Habits of Highly Effective People," offers a straightforward yet powerful method to prioritize tasks effectively. By categorizing tasks based on their urgency and importance, this method helps ensure that the most critical tasks are addressed first, leading to increased productivity and reduced stress. Honestly, you'll find that some of the things you currently prioritize aren't necessary at all for your success and you'll find yourself saying no to much more creating a more successful you who is happier, healthier and more mentally and emotionally fit.

The 4 Square Checklist organizes tasks into four distinct quadrants. The first quadrant is for tasks that are both urgent and important, demanding immediate attention with significant consequences if not completed. These tasks often include crises, pressing problems, or deadline-driven projects. The second quadrant contains tasks that are important but not urgent, crucial for achieving long-term goals and personal growth. These activities involve planning, relationship-building, and preventive measures. The third quadrant consists of tasks that are urgent but not important, requiring immediate attention but offering little contribution to long-term objectives. These tasks are often interruptions, such as non-critical emails or phone calls. Finally, the fourth quadrant is for tasks that are neither urgent nor important, often time-wasters like excessive social media use or unnecessary meetings. Please see the example below.

The effectiveness of the 4 Square Checklist lies in its focus on prioritizing tasks based on their long-term value rather than their immediate urgency. By dedicating time to important but not urgent tasks, you invest in activities that prevent crises and promote sustained success. This balanced approach helps avoid the stress and burnout associated with constantly addressing urgent matters. To implement the 4 Square Checklist, start by listing all tasks you need to accomplish, from work-related projects to personal activities. Assign each task to one of the four quadrants based on its urgency and importance. Be honest about the true value and urgency of each task. Focus on completing first quadrant tasks first due to their

Urgent - Important	Urgent - Not Important
Not Urgent - Important	Not Urgent – Not Important

immediate consequences. Next, allocate time for second quadrant activities, which are vital for long-term success. Minimize time spent on third quadrant tasks and avoid fourth quadrant activities as much as possible. Regularly review and update your 4 Square Checklist to ensure you are consistently focusing on what matters most.

Consider the example of a sales professional using the 4 Square Checklist. First quadrant tasks might include preparing for a crucial sales presentation due tomorrow. Second quadrant tasks could involve building relationships with key clients and developing a long-term sales strategy. Third quadrant tasks might involve responding to non-urgent client emails that could wait, while fourth quadrant activities could include browsing social media during work hours. In personal life, first quadrant tasks might include paying an overdue bill to avoid late fees. Second quadrant tasks could involve scheduling regular exercise and meal planning for better health. Third quadrant tasks might be answering a friend's call about non-urgent plans, while fourth quadrant activities might include watching TV shows so that you keep up to date with the latest reality show drama.

By applying the 4 Square Checklist, you prioritize tasks effectively, reduce stress, and focus on activities that lead to long-term success and personal fulfillment. This method enhances productivity and fosters a balanced and intentional approach to managing your time and energy. The checklist can transform the way you manage your tasks, both professionally and personally. It encourages a shift from reacting to every immediate demand to making thoughtful decisions about how to spend your time. Embrace the 4 square checklist and watch your life become easier and more successful.

Eating the Frog: Tackling Tough Tasks First

In the realm of productivity and personal effectiveness, the concept of "eating the frog" offers a powerful strategy for managing tasks and achieving goals. Coined by author and motivational speaker Brian Tracy, this metaphorical approach encourages individuals to prioritize and tackle their most challenging or unpleasant tasks early in the day. The idea is that by addressing these tasks first, you can boost productivity, reduce procrastination, and enhance overall effectiveness. "Eating the frog" is based on the premise that our tendency to procrastinate often stems from avoiding tasks that are difficult, uncomfortable, or intimidating. These tasks, metaphorically referred to as "frogs," typically require a significant amount of time, effort, or mental energy to complete. Examples include tackling complex projects, making difficult decisions, or handling challenging conversations.

Central to the concept of eating the frog is the 80/20 rule, or the Pareto Principle. This principle posits that roughly 80% of outcomes result from 20% of efforts. Applied to task management, it suggests that a small number of tasks—often the more challenging or critical ones—contribute disproportionately to your overall success and progress. By prioritizing and completing these tasks first, you maximize your impact and move closer to your goals more efficiently. Start each day by identifying the tasks that you've been putting off or avoiding. These are typically tasks that have significant consequences if not completed, or those that contribute the most to your long-term success. Break down your frogs into smaller, actionable steps. Clarify the specific outcomes you want to achieve and the actions required to accomplish them. This approach makes daunting tasks feel more manageable and less overwhelming. Develop a structured plan for tackling your frogs. Allocate dedicated time in your schedule when you are most alert and focused. Use techniques like time-blocking to ensure you have uninterrupted periods for deep work. Commit to starting and completing your frog tasks without distraction. Practice discipline and focus during these dedicated work sessions. Techniques such as the Pomodoro Technique can help maintain concentration and productivity.

Recognize and celebrate your achievements after completing each frog task. Positive reinforcement reinforces the habit of taking on challenges proactively and builds momentum for tackling the next set of tasks. In the context of sales and business, eating the frog is particularly relevant. For instance, if you have a crucial client presentation or a challenging sales pitch, addressing it early in the day can set a positive tone and demonstrate proactive leadership. By tackling difficult tasks first, you position yourself to handle potential obstacles or objections effectively, increasing your chances of success. And remember, if you eat a frog first thing in the morning, the rest of the day feels like a breeze. (Though, to be clear, this doesn't mean you should start adding frogs to your diet!) The point is, once you handle the toughest task of the day, everything else seems more manageable.

Eating the frog is more than just a productivity hack; it's a mindset that promotes resilience, discipline, and proactive behavior. By embracing discomfort and prioritizing challenging tasks, you cultivate a habit of success that extends across all aspects of your life. The frogs on your task list are often the ones that lead to the greatest rewards and achievements. By consistently applying this principle, you can enhance your productivity, achieve meaningful goals, and maintain a sense of accomplishment and fulfillment in your daily endeavors.

Creating a Culture of Love

Building a work culture of love is akin to nurturing a garden: it requires deliberate effort, patience, and a deep understanding of what nourishes and sustains relationships. In this chapter, we delve into the principles and practices that foster a workplace where team members not only work together but genuinely care for each other's well-being and success. Love in the workplace is about more than just camaraderie; it's about empathy, respect, and fostering an environment where individuals feel valued and supported. It's about creating a culture where team members go beyond mere colleagues—they become a work family.

To cultivate love in the workplace, start by fostering deep connections among team members. Encourage open communication and active listening. Be vulnerable and encourage vulnerability. Empower individuals to share their ideas, concerns, and aspirations freely. Create opportunities for team members to bond outside of work, such as organizing team-building activities or outings. Trust and respect are foundational to a loving work culture. Lead by example, demonstrating integrity and fairness in all interactions. Encourage transparency and honesty, ensuring that everyone feels comfortable expressing themselves without fear of judgment. Celebrate diversity and inclusivity, recognizing the unique contributions of each team member. Inspire your team with a shared vision that transcends daily tasks. As Antoine de Saint-Exupéry said in my all-time favorite quote, "If you want to build a ship, don't drum up the men to gather wood, divide the work, and give orders. Instead, teach them to yearn for the vast and endless sea." Encourage team members to see beyond immediate goals and tasks, inspiring them with a compelling vision of the future and the impact of their work.

Show genuine care for the personal and professional growth of your team members. Provide opportunities for learning and development, whether through training programs, mentorship, or skill-building workshops. Support individuals during challenging times and celebrate their successes, fostering a culture where everyone feels empowered to reach their full potential. Create a positive work environment where positivity and optimism thrive. Foster a culture of gratitude and appreciation by recognizing achievements, both big and small. Encourage a healthy work-life balance, promoting well-being and resilience among team members. Lead with compassion and empathy, demonstrating care for each person's holistic health and happiness. Remember, you don't have to have a title to lead, take care of your people regardless of their title and build the culture you dream of.

Leaders play a crucial role in shaping a culture of love. Lead with empathy, compassion, and humility. Listen actively to your team members and demonstrate a genuine interest in their perspectives and experiences. Create a safe space where everyone feels heard and valued, fostering a sense of belonging and trust. In a loving workplace, employees will often support each other through tough times, even sharing humorous moments to lighten the mood. For instance, one might say, "If we can survive the three meetings today, we can survive anything!" These light-hearted interactions can build camaraderie and reduce stress, reminding everyone that they're in it together.

Building a work culture of love requires dedication and ongoing effort, this doesn't just happen, it's orchestrated. By cultivating deep connections, building trust, embracing a shared vision, and supporting personal growth, you create an environment where team members not only thrive professionally but also find fulfillment and happiness in their work. Lead with love, and watch as your team transforms into a community that is resilient, collaborative, and inspired to achieve greatness together.

Self-Care and Signs of Burn Out

In the fast-paced world of work, self-care is often overlooked, yet it's essential for maintaining mental, emotional, and physical well-being. Recognizing the signs of burnout and practicing self-care are crucial for sustaining long-term success and happiness in both personal and professional life. Burnout manifests differently for everyone, but common signs include persistent exhaustion, cynicism or detachment from work, and a sense of ineffectiveness or lack of accomplishment. Physical symptoms may include headaches, insomnia, and changes in appetite. Emotional indicators can range from irritability and anxiety to feelings of hopelessness or detachment from loved ones.

Self-care involves intentional practices that promote health and well-being. It's not just about pampering oneself but also about cultivating habits that support resilience and vitality. This includes adequate sleep, regular exercise, and a balanced diet. Taking breaks throughout the day and disconnecting from work during off-hours are vital for mental recharge. To prevent burnout, it's essential to establish boundaries between work and personal life. Set realistic goals and prioritize tasks to avoid feelings of being overwhelmed. Practice mindfulness and stress-reduction techniques such as meditation or deep breathing exercises. Engage in hobbies or activities that bring joy and relaxation.

The frequency of self-care practices varies from person to person, but consistency is key. Incorporate small, daily habits that promote well-being, such as taking short walks, practicing gratitude, or spending time with loved ones. Schedule regular breaks throughout the year for longer periods of rest and rejuvenation, whether it's a weekend getaway or a week-long vacation. Don't hesitate to seek support from colleagues, friends, or professionals if you're experiencing burnout or high levels of stress. Talking about your feelings and seeking guidance can provide perspective and help alleviate emotional burdens. Build a support network that includes trusted individuals who can offer encouragement and understanding during challenging times.

Self-care is not selfish; it's essential for maintaining a healthy work-life balance and preventing burnout. By recognizing the signs of burnout, prioritizing self-care practices, and seeking support when needed, you can cultivate resilience and sustain your well-being over the long term. Remember, taking care of yourself enables you to perform at your best professionally and enjoy a fulfilling personal life.

Prioritizing self-care can sometimes feel like trying to find time to juggle flaming swords while chewing razor blades and riding a unicycle. But just like with juggling, it gets easier with practice and a few good safety measures! Start by setting realistic goals and boundaries. It's essential to identify what's important and to focus on what can be achieved within a reasonable timeframe. Don't be afraid to say no when necessary to avoid taking on too much. Also, practicing mindfulness and stress-reduction techniques, such as meditation, deep breathing exercises, or yoga, can significantly help manage stress and maintain a sense of balance. Scheduling regular breaks throughout the day for short walks, stretching, or simply stepping away from the computer can prevent burnout and enhance productivity. Lastly, engage in hobbies and activities that bring joy and relaxation to recharge and maintain emotional well-being. You got this, you always have, but you need to take time for yourself so that you can continue at this rigorous pace!

The Power of Inception in Sales

In the cinematic masterpiece *Inception*, the art of inception involves implanting an idea so subtly that it grows and becomes the person's own belief. This ultimately is what I believe lies at the base of psychodynamic marketing from earlier in the book. This concept of inception, though fictional, holds remarkable parallels in the world of sales, where influencing decisions and guiding prospects towards a favorable outcome requires finesse and strategy. Take this with you; you want the prospect to come to the determination that your product is the solution they need and you want to do that with the least amount of influence and pressure as you can. If it can be done so subtly that they don't know they've been influenced then you have in fact used the fictional concept of inception.

In sales, inception isn't about manipulation but rather about subtly guiding prospects towards a decision they genuinely believe is their own. It starts with building trust and rapport, understanding their needs, and empathizing with their challenges. Similar to the movie, where trust is foundational to planting ideas, sales professionals must establish a genuine connection with prospects. This involves active listening, demonstrating expertise, and showing sincere interest in solving their problems.

Imagine a real estate agent who wants to convince a potential buyer that a particular property is their dream home. Instead of pushing the features, the agent paints a picture of how life could be in that home—family gatherings, peaceful mornings, and children playing in the backyard. By evoking emotions and creating a vision aligned with the buyer's aspirations, the agent subtly plants the idea that this property is not just a house but a place where dreams can flourish. In software sales, a salesperson aims to persuade a company to adopt a new cloud-based solution for managing their operations. Instead of bombarding them with technical details, the salesperson shares success stories of similar companies that have streamlined their processes and achieved significant cost savings. By illustrating the benefits and aligning them with the company's goals, the salesperson plants the idea that adopting this software is a strategic move towards efficiency and growth.

Once the idea is planted, nurturing involves consistent follow-up, providing relevant information, and addressing concerns. This reinforces the prospect's belief in the benefits of your solution and helps them visualize the positive outcomes. Successful inception in sales means empowering prospects to make decisions that align with their best interests. By guiding them through a journey of discovery and validation, you enable them to see the value of your offering on their terms, making it their own decision. Ethics play a crucial role in sales inception. Transparency, honesty, and respect for the prospect's autonomy are non-negotiable. Avoid tactics that manipulate or coerce; instead, focus on educating and empowering prospects to make informed choices that benefit them.

Mastering the art of inception in sales requires empathy, creativity, and a deep understanding of your prospect's motivations. By leveraging storytelling, empathy, and ethical practices, you can effectively plant ideas that lead to mutually beneficial partnerships and satisfied customers. Just as in *Inception*, where ideas take root and grow, your sales efforts can foster lasting relationships built on trust and shared success. Plus, who wouldn't want to avoid the paradox of selling themselves into an infinite loop of explanations—like Cobb trying to explain inception to Ariadne, only to be interrupted by his own subconscious projections?

Imagine this: inception in sales is not just real, it's *powerful*! It's the ultimate goal—leading your client to your solution in such a natural way that they don't even realize they're being guided. And here's the key: it's *not* manipulation; it's all about trust. You see, people are skeptical of salespeople, but they're never skeptical of themselves. If I tell myself something, I'm far more likely to believe it than what I read online or hear from someone else. Now picture this working for you—how your mind processes even the most detailed research. It always comes down to those key insights that shape your decisions. Inception in sales takes this process and simply shines a light on the right path, the path that leads your client directly to your solution. You're not just selling—you're empowering them to believe they discovered it on their own. How incredible is that? See what I did there?

Dealing with Different Generations

Have you felt challenged by dealing with different generations - either older or younger? Understanding the unique characteristics and preferences of different generations is crucial for effective selling. Each generation has distinct preferences, communication styles, and values that influence their buying decisions. To sell effectively, it's essential to tailor your approach to meet the unique needs of each group. This chapter explores the characteristics of different generations, why these differences exist, and how to adapt your sales strategies accordingly.

Starting with Baby Boomers, born between 1946 and 1964, this generation grew up during a time of economic prosperity and social change. They value hard work, loyalty, and personal connections. Baby Boomers prefer face-to-face interactions and in-depth conversations. When selling to them, emphasize the quality and reliability of your product. Provide thorough explanations and be prepared to answer detailed questions. Building a personal relationship is key; take the time to understand their needs and show genuine interest in their concerns. Imagine you're pitching a new insurance policy to a Baby Boomer. Instead of relying solely on digital communication, arrange a face-to-face meeting. Highlight your extensive experience and the long-term benefits of the policy. Use testimonials from other satisfied clients to build trust. Avoid rushing the relationship-building process; loyalty and personal connections are paramount to Baby Boomers.

Generation X, born between 1965 and 1980, experienced the rise of technology and economic volatility. They are self-reliant, skeptical, and value efficiency. This generation appreciates clear, concise information and practical solutions. To engage Gen Xers, focus on how your product can save them time and money. Highlight features that offer convenience and practicality. Providing detailed, straightforward information without unnecessary embellishment will resonate well with this group. When selling to Generation X, blend traditional and modern sales techniques. Use technology to streamline processes but don't neglect personal connections. For instance, if you're selling a new software solution, provide data and metrics to support your pitch. Use digital communication tools for efficiency but follow up with a phone call to build a personal connection. Keep your sales approach straightforward and efficient, providing factual information and ROI-focused pitches.

Millennials, born between 1981 and 1996, are digital natives who prioritize experiences and values over material possessions. They expect transparency and authenticity from brands. When selling to Millennials, leverage social media and digital platforms to reach them. Share compelling stories and testimonials that align with their values. Offer personalized experiences and be responsive to their inquiries. Authenticity is crucial; avoid overly polished or insincere marketing tactics. To sell to Millennials, ensure a seamless and engaging buying experience. Be authentic and transparent, and align your brand with their values. Use digital interactions, including social media and personalized emails. Provide interactive content like videos and live chats. For example, if you're selling eco-friendly products, highlight your sustainability efforts and share stories of how your products positively impact the environment. Engage with them through social media and offer personalized interactions to build trust.

Generation Z, born between 1997 and 2012, is the first generation to grow up with smartphones and social media as integral parts of their lives. They value individuality, social justice, and real-time communication. Gen Zers are highly visual and prefer engaging, multimedia content. To connect with this generation, use platforms like Instagram, TikTok, and YouTube to share dynamic and visually appealing content. Emphasize your brand's commitment to social responsibility and inclusivity. Provide quick, direct responses to their questions and feedback. Selling to Generation Z requires proficiency with the latest technology and social media platforms. Show entrepreneurial spirit and creativity. Use multimedia presentations and influencers, and focus on short-form, attention-grabbing content. For instance, if you're launching a new tech gadget, create short, engaging videos showcasing its features on TikTok. Leverage peer recommendations and online reviews to build credibility and trust.

Let's add a little humor. Have you ever noticed how each generation thinks they're the best? Baby Boomers think they're the best because they've seen it all and done it all. Generation X is convinced they're the best because they're the bridge between the old and new worlds. Millennials believe they're the best because they're tech-savvy and value-driven. And Gen Z? They think they're the best because, well, they have TikTok, lolz.

But in all seriousness, understanding the generational differences in the decision-making process is vital for sales success. We're not just selling to Baby Boomers or Gen Xers anymore; Millennials are actually the current number one consumer which will be overtaken by Gen Z in the early 2030s. Knowing who is involved in the decision-making process and how to morph your selling style to align with the person you're selling to will increase your odds of winning. And in sales, there's no prize for second place. That's why we need to sell to win. Embrace the diversity of the generational landscape and leverage it to create meaningful, impactful connections with your audience. By tailoring your strategies to align with their preferences and values, you build trust, foster loyalty, and drive successful outcomes.

Part Three

The Sales Game

Prep and Research - Be Ready, Be Smart

Preparation isn't just a strategy—it's your secret weapon. Much like in the Air Force, where mission success hinges on meticulous planning and thorough reconnaissance, in sales, your ability to gather intelligence and prepare effectively sets the stage for victory. This chapter dive bombs into why preparation and research are crucial in the sales game and provides practical tips to master this essential skill. The importance of prep and research in sales cannot be overstated. Imagine gearing up for a critical mission where your success depends on knowing your terrain, understanding your adversary's strengths and weaknesses, and having a clear strategy to achieve your objectives. In sales, every prospect interaction is akin to a mission. The better prepared you are, the greater your chances of achieving a successful outcome. This preparation not only boosts your confidence but also equips you with the insights needed to tailor your approach and anticipate potential obstacles.

In the military, gathering intelligence is about knowing your adversary inside and out—understanding their vulnerabilities, motivations, and operations. Similarly, in sales, your first step is to understand your customer deeply. Research their industry, company background, challenges, and competitors. Utilize tools like LinkedIn, company websites, and industry reports to gather valuable insights that inform your approach. This level of understanding allows you to position your product or service as the perfect solution to their specific needs. Customizing your approach based on your research is akin to pilots customizing their flight plans based on mission objectives and conditions. Tailor your messaging to resonate with the prospect's needs and priorities. Show them that you've invested time in understanding their challenges and that your solution is uniquely suited to address them. This personalized approach not only demonstrates your expertise but also builds trust and rapport with your prospect.

Anticipating obstacles and preparing for the unexpected is second nature in the military, and it should be in the sales game as well. Predict objections, competitor tactics, and potential roadblocks. Prepare compelling responses backed by data and testimonials. By addressing concerns proactively, you demonstrate confidence and preparedness, reassuring your prospect of your capability to deliver. This level of readiness can be the deciding factor in whether or not you close the deal.

Executing your sales strategy with precision requires a well-structured plan. Develop a sales process that outlines key steps from initial contact to closing the deal. Set clear objectives for each interaction, whether it's a discovery call, demo, or negotiation. Maintain momentum by following up promptly and consistently. Just as a spec ops team executes maneuvers with precision timing, your sales approach should be meticulously planned to ensure a seamless and effective progression through the sales cycle. Reflecting on past experiences can provide valuable lessons in the importance of preparation. Early in my career as a recruiter, I once approached a potential client without researching their industry trends or competitive landscape. The meeting was a disaster. From that experience, I realized that thorough preparation isn't just about ticking boxes—it's about demonstrating respect for your prospect's time and showing them you're serious about helping. This lesson underscored the critical role of preparation in building credibility and trust with clients.

And let's not forget to keep things light. As they say in the Air Force, "If you fail to prepare, you prepare to fail." It's a bit like heading into combat without your gear—sure, you might survive, but your chances of coming out victorious are slim. So, embrace your inner logistics officer (loggie) and get your intel sorted before engaging the training enemy... er, I mean, your prospect! This humorous reminder emphasizes the importance of preparation in a memorable and relatable way. In conclusion, preparation and research are the foundation of successful sales strategies. By investing time in understanding your customer, customizing your approach, and anticipating challenges, you set yourself up for success. Approach each sales opportunity with the same rigor and discipline as a military operation, and watch as your win rate soars. Ready, aim, fire—your preparation will ensure you hit the mark every time.

Lead Generation - Fill Your Funnel

In the ever-evolving world of sales and marketing, lead generation stands as the bedrock of business growth and success. This chapter dives deep into the critical importance of lead generation, empowering strategies to generate leads effectively, and the mindset necessary to believe in oneself and the transformative power of positive thinking. Please listen to me here, you have no business if you have no or even insufficient lead generation. Almost any problem in your business can be solved by increasing the lead generation. Lead generation isn't just about finding potential customers—it's about creating opportunities and forging connections that propel your business forward. It begins with a mindset rooted in belief: belief in your ability to attract, nurture, and convert leads into loyal customers through strategic action and unwavering determination.

Why Lead Generation is Crucial

At its core, lead generation is the process of identifying and cultivating potential customers for your business's products or services. Without leads, there are no prospects to convert into customers, no sales to drive revenue, and ultimately, no business growth. Here's why lead generation is the most essential skill in sales:

1. **Foundation of Sales Success:** Lead generation provides the initial touchpoints that start the sales process. It's the first step in converting prospects into paying customers, making it the lifeblood of any sales strategy.
2. **Sustaining Business Growth:** Consistent lead generation ensures a steady flow of potential customers, which is critical for maintaining and scaling business operations. It keeps the sales pipeline filled and sustains long-term growth. Bad news in the market, generate more leads, bad press - focus on generating more leads.
3. **Targeted Marketing Efforts:** Effective lead generation allows you to focus your marketing efforts on those most likely to be interested in your products or services. This targeted approach improves conversion rates and maximizes the return on investment (ROI) for marketing activities. If you

boost lead generation by just 25% so more than likely just fixing inefficiencies then that 25% increase is a 25% increase in commissions, in your success and in your ability to help people.
4. **Building Relationships:** Generating leads isn't just about making sales; it's about building relationships. By engaging potential customers early and nurturing them through the buying process, you create a loyal customer base that can become advocates for your brand.

The Power of a Positive Mindset in Lead Generation

Belief in your ability to generate leads is foundational. A positive mindset, coupled with strategic action, can transform your lead generation efforts. Here's how:

- **Visualization and Manifestation:** Start by visualizing your success. Picture yourself effectively engaging with prospects, converting leads into customers, and watching your sales grow. This mental rehearsal prepares your mind for success and boosts confidence.
- **Fortitude:** Lead generation can be challenging, with many rejections along the way. A positive mindset helps you remain resilient, viewing each rejection as a step closer to success rather than a setback.
- **Empathy and Authenticity:** Believing in the value you offer allows you to approach prospects with genuine empathy and authenticity. Prospects can sense sincerity, and it builds trust and rapport, making them more likely to engage with you.

Now that we understand the importance of lead generation and the power of a positive mindset, let's explore some practical strategies to master this essential skill:

1. **Email Marketing: Personalization and Connection**

Email marketing remains the leader in lead generation, delivering an astounding average ROI of $42 for every $1 spent (HubSpot). Craft personalized emails that speak directly to the needs and aspirations of your prospects. Infuse your messages with positivity and a genuine desire to help, not just engage but inspire action and build lasting relationships.

2. **Education-Based Marketing: Becoming a Trusted Advisor**

Education-based marketing positions you as a trusted advisor in your industry. Share valuable insights, webinars, or e-books that empower your prospects. Believe in the value you offer and the transformational impact it can have on those who engage with your content.

3. **Social Media Marketing: Amplifying Your Influence**

Social media isn't just a tool; it's a stage where your belief in yourself and your brand can shine. With 54% of social media users turning to these platforms for product research (Sprout Social), your positive presence can attract attention, foster engagement, and inspire confidence in your audience. Share stories, connect authentically, and watch your influence grow.

4. **Grassroots Efforts: Cultivating Local Impact**

Grassroots marketing leverages local connections and community engagement as powerful catalysts for growth. Participate in local events, sponsor causes you believe in, and forge genuine relationships. Believe in the ripple effect of your actions within your community.

5. **Out-of-the-Box Strategies: Unleashing Your Creativity**

Unleash your creativity and explore unconventional paths to lead generation. Create interactive experiences that captivate and engage your audience, showcasing your products in ways that spark imagination and excitement. Collaborative partnerships with like-minded businesses or influencers can amplify your reach and impact, inspiring new audiences to believe in what you offer.

Certain strategies consistently prove their worth in lead generation:

- **Content Marketing:** Sharing valuable content positions you as a beacon of knowledge and solutions. DemandMetric reports a 3x higher lead generation rate at 62% lower cost compared to traditional methods.
- **SEO Mastery:** Optimize your online presence to ensure that those seeking solutions find you. HubSpot statistics show a 14.6% close rate from SEO leads, highlighting the power of being found when it matters most.

- **Harnessing Referrals:** Believe in the power of word-of-mouth. Nielsen reveals that 84% of consumers trust recommendations from friends and family, making referral programs a potent tool in your arsenal.

Lead generation is not merely a strategy—it's a belief system. It's about trusting in your ability to make meaningful connections, offer genuine value, and positively impact the lives of your prospects. By harnessing the power of positive thinking and manifestation, you transform challenges into opportunities and dreams into realities. Believe in yourself, believe in your vision, and watch as your efforts yield success beyond measure. In the end, lead generation is the gateway to sustainable business growth, long-term relationships, and a thriving sales career.

Understanding Your Client Base

Understanding your client base is not just a strategic advantage; it's the cornerstone of successful sales and lasting relationships. At the heart of every successful sales effort lies a deep understanding of your client base. This knowledge goes beyond demographics and transactional data; it encompasses their challenges, aspirations, preferences, and pain points. When you truly understand your clients, you can tailor your approach, messaging, and solutions to meet their specific needs and exceed their expectations.

Clients are more likely to trust and engage with sales professionals who demonstrate an understanding of their industry, challenges, and goals. By investing time in researching and understanding your client base, you show genuine interest and commitment to their success. This builds credibility and fosters a stronger connection, laying the groundwork for fruitful partnerships. Every client is unique, with distinct preferences and priorities. Understanding your client base allows you to personalize your interactions and offerings, creating a tailored experience that resonates deeply. Whether it's adapting your product features or adjusting your sales pitch, personalization demonstrates attentiveness and enhances the perceived value of your solutions.

A deep understanding of your client base enables you to anticipate their needs and offer proactive solutions before they even articulate them. By staying attuned to industry trends, challenges, and upcoming opportunities, you position yourself as a trusted advisor who adds strategic value. This proactive approach not only addresses immediate concerns but also cultivates long-term loyalty. Research and analysis are essential starting points. Begin by conducting thorough research into your target market and client segments. Utilize market research, customer surveys, and analytics to gather insights into their preferences, behaviors, and pain points. Engage directly with your clients through conversations, focus groups, and feedback sessions. Actively listen to their concerns, aspirations, and feedback to gain a deeper understanding of their motivations and expectations. Segment your client base into distinct groups based on demographics, behavior, and needs.

Develop detailed buyer personas that encapsulate the characteristics and challenges of each segment, guiding your sales and marketing strategies. Client preferences and market dynamics evolve over time. Stay agile by continuously learning about your client base, adapting your strategies, and refining your approach based on new insights and feedback.

Consider the example of a technology solutions provider. By understanding their client base of small businesses seeking scalable IT solutions, they tailored their offerings with flexible pricing models and personalized support. This approach led to increased client retention and expanded market share. Similarly, a healthcare consultant specializing in compliance services deepened their understanding of client needs by conducting industry-specific workshops and offering customized compliance audits. This proactive approach not only enhanced client satisfaction but also generated referrals and repeat business. Understanding your client base is not just a strategy; it's a commitment to building meaningful relationships and delivering exceptional value. By investing in comprehensive research, active engagement, and continuous adaptation, you can anticipate needs, personalize solutions, and foster long-term loyalty. Embrace the journey of understanding your clients, and watch as your sales efforts transform into impactful partnerships.

Mastering the Art of Prospecting

Prospecting (lead generation) is the lifeblood of sales, the initial step that opens doors to potential clients and opportunities. Understanding the fundamental value of prospecting is crucial to maintaining a robust sales pipeline and ensuring a steady flow of qualified leads and opportunities. Effective prospecting is about identifying prospects who align with your ideal customer profile (ICP) and have the potential to become long-term partners, thus expanding your network, generating qualified leads, and building relationships.

The first step to effective prospecting is defining your target customer profile (TCP). This profile outlines the characteristics such as industry, company size, demographics, challenges, and buying behavior of your ideal client. Refining your TCP using existing customer data and market research will provide a clear target for your prospecting efforts. Once you have a clear TCP, the next step is to research and identify prospects. Utilize various sources and methods to find potential clients. Online research using search engines, social media platforms, and industry directories can help identify companies and individuals within your target market. Networking at industry events, conferences, and gatherings allows you to connect with decision-makers and influencers. Additionally, leveraging your existing network and asking satisfied customers for referrals can lead to high-quality prospects.

Not every identified prospect will be a good fit for your products or services, so it's essential to qualify your prospects. Assess factors such as the prospect's need for your offering, their budget, their authority to make purchasing decisions, and their timeline for making a decision. This qualification process ensures that you focus your efforts on prospects who are most likely to convert into paying customers. Engaging and initiating contact with prospects requires a personalized and value-driven approach. Cold calling and emailing with compelling messages that address specific needs can grab attention and communicate value succinctly. Content marketing, through sharing relevant blog posts, whitepapers, or case studies, can demonstrate your expertise and offer solutions to their pain points.

Social selling on platforms like LinkedIn can also help build relationships over time by sharing insights and engaging with prospects.

Building trust and rapport with prospects takes time and a nurturing strategy. Consistent follow-up through personalized emails, phone calls, or social media interactions keeps you top-of-mind. Providing additional resources, insights, or industry updates shows your commitment to their success. Listening actively to feedback and adjusting your approach based on their responses and evolving needs further solidifies these relationships. Tracking and measuring progress is essential to refining your prospecting efforts. Use CRM tools and sales analytics to monitor conversion rates, assess the health of your sales pipeline, and evaluate the ROI of different prospecting methods and channels. This data-driven approach allows you to optimize your strategies over time, ensuring continuous improvement and effectiveness.

Case studies highlight the impact of effective prospecting. For instance, a software solutions provider increased their sales pipeline by 30% within six months by defining a detailed TCP and leveraging targeted email campaigns. Similarly, a financial consultant achieved a 40% increase in client acquisition over the year through consistent networking and referral programs. These examples underscore the importance of a structured prospecting approach in driving business growth. Prospecting is not just about finding leads; it's about laying the groundwork for meaningful relationships and driving business growth. By defining your TCP, researching and identifying prospects, qualifying leads, engaging effectively, nurturing relationships, and tracking progress, you can identify qualified leads, build trust, and close more deals. Embrace prospecting as a vital skill that fuels your success in sales. Remember, the journey of prospecting is an ongoing process that requires dedication, strategy, and continuous refinement to achieve lasting success in the competitive world of sales.

Book Four

Mastering Marketing

Innovative Lead Generation Techniques

Lead generation is the cornerstone of successful recruiting, sales, every type of marketing effort, everything, ensuring that recruiters and salesmen can continually meet their quotas and attract high-quality candidates. In military recruiting for example, lead generation involves identifying and engaging with potential recruits who have the right qualifications, interests, and motivations to join the armed forces. Without an effective lead generation strategy, recruiters may struggle to find candidates, leading to a shortfall in enlistments and ultimately impacting the overall readiness and strength of the military. Consistently generating leads ensures that recruiters always have a pool of prospective candidates to engage with, increasing the likelihood of meeting enlistment goals.

Statistics highlight the critical role of lead generation in military recruiting. For instance, the U.S. Army has reported that recruiters who actively focus on generating leads are significantly more successful in meeting their enlistment targets. According to the Department of Defense, recruiters who use proactive lead generation methods, such as social media outreach, community engagement, and targeted advertising, can achieve their quotas up to 25% more efficiently than those who rely solely on walk-ins or referrals. Moreover, a RAND Corporation study found that innovative lead generation strategies, including the use of digital platforms and data analytics, can enhance recruiter productivity by as much as 30%, demonstrating the substantial impact of a focused approach.

Conversely, neglecting lead generation can lead to significant challenges in military recruiting. Recruiters who fail to prioritize lead generation often struggle to find enough qualified candidates, leading to missed targets and increased pressure on recruitment efforts. The military faces ongoing recruitment challenges, with the Department of Defense noting that approximately 70% of young Americans are ineligible for military service due to various factors such as health, education, and legal issues. This makes effective lead generation even more critical, as recruiters need to identify and engage the remaining 30% who are eligible. By leveraging diverse lead generation strategies, including online marketing, community outreach, and partnerships with educational institutions, successful recruiters can ensure a steady flow of qualified candidates, helping to maintain the strength and readiness of the armed forces.

Traditional Lead Generation Methods

Cold Calling: This involves reaching out to potential customers who haven't expressed prior interest in your product. It's direct but often met with resistance.

Direct Mail: Sending physical promotional materials to potential customers. It's tangible and can be personalized but will probably end up in the trash.

Networking Events: Attending industry conferences, trade shows, career fairs and local business events to meet potential leads face-to-face. It builds personal connections but can be time-consuming.

Referrals: Encouraging existing customers to refer new leads. It leverages trust and has a high conversion rate but depends on the satisfaction of current clients. Referral generation is the best lead generation technique. Use it, hone it, master it for ultimate success. Referral generation comes with a testimonial and more than likely a qualified lead because people often flock to other people like themselves. If your referral is a successful consumer then it's likely their referral will share the same attributes.

Print Advertising: Placing ads in newspapers, magazines, and industry journals. It reaches a broad audience but can be expensive and hard to track.

Radio and TV Ads: Broadcasting commercials to a wide audience. It offers high visibility but is costly and less targeted.

Bus Ads: We started doing bus ads in the past year and they are surprisingly less expensive for the ROI and visibility than you would imagine. Definitely recommend taking a look.

Digital Lead Generation Methods

Education Content Marketing: Creating and sharing valuable content to attract and engage potential leads. It's cost-effective and builds authority but requires time to see results.

Email Marketing: Sending targeted email campaigns to potential leads. It allows for personalization and tracking but can be seen as spam.

Social Media Marketing: Using platforms like Facebook, LinkedIn, and Twitter to connect with potential leads. It's highly engaging but requires consistent effort.

SEO (Search Engine Optimization): Optimizing your website to rank higher in search engine results. It attracts organic leads but takes time to implement.

PPC (Pay-Per-Click) Advertising: Paying for ads that appear in search engine results or on social media. It offers quick results but can be expensive.

Webinars: Hosting online seminars to educate potential leads. It builds authority and captures interested leads but requires preparation.

Landing Pages: Creating specific pages designed to capture lead information. It's highly targeted but requires good design and copywriting.

Retargeting: Using cookies in cache to display ads throughout the prospects' internet time to continuously market inexpensively though appearing to be in most places in the market through massive marketing campaign.

Innovative Lead Generation Methods

Influencer Partnerships: Collaborating with influencers to reach their audience. It leverages trust but can be expensive.

Affiliate Marketing: Partnering with affiliates who promote your product for a commission. It expands reach but requires good affiliate management.

Podcasting: Creating podcasts to discuss topics relevant to your audience. It builds authority and engagement but takes time to build an audience.

Online Courses: Offering free courses that provide value and capture leads. It establishes expertise but requires significant effort to create.

Quizzes and Surveys: Engaging potential leads with interactive content. It's fun and informative but requires good design.

Customer Reviews and Testimonials: Leveraging positive feedback from existing customers to attract new leads. It builds trust but depends on customer satisfaction.

Networking Groups: Joining or creating groups where potential leads gather. It builds connections but requires active participation.

Public Speaking: Giving talks at industry events to showcase your expertise. It builds authority but requires confidence and skill.

Freemium Models: Offering a free version of your product to attract users who may later convert to paying customers. It provides value but requires a compelling upgrade path.

Examples of Lead Generation Methods

Cold Calling: A real estate agent calls homeowners in a specific neighborhood to inform them about market trends and offers free home evaluations.

Content Marketing: A software company publishes a series of blog posts and eBooks about the latest trends in cybersecurity, attracting IT managers looking for solutions.

Email Marketing: An e-commerce store sends personalized email recommendations based on previous purchases and browsing history to re-engage past customers.

Social Media Marketing: A fashion brand uses Instagram to showcase their latest collection and runs targeted ads to attract fashion-conscious users.

SEO: A local bakery optimizes their website with keywords like "best cupcakes in [City]" to appear in local search results and attract nearby customers.

PPC Advertising: A digital marketing agency runs Google Ads targeting businesses looking to improve their online presence.

Webinars: A financial advisor hosts a webinar on retirement planning, capturing leads interested in long-term financial security.

Landing Pages: A fitness coach creates a landing page offering a free workout plan in exchange for email addresses.

Retargeting: An online retailer installs a cookie when a prospect visits their website. The prospect then sees ads on Facebook, Instagram, Google homepage, etc. appearing to have a large marketing campaign though the marketing effort is displaying directly to that person.

Influencer Partnerships: A skincare brand collaborates with a beauty influencer to promote their new product line, reaching a large audience.

Affiliate Marketing: A tech company partners with bloggers who review and recommend their products, earning a commission on sales generated.

Podcasting: A business consultant launches a podcast discussing strategies for small business growth, attracting entrepreneurs seeking advice.

Online Courses: A marketing expert offers a free online course on social media strategies, capturing leads interested in advanced training.

Quizzes and Surveys: A travel agency creates a fun quiz, "What's Your Perfect Vacation Destination?" and captures lead information upon completion.

Customer Reviews and Testimonials: An online store highlights customer reviews and testimonials on their homepage to build trust with new visitors.

Networking Groups: A financial planner joins a local business networking group, meeting potential clients looking for financial advice.

Public Speaking: A startup founder speaks at a tech conference, sharing insights on innovation and attracting potential investors and partners.

Freemium Models: A project management tool offers a free version with basic features, encouraging users to upgrade for advanced functionality.

Ranking Lead Generation Methods by Success Rate

High Success Rate: Referrals, Email Marketing, Content Marketing, SEO, Social Media Marketing, Webinars, Retargeting

Moderate Success Rate: PPC Advertising, Influencer Partnerships, Affiliate Marketing, Networking Events, Landing Pages, Customer Reviews and Testimonials, Public Speaking

Variable Success Rate: Cold Calling, Direct Mail, Print Advertising, Radio and TV Ads, Podcasting, Online Courses, Quizzes and Surveys, Networking Groups, Freemium Models

Lead generation is a multifaceted process requiring a mix of traditional, digital, and innovative methods to ensure a consistent flow of prospects. By understanding the strengths and weaknesses of each method and tailoring your approach to your target audience, you can optimize your lead generation efforts and achieve higher conversion rates. Investing time and resources in the right strategies will pay off in the long run, providing a steady stream of potential customers eager to engage with your brand.

Email Marketing Funnels: Nurturing Leads to Conversion

Email marketing is a powerful tool in the arsenal of any salesperson. It allows for direct communication with potential and existing customers, providing valuable content and gradually nurturing leads through a well-defined funnel until they are ready to make a purchase. Let's delve into the intricacies of email marketing funnels, discussing how to create them, why they work, and giving practical examples to illustrate their effectiveness. An email marketing funnel is a systematic approach to guide subscribers through a series of steps that gradually build trust, provide value, and ultimately lead to conversion. Unlike one-off email campaigns, an email marketing funnel is designed to move prospects from initial awareness to a final decision, often resulting in a sale. The funnel typically consists of several stages, each with its own goals and types of content.

Email marketing funnels are effective because they allow for personalized, targeted communication. By segmenting your audience and sending tailored messages based on their interests and behavior, you can significantly increase engagement and conversion rates. Additionally, email marketing is cost-effective, easily measurable, and can be automated, saving you time and resources while maintaining a consistent connection with your audience.

Building an Effective Email Marketing Funnel

Stage 1: Awareness

At the top of the funnel, your goal is to capture the attention of potential leads and introduce them to your brand. This is typically done through lead magnets—valuable pieces of content or offers that entice people to subscribe to your email list. Examples include eBooks, whitepapers, free trials, discounts, or access to exclusive content. For instance, a fitness coach might offer a free 7-day workout plan in exchange for an email address. This lead magnet should be highly relevant to your target audience and provide immediate value.

Stage 2: Interest

Once you've captured a lead's attention, the next step is to nurture their interest. This stage involves sending a series of welcome emails that introduce your brand, share your story, and highlight the benefits of your products or services. The goal is to build a relationship and establish trust. For example, the fitness coach might send a welcome email that introduces themselves, followed by emails with tips on fitness and nutrition, client success stories, and additional free resources. These emails should be engaging, informative, and designed to keep the lead interested and eager to learn more.

Stage 3: Consideration

As leads move down the funnel, they enter the consideration stage, where they evaluate your offerings more closely. This is where you provide more detailed information about your products or services, address common objections, and highlight your unique selling points. The fitness coach might send emails that delve into the specifics of their training programs, share testimonials from satisfied clients, and compare their approach to competitors. You can also include case studies, product demos, and detailed guides to help leads understand how your solution meets their needs.

Stage 4: Intent

At this stage, leads are showing clear signs of intent to purchase. Your emails should focus on removing any remaining barriers to conversion. This might involve offering limited-time discounts, free trials, or personalized consultations. The fitness coach could send an email offering a discount on their premium training program for a limited time, along with a link to schedule a free consultation call. The goal is to create a sense of urgency and provide an incentive for the lead to take the next step.

Stage 5: Decision

The final stage of the funnel is where the lead makes a decision to purchase. Your emails should make the buying process as smooth and straightforward as possible. Provide clear calls to action, easy payment options, and reassurances about their purchase. For example, the fitness coach might send a final email thanking the lead for considering their program, reiterating the benefits, and providing a direct link to sign up. Including a money-back guarantee or highlighting any risk-free aspects can also help alleviate last-minute hesitations.

Stage 6: Post-Purchase

The funnel doesn't end with the purchase. Post-purchase emails are crucial for maintaining customer satisfaction, encouraging repeat business, and turning customers into advocates. These emails can include thank you messages, onboarding information, tips for getting the most out of their purchase, and requests for feedback or reviews. The fitness coach might send an email thanking the new client for joining their program, providing a detailed plan for the first week, and inviting them to join a private community for additional support. Regular follow-up emails can help keep the client engaged and satisfied with their decision.

Example of an Email Marketing Funnel

To illustrate, let's create a fictional email marketing funnel for a company selling eco-friendly household products.

Awareness: The company offers a free eBook on "10 Simple Ways to Make Your Home Eco-Friendly" in exchange for email sign-ups.

Interest: The welcome email series introduces the company's mission to reduce plastic waste, shares the founder's story, and provides tips on sustainable living.

Consideration: Subsequent emails highlight the benefits of their products, share customer testimonials, and compare their products to less sustainable options.

Intent: The company sends an email offering a limited-time discount on their best-selling product bundle, along with a link to a product demo video.

Decision: A final email simplifies the purchase process, includes a direct link to buy, and reassures the lead with a satisfaction guarantee.

Post-Purchase: After the purchase, the company sends a thank you email, an onboarding guide on how to use the products, and an invitation to join a loyalty program for exclusive offers and updates.

An essential aspect of email marketing funnels is tracking their performance and optimizing them for better results. Key metrics to monitor include open rates, click-through rates, conversion rates, and unsubscribe rates. Analyzing these metrics helps you identify areas for improvement, such as tweaking subject lines, refining content, or adjusting the timing of your emails. For example, if you notice a high open rate but a low click-through rate, you might need to work on making your email content more engaging or your calls to action more compelling. If you see a high unsubscribe rate after a particular email, it may indicate that the content wasn't relevant or valuable to your audience.

Email marketing funnels are a powerful strategy for nurturing leads and driving conversions. By understanding the different stages of the funnel and creating targeted, engaging content for each stage, you can build strong relationships with your leads and guide them smoothly towards making a purchase. Investing time and effort into building and optimizing your email marketing funnel will pay off in increased engagement, higher conversion rates, and ultimately, more satisfied customers.

Education Based Marketing - Teach to Sell

Education touch marketing is a powerful strategy that integrates informative content with direct outreach to engage potential recruits or customers meaningfully. By focusing on educating prospects about the opportunities and benefits, recruiters and salespeople can build trust and credibility, positioning their offer as a desirable choice. This approach not only attracts interest but also empowers prospects with knowledge, fostering a deeper connection and commitment. At its core, education touch marketing is about providing value through consistent, informative communication. Instead of solely focusing on closing a sale or enlistment, this strategy emphasizes educating prospects about various aspects of the product, service, or career path. This can be achieved through multiple channels, such as emails, social media, webinars, and in-person events. By offering valuable content, recruiters and salespeople can keep potential recruits or customers engaged and interested over time, even if they are not immediately ready to commit.

One of the key advantages of education touch marketing is its ability to nurture leads over a longer period. Prospects often need time to consider their options, discuss with family and friends, and decide if the offer aligns with their goals. Let's remember earlier in the book where we found that only 2-3% of buyers are ready today where the rest of people who are going to buy need to be touched up to 12 times before making a commitment. By maintaining regular contact and providing educational content, recruiters and salespeople can stay top-of-mind and gradually address any concerns or misconceptions potential recruits or customers may have. This ongoing engagement helps build a strong relationship, increasing the likelihood that when prospects are ready to make a decision, they will choose you or your product.

For instance, a military recruiter might implement an education touch marketing campaign by starting with an introductory email series that explains the various branches of the military, the enlistment process, and the benefits of service, such as educational scholarships, career training, and travel opportunities.

Following this, the recruiter could share success stories of current and former service members, highlighting their career progression, educational achievements, and personal growth. Similarly, a salesperson could start with an email series about the product's features, benefits, and unique selling points, followed by testimonials from satisfied customers and case studies showing successful implementations.

This strategy is highly effective because it leverages the power of information to build a foundation of trust and interest. Potential recruits or customers are more likely to respond positively when they feel informed and respected, rather than simply being targeted with hard-sell tactics. By educating them, recruiters and salespeople can also ensure that new enlistees or customers have a realistic understanding of what to expect, leading to better retention and satisfaction rates. Furthermore, education touch marketing can be tailored to address specific concerns and interests of different demographics. For example, younger recruits might be more interested in hearing about educational benefits and career training programs, while older recruits or those with families might prioritize healthcare benefits and housing allowances. Similarly, different customer segments might value different product features or benefits. By segmenting the audience and personalizing the content, recruiters and salespeople can make their messages more relevant and compelling.

The impact of education touch marketing extends beyond just attracting recruits or customers. It also plays a crucial role in shaping public perception. By consistently sharing positive and informative content, recruiters and salespeople can build a reputation as transparent and trustworthy professionals. This not only aids in recruitment or sales efforts but also fosters broader community support and engagement. A case in point is the U.S. Army's "March2Success" program, which provides free online test preparation and career exploration tools to help students improve their academic skills. While the primary goal is to assist students, it also serves as an excellent education touch marketing tool. Students who benefit from the program gain a positive impression of the Army, and when considering their future, they are more likely to view the Army as a supportive and beneficial option. Similarly, a company offering free webinars or whitepapers on industry trends can position itself as a thought leader, making potential customers more likely to choose its products or services.

Another example is the use of social media platforms to share educational content and engage with potential recruits or customers. Recruiters and salespeople can create informative videos, blog posts, and infographics that explain different aspects of military life, product features, career paths, and benefits. By responding to comments and questions on these platforms, they can foster a sense of community and accessibility, making the military or product more appealing to digital-savvy prospects.

In conclusion, education touch marketing is a vital strategy for military recruiters and salespeople of all walks. By focusing on providing valuable information and maintaining consistent communication, they can build trust, nurture leads, and ultimately attract and retain high-quality recruits or customers. This approach not only enhances recruitment or sales efforts but also contributes to a positive public image and a more informed and committed force or customer base. Through thoughtful implementation of education touch marketing, recruiters and salespeople can ensure a steady flow of qualified and motivated individuals ready to engage.

Retargeting for Results - Using Cookies

In the digital age, where the majority of consumer interactions happen online, retargeting has emerged as a crucial strategy add-on for sales professionals. This method leverages internet cookies to re-engage potential customers who have previously shown interest in a product or service but have not yet made a purchase. By understanding and utilizing retargeting, sales professionals can significantly increase their chances of converting leads into customers. At its core, retargeting involves placing a small piece of code, known as a pixel, on a website. This pixel drops an anonymous browser cookie on the visitor's device, which tracks their behavior and interests. When these potential customers browse other websites or social media platforms, the cookies trigger targeted ads that remind them of the product or service they previously viewed. This persistent yet subtle reminder can nudge them towards completing their purchase.

The psychology behind retargeting is straightforward: familiarity breeds trust. When consumers see a product multiple times, they are more likely to remember it and develop a sense of familiarity. This repeated exposure helps to build trust and confidence in the brand, making it more likely that the consumer will eventually make a purchase. Retargeting capitalizes on this principle by ensuring that the brand remains visible to the consumer even after they have left the website. Retargeting is particularly effective because it targets individuals who have already expressed an interest in the product or service. These individuals are often further along in the purchasing funnel compared to new prospects. They have demonstrated a clear interest by visiting the website, viewing specific products, or adding items to their cart. By retargeting these individuals, sales professionals can focus their efforts on leads that are more likely to convert, thereby maximizing their return on investment.

For instance, consider an online clothing retailer. A visitor browses the website, looks at a few items, and then leaves without making a purchase. Through retargeting, the retailer can serve ads showcasing those exact items or similar ones to the visitor as they browse other websites or social media. This personalized approach reminds the visitor of their interest and can prompt them to return to the retailer's site to complete their purchase. Another powerful aspect of retargeting is its ability to provide personalized ad experiences. By analyzing the data collected through cookies, sales professionals can segment their audience based on behavior and preferences. For example, someone who spent a significant amount of time looking at winter jackets might be retargeted with ads for winter apparel, while another visitor who looked at running shoes might see ads for athletic gear. This level of personalization increases the relevance of the ads, making them more likely to capture the consumer's attention and drive conversions. I'm sure you have felt the feeling of ads following you around to everything that you visit, well that's retargeting. You may think that it's a bit unsettling but at the end of the day, it works, and that's why major corporations use it. That and it's extremely inexpensive.

One of the most compelling advantages of retargeting is its cost-effectiveness. Traditional advertising methods, such as television or print ads, cast a wide net, reaching a broad audience that may or may not be interested in the product. In contrast, retargeting focuses on individuals who have already shown interest, leading to higher conversion rates at a lower cost. According to a study by the Network Advertising Initiative, retargeted ads are 76% more likely to be clicked on than regular display ads, highlighting their efficiency and effectiveness. A real-world example of successful retargeting comes from the travel industry. A potential traveler might visit a website to look at vacation packages but leave without booking. Through retargeting, the travel company can serve ads featuring the destinations the traveler viewed, special offers, or testimonials from satisfied customers. This strategy keeps the travel company top-of-mind and can persuade the potential traveler to return and book their trip.

However, while retargeting is a powerful tool, it must be used judiciously to avoid overwhelming or annoying potential customers. There is a fine line between reminding and bombarding. Overexposure to the same ads can lead to ad fatigue, where consumers become annoyed and actively avoid the brand. To prevent this, sales professionals should carefully manage the frequency and timing of retargeted ads, ensuring they remain helpful and relevant rather than intrusive.

Moreover, transparency is crucial. Consumers should be aware that their online behavior is being tracked and used for retargeting purposes. Clear privacy policies and opt-out options can help build trust and reassure consumers that their data is being used responsibly. By being upfront about data usage, brands can enhance their credibility and foster positive relationships with their audience. In conclusion, retargeting is an essential strategy for sales professionals in the digital age. By leveraging internet cookies to track and re-engage potential customers, sales teams can increase their chances of converting leads into customers. This approach not only enhances brand visibility and familiarity but also allows for personalized ad experiences that resonate with consumers. When executed thoughtfully, retargeting can be a cost-effective and highly efficient tool in the sales arsenal, driving higher conversion rates and maximizing return on investment. Through strategic use of retargeting, sales professionals can ensure their brand stays top-of-mind and remains competitive in the ever-evolving digital marketplace.

Shotgun Approach: Broad Reach Big Impact

In the world of sales, precision is often touted as the key to success. Crafting the perfect message, targeting the ideal customer, and timing everything just right can indeed yield excellent results. However, there's another approach that can be equally, if not more, effective: shotgun marketing. This strategy involves spreading a wide net, akin to firing a shotgun blast, to reach as many potential customers as possible. The philosophy here is simple: sales is a numbers game, and by increasing the volume of outreach, you increase the chances of making a sale. Shotgun marketing operates on the principle that, in many cases, 90% perfect and ten times faster is better than striving for perfection. In a highly competitive market, waiting to craft the perfect message can lead to missed opportunities. Instead, getting your message out to a large audience quickly can yield immediate results. This approach leverages the law of large numbers, which suggests that the more attempts you make, the higher your probability of success.

Imagine you are a recruiter trying to fill multiple positions. Instead of meticulously crafting individual messages for each potential recruit, you send out a well-crafted but broadly applicable message to a large pool of candidates. Some may not respond, but others will, and those responses are your hits. By not spending excessive time on each individual message, you can reach a larger audience in less time, increasing the overall number of responses. I teach this as it's akin to fishing. Well, I guess it would be closer to throwing a cast net. Throw out the net, get a great cast and pull in what you catch.

The effectiveness of shotgun marketing lies in its ability to maximize outreach. In the context of sales, this means utilizing multiple channels to broadcast your message. Email campaigns, social media advertising, cold calling, and direct mail can all be part of a comprehensive shotgun marketing strategy. Each of these channels casts a wide net, ensuring that your message reaches a diverse audience. I also figured out how to mass text using Microsoft Word email merge and the email to phone number email addresses. If you don't know what I am talking about then this paragraph is worth the purchase price multiple times over. Google email texts to phone carriers and you'll get a list of AT&T, Verizon, T-Mobile, etc. Use excel formulas to take your phone number lists and concatenate all of that data. You now have a list that can be email merged to, that will create individual text messages and send them to your prospect list. While not every interaction will result in a sale, the cumulative effect of these efforts can lead to a significant increase in conversions.

A key advantage of shotgun marketing is its ability to quickly gather data and insights. By casting a wide net, you can quickly see which messages resonate with which segments of your audience. This feedback allows you to refine and adjust your strategy on the fly, improving effectiveness over time. For instance, if a particular email subject line generates a high open rate, you can use similar lines in future campaigns to maintain engagement. To illustrate, consider a military recruiter aiming to meet quarterly enlistment goals. Instead of targeting a select few candidates with tailored messages, the recruiter sends out a broad, compelling message to a large group of potential recruits. This message highlights the benefits of joining the military, addresses common concerns, and provides a clear call to action. While many recipients may not respond, those who do are likely interested and more likely to convert. The sheer volume of outreach ensures that the recruiter can meet or exceed their enlistment targets.

Shotgun marketing also benefits from the element of surprise. Sometimes, potential customers or recruits are not actively seeking your product or service but can be persuaded by a compelling message that lands in their inbox or social media feed to look into what value you add. By reaching out to a broad audience, you capture the interest of individuals who may not have otherwise considered your offering. However, it's important to balance quantity with quality. While shotgun marketing emphasizes volume, the messages should still be well-crafted and relevant to the audience. Generic or poorly constructed messages can backfire, leading to disengagement and negative perceptions of your brand. Therefore, it's crucial to find a balance where the message is broad enough to appeal to a wide audience but specific enough to capture interest and prompt action. I do want to point out something about purposeful errors in marketing. While it seems counterintuitive, there is actually studies that have found prospects are more likely to open emails with a small error like "their" instead of "there" in the subject line over perfectly spelled or grammatically correct. I assume this is because it's more noticeable and sticks out for the reticular activating system to pick up over the constant tsunami of everyday information we typically receive.

Another aspect to consider is the integration of shotgun marketing with more targeted approaches. While shotgun marketing casts a wide net, follow-up strategies can be more personalized and targeted. For example, after an initial broad outreach, you can segment responses and tailor subsequent communications based on the recipient's behavior and interests. This hybrid approach leverages the strengths of both shotgun and targeted marketing, ensuring maximum reach and engagement. One of my best salesmen used this hybrid approach to send messages to colleges and where I would send a message to the whole school, he opted to send tailored messages to each major. So still a shotgun method just using buckshot over birdshot. His method was much more effective in conversion rate than mine and something I highly recommend you give a shot at using your email lists.

In summary, shotgun marketing is a powerful strategy for sales professionals who understand that volume overpowers precision. By casting a wide net and reaching a large audience quickly, you increase the chances of making a sale. This approach leverages the law of large numbers, maximizes outreach, and provides valuable data for refining your strategy. While it's important to balance quantity with quality, the overarching goal is to increase the number of touchpoints with potential customers, thereby boosting the probability of success. In the fast-paced world of sales, embracing the shotgun marketing approach can lead to significant gains and a more robust sales pipeline.

Crafting Captivating Sales Copy

Sales copy is the lifeblood of any successful marketing campaign. It's the art of using words to persuade potential customers to take a specific action, whether that's making a purchase, signing up for a newsletter, or requesting more information. Crafting compelling sales copy is both an art and a science, requiring a blend of creativity, psychology, and data-driven insights. One of the foundational tools in creating successful sales copy is the use of swipe files. Swipe files are collections of tested and proven advertising and sales letters. They serve as a source of inspiration and guidance, allowing you to see what has worked in the past and apply those principles to your own copy. By analyzing these examples, you can identify patterns, techniques, and phrasing that resonate with audiences and drive conversions.

Research is another crucial element in crafting effective sales copy. Understanding your target audience is paramount. You need to know their pain points, desires, and objections to tailor your message accordingly. Researching the best headlines is a great starting point because the headline is often the first thing a potential customer sees. A compelling headline can grab attention and entice the reader to continue engaging with your content. Statistics show that headlines play a significant role in the success of sales copy. For example, studies have found that 80% of people will read a headline, but only 20% will read the rest of the content. This underscores the importance of crafting a powerful, attention-grabbing headline. Consider using numbers, questions, or a sense of urgency to make your headlines more compelling. Here are some examples of headlines that work:

- "10 Ways to Double Your Sales in 30 Days"
- "Are You Making These Common Sales Mistakes?"
- "How to Achieve Financial Freedom in Just 5 Steps"
- "Unlock the Secrets to a Successful Business"
- "Limited-Time Offer: Save 50% on Your Purchase Today"

Little-known facts and surprising statistics can also enhance the effectiveness of your sales copy. People are naturally drawn to new and intriguing information. Including such details can make your content more engaging and persuasive. For example, did you know that using the word "you" in sales copy can increase engagement by 34%? This is because it personalizes the message and makes the reader feel directly addressed. Another key aspect of successful sales copy is storytelling. Humans are wired to respond to stories. A well-told story can create an emotional connection, making your message more memorable and impactful. Consider weaving narratives into your sales copy that highlight the benefits of your product or service. Share customer success stories or case studies that demonstrate tangible results. This not only builds credibility but also helps potential customers envision themselves experiencing the same benefits.

Imagine a sales copy for a fitness program. Instead of simply listing the features of the program, you could tell the story of a person who transformed their life through the program. Describe their struggles, the turning point, and the ultimate success they achieved. This narrative approach makes the copy more relatable and inspiring, increasing the likelihood of conversion. Including social proof is another effective technique. People tend to follow the actions of others, especially when they are uncertain. Testimonials, reviews, and endorsements from satisfied customers can significantly boost the credibility of your sales copy. Highlighting these elements can reassure potential customers that others have had positive experiences with your product or service, making them more likely to take action.

Psychology also plays a crucial role in successful sales copy. Understanding psychological triggers can help you craft messages that resonate on a deeper level. Scarcity and urgency are powerful motivators. By implying that an offer is limited or time-sensitive, you can prompt immediate action. For example, phrases like "limited-time offer" or "only a few spots left" create a sense of urgency that can drive conversions. Additionally, the principle of reciprocity can be leveraged in sales copy. When you give something of value to your audience, they feel compelled to return the favor. Offering free resources, such as e-books, webinars, or trials, can create a sense of obligation, encouraging potential customers to reciprocate by making a purchase.

One of the coolest tips and tricks in email marketing piqued my interest in going down the rabbit hole of psychology in sales. You see, email marketing is full of subtle tactics that take advantage of psychological triggers, and something as seemingly trivial as a misspelling in the subject line can have a surprisingly powerful effect. Consumers are more likely to open emails with such errors for a few key reasons, one of which is how it disrupts patterns. When scanning through an inbox filled with perfectly structured subject lines, our brains naturally pick out anomalies. A misspelled word catches the eye because it breaks the familiar and expected flow. This tactic, known as "pattern interruption," sparks curiosity. The reader is left wondering whether the error was intentional, whether it changes the meaning of the content, or if there's something unique about the message, maybe they wonder if the writer is just an idiot?

In a world driven by automation and polished digital communication, misspellings also lend a sense of authenticity. Imperfections make the content feel more human, as if a real person hurriedly crafted the email. In contrast to the robotic precision of many marketing campaigns, this "human touch" makes the message more relatable. It implies the sender is just like the reader, prone to small mistakes, and, as a result, the content becomes more trustworthy and engaging. A misspelling also helps differentiate a message from the flood of generic spam. Most spam emails follow a highly polished, formal structure, often laden with impersonal tones and carefully engineered phrases. By adding a touch of imperfection, the email feels less scripted, which can make it seem more genuine or even humorous. This small but intentional flaw invites the reader to pause and examine the content more closely.

On another level, urgency can be implied through a simple typo. The reader might infer that the email was sent in haste, which could mean that the content inside is time-sensitive or highly relevant. This rush to communicate adds a layer of importance, suggesting that the sender had to get the message out quickly, errors and all, to ensure the recipient didn't miss out on something valuable. Novelty, too, plays a key role. Humans are inherently attracted to things that stand out as new or unexpected, and when an email subject line disrupts the monotony of polished marketing copy, it increases the likelihood of it being opened. However, this tactic should be used with caution. While a subtle misspelling can trigger curiosity and engagement, overdoing it can backfire, making the sender appear unprofessional or careless. Balance is key in ensuring that this strategy enhances rather than detracts from the email's effectiveness. In a crowded inbox, it's the calculated use of curiosity, authenticity, and novelty that ultimately grabs attention.

Moreover, successful sales copy often taps into the reader's emotions. People make purchasing decisions based on emotions and then justify them with logic. Identifying and addressing the emotional needs and desires of your audience can make your copy more persuasive. For instance, if you're selling a luxury watch, emphasize the feelings of prestige, confidence, and success that come with owning the watch, rather than just its technical specifications. Creating a strong call to action (CTA) is another critical component. Your CTA should be clear, concise, and compelling, guiding the reader toward the desired action. Use action-oriented language and make the benefits of taking that action immediately apparent. For example, instead of saying "Submit your form," a more effective CTA would be "Get Your Free Consultation Now." I personally like the "Buy Now on Amazon!" because it says this is legitimate, on Amazon, so let's get it. Maybe I just buy too much on Amazon.

A/B testing can further enhance the effectiveness of your sales copy. This involves creating two versions of your copy and testing them against each other to see which performs better. Elements to test include headlines, CTAs, body text, and visuals. By continually refining your copy based on real-world data, you can optimize your messaging to maximize conversions. In conclusion, crafting successful sales copy requires a strategic blend of research, psychology, storytelling, and data analysis. By utilizing tools like swipe files, researching effective headlines, and incorporating compelling stories and social proof, you can create persuasive messages that drive action. Throw in a misspelling salience and focus on understanding the emotional triggers and psychological principles that influence purchasing decisions to further enhance the impact of your copy. Through continuous testing and refinement, you can develop sales copy that not only captures attention but also converts leads into loyal customers.

Mastering Social Media Marketing

In today's fast-paced sales landscape, mastering social media is not just beneficial—it's essential for your success. Social media platforms like Facebook, Instagram, Twitter, LinkedIn, and TikTok are not just places for sharing selfies and memes; they're powerful tools to connect directly with your potential customers. These platforms boast billions of active users, offering you unprecedented opportunities to build relationships, showcase your expertise, and ultimately, close deals. Imagine social media as your virtual storefront. It's where you get to shape how others perceive you and your offerings. Consistency is key here. Your profile should reflect your professional image—clear, compelling, and aligned with your sales goals. Use engaging content to demonstrate your knowledge and value. Whether it's sharing industry insights, success stories, or tips and tricks, every post should reinforce your expertise and credibility.

To succeed in social selling, start with a solid content strategy. Tailor your messages to resonate with each platform's unique audience. For instance, LinkedIn is ideal for professional networking and B2B sales, while Instagram might be better suited for visual storytelling and reaching a younger demographic. Use a mix of content formats—videos, infographics, and customer testimonials—to keep your audience engaged and coming back for more. Harness the power of targeted advertising. Social media platforms offer sophisticated ad targeting options based on demographics, interests, and behaviors. Invest in targeted ads to reach your ideal customers efficiently. Use analytics tools to track the performance of your campaigns. Pay attention to metrics like engagement rates, click-through rates, and conversions. This data will guide you in refining your approach and maximizing your ROI.

While social media presents incredible opportunities, it also comes with challenges. Negative feedback, misunderstandings, or viral missteps can impact your reputation. Always prioritize authenticity and transparency. Address issues promptly and professionally. Remember, every interaction is a chance to build trust and strengthen your brand. Social media is not just about likes and shares—it's about building meaningful connections and driving sales. By mastering these platforms, you can elevate your sales game, expand your network, and achieve your career goals. Stay proactive, stay engaged, and always strive to provide value. Social media is your stage—make sure your performance shines bright.

Perception plays a pivotal role in social media marketing, influencing how brands are perceived by their audience and stakeholders. In the digital realm, where information spreads rapidly and opinions are formed quickly, managing perception is essential for maintaining a positive brand image. Brands must carefully curate their content, visuals, and messaging to align with their values and resonate with their target audience. Authenticity is paramount in shaping perception on social media. Audiences value transparency and honesty from brands, and any inconsistencies between a brand's online persona and real-world actions can erode trust. Positive perception can be enhanced through consistent branding, engaging storytelling, and proactive community management. By actively listening to feedback and addressing concerns promptly, brands can foster a favorable perception that encourages loyalty and advocacy among followers.

In contrast, missteps or controversies on social media can quickly tarnish a brand's reputation. Negative perception can arise from insensitive posts, poor customer service responses, or public relations crises. Brands must be vigilant in monitoring social media sentiment and prepared to respond swiftly and sincerely to mitigate reputational damage. Ultimately, perception in social media marketing hinges on authenticity, responsiveness, and strategic communication that resonates with the audience's values and expectations. To stay relevant in the ever-changing social media landscape, it's crucial to keep up with the latest trends and platforms. Begin by staying informed through industry news, blogs, and social media influencers who specialize in digital marketing and social media trends. Websites like Social Media Examiner, HubSpot, and Marketing Land are excellent resources for staying updated on the latest developments. Don't hesitate to experiment with new social media platforms that are gaining popularity; early adoption can give you a competitive edge and help you connect with audiences that might be migrating to these new spaces. Additionally, use social media analytics to understand where your audience spends their time. Platforms like Google Analytics, Facebook Insights, and Twitter Analytics provide valuable data on your audience's preferences and behaviors.

Engaging with your community by actively participating in social media groups, forums, and discussions related to your industry is another effective strategy. This not only builds your reputation but also provides insights into emerging trends and platforms. Monitor your competitors' social media activities to see which platforms and strategies they are using effectively, as this can provide inspiration and help you identify gaps or opportunities in your own approach. Leverage tools like Hootsuite, Buffer, and Sprout Social to manage your social media presence across multiple platforms. These tools offer analytics and trend reports to help you stay ahead of the curve. Lastly, invest in continuous learning by attending webinars, workshops, and conferences focused on social media marketing. This commitment to ongoing education ensures you stay updated on best practices and innovative strategies, keeping your social media efforts effective and relevant in the dynamic digital landscape.

Part Five

Overcoming Challenges

Thriving Amidst Competition

Sales is competitive, so mastering your understanding of competitors isn't just about gathering data—it's a strategic journey that combines external research with introspection and proactive planning. This chapter serves as your guide to navigating the complexities of competition, empowering you to leverage insights and overcome challenges effectively. Begin your journey by diving deeper into your competitors' landscape. It's more than knowing their products or pricing—it's about understanding their reputation, customer satisfaction levels, market positioning and more. Look for customer reviews, testimonials, and industry analyses to uncover insights that go beyond the obvious. Ask yourself: What do customers value most about my competitors? How do my competitors handle customer service and support? What are their strengths and weaknesses in delivering their promises? This holistic approach will provide a comprehensive view of where your competitors stand and where opportunities for differentiation lay.

Armed with insights from your research, it's time to craft your strategic game plan. Focus on highlighting your unique strengths and value proposition that set you apart in the marketplace. Consider your agility, customer-centric approach, or innovative solutions that address specific pain points your competitors might overlook. Outline your game plan by emphasizing your responsiveness and adaptability to customer feedback, highlighting personalized solutions that cater to individual client needs, and showcasing your commitment to superior customer service and support. By articulating your strengths clearly, you position yourself not just as a competitor but as a preferred choice for potential clients seeking genuine value and reliable partnership.

Competitive environments often trigger internal challenges such as imposter syndrome—a feeling of inadequacy despite evidence of competence. Recognize that these feelings are natural and common among high achievers. Combat imposter syndrome by acknowledging your accomplishments and strengths, setting realistic goals for improvement and growth, and seeking feedback and support from mentors or peers. By nurturing a positive self-image and focusing on continuous learning, you enhance your resilience and confidence in navigating competitive pressures. Beyond traditional metrics, consider factors often overlooked in competitive analyses, such as customer loyalty and retention strategies, long-term relationship building and trust cultivation, and emerging trends or disruptive innovations in the industry. These insights provide a nuanced understanding of market dynamics and potential opportunities for innovation and differentiation.

Mastering your understanding of competition isn't just about gaining knowledge—it's a journey of self-discovery and strategic alignment. Embrace the challenges and opportunities that come with competition, leveraging insights to propel your personal and professional growth. Stay adaptable and open to evolving market trends, celebrate successes and learn from setbacks, and continuously refine your strategies based on new insights and feedback. By adopting a proactive and reflective approach to understanding your competition, you position yourself not only to compete but to thrive in dynamic and competitive markets. Embrace this journey with confidence and determination, knowing that each step brings you closer to achieving your sales goals and personal aspirations.

Sales Stigmas - Changing Perceptions

Navigating the landscape of sales often involves confronting and overcoming stigmas—preconceived notions or stereotypes that can hinder your success. I absolutely hate the stigma of the snake oil salesman or slimy salesman. I hate the thought that people think all salesmen lie. I hate it because I know in my heart that I am just trying to help you and by helping you then together we both succeed. This isn't a zero-sum game, there is definitely room for all of us to eat at this table. This chapter explores effective strategies for overcoming stigmas and includes a motivational anecdote to inspire resilience and determination in your sales journey.

Stigmas in sales can arise from various sources, including negative perceptions about salespeople, industry biases, or misconceptions about specific products or services. These stigmas can create barriers to trust and credibility, making it challenging to build meaningful client relationships and secure sales. Combat stigmas by demonstrating authenticity and transparency in your interactions. Be genuine about your intentions, communicate openly, and address any concerns or misconceptions directly. Proactively educate clients about your product or service to dispel myths or misinformation. Provide clear and accurate information, backed by evidence and customer testimonials, to build credibility and trust. Shift the conversation away from stigmas by emphasizing the tangible value and benefits your offering provides. Showcase how your solution solves specific problems or enhances the client's experience, demonstrating its relevance and importance. This is one of the main aspects of the salesman's paradox sales system. I'm teaching you how to help the client come to the decision that the product is the solution they need so that you are not having to "sell" to them in the traditional sense.

You need to tailor your approach to each client's needs and preferences. Listen actively, empathize with their concerns, and offer personalized solutions that address their unique challenges. This personalized approach reinforces your commitment to their success, overriding any negative perceptions. Maintain a high standard of professionalism in every interaction but not overly stuffy. Once your rapport is built and both of your walls have come down, be yourself, be transparent and helpful. Demonstrate reliability, integrity, and a customer-first mindset to differentiate yourself positively from stigmatized stereotypes.

Sarah, a determined sales professional, faced a daunting challenge when she joined a company known for aggressive sales tactics and high turnover rates. Despite her genuine passion for helping clients, she encountered skepticism and resistance from prospects who had been burned by previous salespeople. One particular client, Mr. Johnson, was initially reluctant to engage with Sarah due to his past negative experiences. He voiced concerns about pushy sales tactics and exaggerated promises that had left him dissatisfied with previous vendors. Instead of being discouraged, Sarah saw an opportunity to change Mr. Johnson's perception. She took the time to listen attentively to his concerns, acknowledging the validity of his past experiences while assuring him of her commitment to a different approach. Over several meetings, Sarah patiently educated Mr. Johnson about her company's solutions, focusing on their reliability, transparent pricing, and track record of client success stories. She invited him to speak directly with satisfied customers and encouraged him to ask tough questions, demonstrating her company's transparency and integrity. Gradually, Mr. Johnson's skepticism began to wane as he witnessed Sarah's genuine efforts to address his concerns and provide value-driven solutions. Impressed by her professionalism and sincerity, he eventually became not only a client but also a vocal advocate for Sarah's services within his network. Sarah's story illustrates the transformative power of fortitude, integrity, authenticity, and a client-centered approach in overcoming stigmas. By staying true to her values and focusing on building trust, she not only broke through initial skepticism but also turned a skeptical prospect into a loyal client and advocate.

Overcoming stigmas in sales requires resilience, empathy, and a proactive strategy to challenge misconceptions and build trust. By embracing authenticity, educating clients, emphasizing value, and maintaining professionalism, you can effectively navigate and overcome stigmas, paving the way for meaningful client relationships and sustainable success in sales.

Navigating Outside Influences

In the dynamic world of sales, external influences can significantly impact the decision-making process of your potential clients. Understanding and effectively managing these influences is crucial for maintaining control over the sales conversation and ultimately securing successful outcomes. This chapter explores various external factors that can affect sales interactions and provides strategies to navigate them effectively. External influences in sales encompass a wide range of factors, including media and news, friends and family, economic conditions, competing priorities, and cultural and social norms. Current events, industry news, and media coverage can shape client perceptions and influence their buying decisions. Recommendations and opinions from trusted individuals can sway a client's preferences and priorities. Market fluctuations, economic stability, and financial trends can impact a client's willingness to invest or make purchasing decisions. Personal or business-related commitments, deadlines, and competing projects may divert a client's attention and influence their purchasing timeline. Cultural values, social trends, and peer influences can shape client preferences and behaviors.

To stay informed and proactive, keep abreast of relevant news and industry developments that may impact your clients. Anticipate potential concerns or questions related to current events and be prepared to address them proactively during your sales conversations. Establish trust by demonstrating your expertise, reliability, and commitment to delivering value. Leverage testimonials, case studies, and references from satisfied clients to build credibility and alleviate concerns influenced by external factors. Emphasize how your product or service addresses specific client needs and provides tangible benefits. Illustrate the positive impact of your solution, regardless of external challenges or distractions. Tailor your sales approach to align with the client's unique circumstances and preferences. Acknowledge and respect external influences such as personal priorities or financial considerations, and position your offering as a valuable solution that complements their existing commitments. Be prepared to address objections that may arise from external influences, such as budget constraints or competitive offers. Listen actively, empathize with their concerns, and provide solutions that alleviate their uncertainties.

Mark, a seasoned sales executive, faced a challenging sales pitch to a potential client who expressed hesitancy due to economic uncertainties highlighted in recent news reports. The client, Mr. Thompson, voiced concerns about budget constraints and the potential impact of market volatility on their investment decisions. Instead of dismissing Mr. Thompson's concerns, Mark acknowledged the validity of his worries and took a proactive approach. He scheduled additional meetings to provide updated market analysis, demonstrating his commitment to staying informed and addressing current economic conditions directly. During these meetings, Mark focused on showcasing the long-term benefits and return on investment of his company's services, emphasizing stability, reliability, and competitive advantage despite external economic fluctuations. He leveraged success stories from similar clients who had achieved significant results during challenging economic periods. Through consistent communication, transparency, and personalized attention to Mr. Thompson's specific concerns, Mark successfully navigated external influences and secured a partnership that exceeded the client's expectations. By demonstrating resilience and adaptability in addressing external factors, Mark strengthened client confidence and solidified long-term business relationships.

Effectively navigating external influences in sales requires strategic foresight, proactive communication, and a client-centered approach. By understanding the impact of media, personal relationships, economic conditions, and cultural norms on client decisions, you can tailor your sales strategy to address concerns, build trust, and highlight the value of your offering. Embrace challenges as opportunities to showcase your expertise and commitment to client success, positioning yourself as a trusted advisor and partner in their decision-making process. By doing so, you will not only overcome external influences but also turn them into a competitive advantage, leading to more successful and lasting client relationships.

Balancing Needs vs. Wants

Understanding the distinction between needs and wants is essential for guiding successful interactions and closing deals effectively. While needs address fundamental requirements for survival or function, wants are desires or preferences that enhance quality of life or fulfill aspirations. The challenge for sales professionals often lies in bridging the gap between wants and needs, particularly when presenting products or services that fulfill desires rather than necessities. Identifying whether a potential customer views your offering as a want or a need requires keen observation and effective questioning during the engagement phase. Needs are typically associated with practicality and immediate benefits, addressing specific pain points or solving critical problems. In contrast, wants appeal to desires, aspirations, or lifestyle enhancements, offering unique experiences or emotional satisfaction.

To successfully navigate this distinction, sales professionals must emphasize the value and benefits of their product or service in a way that resonates with the customer's priorities and motivations. This involves highlighting not only the functional aspects but also the emotional and aspirational benefits that fulfill the customer's desires and align with their personal or professional goals. Making a want feel like a need involves framing the offering in a way that emphasizes its importance and relevance to the customer's life or business.

This can be achieved by:

Demonstrating Value Proposition: Clearly articulate how your product or service addresses specific wants or desires, enhancing the customer's quality of life, productivity, or enjoyment.

Highlighting Unique Benefits: Emphasize unique features or benefits that differentiate your offering from competitors and align with the customer's preferences or aspirations.

Creating Urgency: Instill a sense of urgency by highlighting limited-time offers, exclusive benefits, or opportunities that reinforce the immediate value of acting now rather than later.

Building Emotional Connection: Appeal to the customer's emotions by sharing success stories, testimonials, or case studies that illustrate how your offering has positively impacted others in similar situations.

Ultimately, closing the sale hinges on understanding and addressing the customer's underlying motivations and priorities, whether they are driven by needs or wants. By effectively communicating the value, benefits, and unique advantages of your product or service, you can bridge the gap between desires and necessities, compelling the customer to make a confident and informed decision to purchase. In conclusion, while needs and wants may differ in urgency and necessity, successful sales professionals recognize the power of addressing both in a way that aligns with the customer's personal or business objectives. By mastering the art of distinguishing between needs and wants, and effectively positioning your offering to fulfill both, you can enhance customer satisfaction, loyalty, and ultimately achieve consistent sales success.

Part Six

5 E's of "The Sell"

Alright, let's get into it! The succinct and most important section of this book, the step-by-step instructions, the 5E's framework—the Entry, Extraction, Engagement, Excitement, and Ending—serve as a comprehensive guide to navigate the intricate stages of the sales process. Each phase is crucial for building trust, understanding client needs, showcasing your product's value, creating enthusiasm, and ultimately securing a successful deal. Mastering these phases ensures that you approach sales with a structured, effective, and client-centric strategy.

The Entry phase is the initial point of contact where first impressions are formed, and relationships begin to develop. This phase sets the tone for the entire sales process and involves creating a positive and memorable first impression, establishing rapport, and setting the stage for a productive conversation. It's essential to prepare thoroughly, understand the prospect's background, and tailor your approach to resonate with their specific needs and priorities. The Extraction phase delves deeper into understanding the prospect's true needs, challenges, and motivations. This is where you gather valuable insights through effective questioning and active listening. By uncovering the root of their problems (pain points) and identifying their goals (wants, needs and desires), you can position your product or service so that the prospect determines it is their best solution. Empathy and sensitivity are crucial here, as they help build a supportive environment where the prospect feels comfortable sharing their concerns.

Engagement is the phase where you demonstrate how your product or service can solve the prospect's identified challenges. This involves highlighting key features and benefits, tailoring your presentation to the prospect's specific situation, and using real-world examples and use cases. By engaging in an interactive dialogue, you can address any concerns or objections proactively and ensure that the prospect sees the practical benefits of your offering. Excitement is about building enthusiasm and commitment towards moving forward with your solution. This phase leverages testimonials, success stories, and envisioning future positive outcomes. By creating a vision of how your product or service can significantly impact the prospect's business or life, you foster a sense of anticipation and readiness to proceed. Active listening and adaptation are key to maintaining engagement and excitement throughout this phase.

The Ending phase is where you solidify the commitment, address any final concerns, and secure the deal. This phase includes effective closing techniques, proactive follow-up, and addressing buyer's remorse. It's also an opportunity to cultivate referrals and advocacy by exceeding expectations and delivering exceptional value. Celebrating success and creating advocates ensure long-term relationships and future growth opportunities.

E1 – Creating an Impactful Entry

We start off the E's with the entry, the entry phase of a sales interaction sets the tone and foundation for the entire process. It is the crucial moment where first impressions are formed, relationships begin to develop, and the groundwork for trust and rapport is laid. Mastering the art of entry requires finesse, preparation, and a deep understanding of both your prospect and the context of the meeting. Entering a sales meeting is akin to stepping onto a stage where you are the protagonist of your narrative. Your appearance, demeanor, and initial words should exude confidence, professionalism, and warmth. A firm handshake, genuine smile, and respectful greeting establish a positive tone and convey sincerity from the outset. Imagine your entrance as the opening scene of a captivating performance. Every detail matters, from your attire to your body language. Dress appropriately for the occasion, as this reflects your respect for the prospect and the importance you place on the meeting. Maintain an open posture and make eye contact to project confidence and approachability. Your initial words should be carefully chosen to convey enthusiasm and a genuine interest in the prospect's needs.

My administrator or I would typically ask the client to have a seat in the waiting room and review my testimonial binder while I got ready for the meeting or finished up what I was doing. Even if I wasn't doing anything pressing, I still did this for the psychological principles at play. By asking the client to have a seat and offering the testimonial binder and asking if they'd like a bottle of water, you are establishing that you are professional and your time is valuable. If they read the testimonial binder then you are lowering their defense mechanisms prior to the meeting even starting to allow for a faster paced rapport building and by offering the water, even if they decline, you are engaging the reciprocity principle where they now subconsciously owe you something due to your generosity. Shake their hand firmly and consider the two-handed handshake grip to show that you truly care. As you enter your office, stand behind your desk until they sit indicating that they are your guest but you are still in charge.

Preparation is paramount in the entry phase. Before meeting a prospect, thorough research on their background, industry trends, and potential pain points provides invaluable insights. This knowledge not only demonstrates your commitment but also allows you to tailor your approach and conversation to resonate with their specific needs and priorities. In-depth preparation involves more than just skimming through the company's website. Utilize various resources such as industry reports, news articles, and social media profiles to gather comprehensive information about the prospect. Understand their market position, recent achievements, and challenges they may be facing. By doing so, you equip yourself with the context needed to engage meaningfully and position your solution as the best solution.

The physical environment and setting play a significant role in the entry phase as well. Whether you are meeting in person or virtually, ensure the space is conducive to open communication and engagement. Consider factors such as lighting, seating arrangement, and minimal distractions to foster a focused and comfortable atmosphere. For in-person meetings, choose a quiet, well-lit location that encourages dialogue. Arrange seating in a way that promotes a conversational rather than confrontational dynamic. For virtual meetings, ensure your background is professional and free from distractions, and test your technology beforehand to avoid any technical issues.

Effective entry involves more listening than speaking. Start by defining the purpose as you are not there to waste their time and as you begin to ask your open-ended questions begin active listening. By actively listening to your prospect's initial comments, questions, and concerns, you demonstrate respect and a genuine interest in understanding their perspective. Reflecting back their concerns or interests shows empathy and begins to establish a foundation of trust. Active listening requires full engagement with the prospect. Nod to show understanding, and use verbal affirmations such as "I see" or "That's interesting" to encourage them to continue. Also, remember that up to 93% of communication is non-verbal, as expressed in the Mehrabian Communication Model - 7% verbal, 38% vocal (tone, intonation), and 55% non-verbal (body language, facial expressions). When responding, paraphrase their points to confirm your understanding and show that you value their input. This not only builds rapport but also provides valuable insights into their needs and expectations.

Finding common ground early in the conversation helps to establish rapport and create a connection. Whether through shared experiences, mutual contacts, or industry insights, identifying commonalities builds a sense of camaraderie and reduces barriers between you and the prospect. Look for opportunities to relate to the prospect on a personal or professional level. Mention any mutual connections or similar experiences you might share. Discuss industry trends or challenges that you both are familiar with. This approach humanizes the interaction, making it easier to build a trusting relationship. Every entry into a sales conversation should be tailored to the individual prospect. Acknowledge their unique challenges, aspirations, and goals based on your pre-meeting research. By addressing their specific needs from the outset, you demonstrate attentiveness and position yourself as a trusted advisor capable of delivering personalized solutions. Personalization goes beyond using the prospect's name. Incorporate specific details about their business and industry into your conversation. Reference recent events or trends that are relevant to them. This level of detail shows that you are not just another salesperson but a knowledgeable partner invested in their success.

Confidence in yourself and your offering is contagious. It instills trust and reassures the prospect of your competence and reliability. Authenticity, paired with confidence, allows you to genuinely connect with the client on a human level, fostering a more meaningful and productive dialogue. Speak with conviction about the value your product or service can bring. Be honest about what you can and cannot deliver. Authenticity builds trust and credibility, while confidence reassures the prospect that you are capable of helping them achieve their goals. Avoid overpromising, and instead, focus on realistic outcomes and the tangible benefits of your offering.

Mastering the art of entry in sales requires meticulous preparation, genuine interest, and a focus on building trust and rapport from the first moment of contact. Remember that you get 7-30 seconds to create the initial impression and set the tone for the meeting per some of the greatest social psychology minds of our generation. By creating a positive first impression, actively listening, and tailoring your approach to address the prospect's specific needs, you set the stage for a successful sales journey. The entry phase not only establishes the foundation for future interactions but also positions you as a knowledgeable and empathetic partner dedicated to achieving mutual success. By embracing these principles, you can transform initial meetings into opportunities to build lasting relationships and drive meaningful results. Remember, the entry phase is not just about making a good impression—it's about laying the groundwork for a partnership built on trust, understanding, and shared goals.

To recap, at this point you have; done your research before the meeting, you have had the client sit and wait for you, read your testimonials, and engaged in reciprocity by offering a refreshing beverage. Then as you enter your office, you have shaken hands with the two-handed handshake - one in hand, one on forearm, with perfect eye contact saying that you are warm, open and here to help. You stand until they sit indicating you are in charge of the meeting and open the conversation with rapport building followed by a meeting focus statement. You have now engaged multiple psychological principles and have built quick and strong rapport. You are now ready for the next phase of the E's, E2 - Extraction.

E2 - Extracting Valuable Insights

The extraction phase stands as a pivotal moment where understanding the prospect's true needs, challenges, and motivations becomes paramount. This phase is about diving deep, uncovering valuable insights, and guiding the conversation towards identifying the real issues that your

product or service can effectively address. Effective extraction begins with asking insightful questions that penetrate beyond surface-level inquiries. These questions should be crafted to uncover the prospect's pain points, wants, needs, goals and aspirations. For example, consider a scenario where a software sales consultant is meeting with a prospective client from a logistics company. Instead of asking generic questions about their software needs, the consultant dives deeper: "I understand that logistics coordination can be complex. Could you share with me the specific challenges your team faces when managing inventory across multiple warehouses?" This kind of question shows that you have done your homework and are genuinely interested in understanding their specific situation.

Asking probing questions requires empathy and sensitivity to the prospect's situation. It's important to frame questions in a way that demonstrates genuine interest in understanding their challenges rather than simply gathering information. By approaching the conversation empathetically, you create a supportive environment where the prospect feels comfortable sharing their concerns and goals. For instance, instead of asking, "What's wrong with your current supplier?" you might say, "It sounds like reliability is crucial for your operations. Can you tell me more about your experiences and what you're looking for in a supplier?"

Pain statements are powerful tools when used positively to guide the conversation towards solutions. Instead of dwelling on negatives, reframe pain points as opportunities for improvement or growth. For instance, if the prospect expresses frustration with their current supplier's lack of responsiveness, you could say, "It sounds like having a reliable partner who responds promptly to your needs is crucial. How would having real-time support enhance your team's efficiency and overall satisfaction?" This not only acknowledges their pain but also opens up a discussion about how your solution can address it. Active listening plays a critical role in the extraction phase as well. It involves not only hearing but also comprehending and empathizing with what the prospect is communicating. Reflecting back their concerns and insights demonstrates your attentiveness and commitment to understanding their perspective fully. For example, you might say, "I hear that managing inventory across multiple locations is a significant challenge for your team. What specific outcomes are you hoping to achieve with a new solution?"

Often, prospects may not articulate all their needs upfront. Skilled extraction involves uncovering these hidden needs through attentive listening and thoughtful questioning. By digging deeper into their challenges and objectives, you can identify opportunities where your product or service can make a significant impact. For example, if a prospect mentions a general frustration with their current system, ask follow-up questions like, "Can you walk me through a typical day using your current system? Where do you encounter the most friction?" You want to go multiple layers deep just like the movie Inception we mentioned earlier. Try to go three, four, even five layers deep like you are trying to get to the root cause of the issue. If you have experience in project management or Lean Six Sigma, now is the time to let that skillset shine!

Once you've gathered insights, guide the conversation towards exploring how your offering can address their specific challenges and goals. Position yourself as a strategic partner invested in their success by presenting tailored solutions that align with their identified needs and aspirations. For instance, if a logistics company struggles with inventory visibility, you might discuss how your software's real-time tracking features can streamline operations and reduce errors. Throughout the extraction phase, maintain a positive and supportive atmosphere. Even when discussing challenges, emphasize the potential for improvement and positive outcomes. This approach reassures the prospect and reinforces your role as a proactive problem-solver. For example, you might say, "While it sounds like inventory management has been a headache, I'm confident that with the right tools, we can turn this around and significantly improve your efficiency."

Here's a quick story to illustrate the extraction phase. In a recent sales meeting, a logistics software consultant engaged with a potential client who struggled with inventory management inefficiencies. By asking probing questions about their current process and pain points, the consultant uncovered that the client's biggest challenge was real-time visibility across multiple warehouses. Through active listening and empathetic understanding, the consultant proposed a solution that integrated advanced tracking and reporting features, addressing the client's need for streamlined operations and improved inventory accuracy. This tailored approach not only addressed the client's immediate concerns but also positioned the consultant as a trusted advisor invested in their long-term success.

Mastering the extraction phase in sales requires a combination of strategic questioning, empathetic listening, and a positive mindset. By skillfully probing for insights, understanding the prospect's true needs, and guiding the conversation towards solutions, you set the stage for a collaborative and productive sales journey. Approach each interaction with empathy and a genuine desire to help, and you'll build trust, uncover hidden opportunities, and ultimately achieve successful outcomes for both you and your client.

E3 - Engaging with Purpose

Once you've identified the real issues and challenges faced by your prospect through effective extraction, the next crucial step in the sales process is to demonstrate how your product or service can effectively solve these problems. Engaging with your product in a way that resonates with the prospect's needs and objectives is key to moving towards a successful sale. Before diving into product details, reaffirm your understanding of the prospect's pain points and challenges. Summarize what you've gathered from the extraction phase to ensure alignment and demonstrate your attentiveness. This step not only reinforces your commitment to addressing their specific needs but also sets the stage for a focused and productive discussion.

Present your product or service as a solution by highlighting its key features and benefits that directly address the prospect's identified challenges. Focus on how these features translate into tangible advantages and outcomes for their business. For example, if your software solution enhances operational efficiency, quantify potential time savings or cost reductions. This approach helps the prospect see the direct impact of your offering on their pain points. Customize your presentation to resonate with the prospect's industry, business model, and objectives. Use case studies, testimonials, or relevant examples to illustrate how similar clients have successfully utilized your product to overcome challenges similar to theirs. This personalized approach reinforces the relevance and applicability of your solution to their specific situation. Utilize use cases or demonstrations to show the prospect how your product functions in real-world scenarios. Walk them through specific workflows or functionalities that directly address their pain points. This hands-on approach not only showcases the capabilities of your offering but also allows the prospect to visualize its impact on their operations.

Anticipate potential concerns or objections that may arise and address them proactively during your engagement. Be transparent about limitations or considerations while emphasizing the overall value and benefits. People appreciate when you don't try to provide your solution as infallible or as the greatest thing since sliced bread. You can love your product or service through its downsides and that comes off as authentic and true. Use your knowledge gained from the extraction phase to tailor your responses and reassure the prospect of your solution's suitability. By the way did you know that it took years for people to adopt sliced bread? Google it, it struggled for about 2 years until Wonderbread adopted it and helped market it into its wild success. Sorry for the tangent, you should engage the prospect in an interactive dialogue throughout the presentation. Remember you are on a team working together to accomplish the same mission. Encourage questions, feedback, and discussions to ensure mutual understanding and alignment. Actively listen to their input and concerns, and adjust your presentation accordingly to maintain their interest and address any additional insights they provide.

In conclusion, engaging with your product to solve customer challenges requires a strategic approach that combines understanding, customization, and effective communication. By presenting your product as a tailored solution to the prospect's identified pain points, you demonstrate value and build confidence in your ability to deliver results. Remember you are not selling your product or service, rather you are positioning your answer to allow the client to come to the conclusion that your solution is ultimately the only feasible one that exists. Approach each engagement with a focus on addressing the specific needs and illustrating the practical benefits of your offering, and you'll pave the way for a successful sales conversion based on mutual understanding and alignment.

E4 - Generating Excitement & Anticipation

The excitement phase of the sales process is where the groundwork laid in understanding the prospect's challenges and allowing them to find your solution culminates in building enthusiasm and commitment towards moving forward. This phase focuses on leveraging testimonials, reinforcing alignment, and subtly guiding the prospect towards envisioning the positive outcomes of choosing your product or service. Here's how to effectively create excitement and momentum towards closing the sale. Harness the power of testimonials and success stories to build credibility and inspire confidence in your solution. Share case studies or quotes from satisfied customers who have achieved significant results by using your product or service. Highlight specific benefits and outcomes that resonate with the prospect's needs, reinforcing the value of choosing your solution. For instance, if your solution has helped similar companies achieve measurable improvements, detail those successes to illustrate the potential impact on your prospect's business.

Revisit the prospect's identified challenges and pain points to reaffirm how your solution addresses these issues effectively. Emphasize the unique benefits and advantages that set your product apart from competitors. Align your presentation with their goals and objectives, demonstrating a clear path towards achieving desired outcomes through your offering. This alignment shows that you have listened and understood their needs, and it reinforces the relevance of your solution. Engage the prospect in envisioning the future state with your solution integrated into their operations. Use language that invites them to visualize the positive impact and benefits of adopting your product or service. Guide the conversation towards exploring how their business will thrive and grow with your solution, subtly planting the idea that choosing your offering is the natural next step towards success. This vision-casting helps prospects see beyond the immediate transaction to the long-term benefits of your solution.

Throughout the excitement phase, maintain active listening and adapt your approach based on the prospect's reactions and feedback. Utilize psychological principles like the micro-expressions addressed earlier to ensure you have captured their interest and hopefully their heart. Address any remaining questions or concerns promptly and confidently. By demonstrating responsiveness and attentiveness, you reinforce your commitment to their satisfaction and build trust in your ability to deliver results. Stay one notch more excited than them so that you are leading and not drifting away and losing them. This adaptability shows that you are not just selling a product but are invested in solving their problems.

Quick story would be something like; In a recent sales presentation for a marketing automation platform, a sales representative shared a testimonial from a client in a similar industry. The testimonial highlighted how the platform significantly increased lead conversion rates and improved campaign ROI. By illustrating tangible results and demonstrating how the platform could similarly benefit the prospect's business, the representative effectively sparked excitement and interest in exploring further. This hypothetical underscores the importance of using real-world success stories to validate your claims and build enthusiasm.

Creating excitement in the sales process is about building momentum and confidence towards closing the sale. By leveraging testimonials, reinforcing alignment with the prospect's goals, and guiding them towards envisioning positive outcomes with your solution, you inspire enthusiasm and readiness to move forward. Approach each interaction with a focus on demonstrating value, addressing concerns proactively, and subtly influencing their decision-making process. Through strategic engagement and genuine enthusiasm, you can effectively navigate the excitement phase and secure a successful outcome for both you and your client.

In conclusion, the excitement phase is critical for translating the groundwork of understanding and presentation into genuine interest and commitment from your prospect. By effectively utilizing testimonials, aligning with the prospect's goals, and maintaining active and responsive engagement, you build a compelling case for your solution. This phase not only locks the prospect into your positive decision but also fosters a sense of anticipation and eagerness to move forward, setting the stage for a successful close and long-term partnership.

E5 - Memorable Ending - Perfect Close

Congratulations on reaching the final phase of the sales process! This is where all your hard work and strategic efforts come together to secure a successful outcome and lay the foundation for lasting relationships with your clients. The ending phase is crucial for solidifying commitment, addressing concerns, and ultimately creating advocates who champion your product or service. Let's explore how to navigate this phase with confidence and celebrate your achievements along the way.

As you approach the close, consider utilizing the assumptive close, a powerful technique that confidently assumes the prospect is ready to move forward. For instance, you might say, "Based on our discussion, it sounds like our solution aligns perfectly with your needs. Let's go ahead and proceed with the next steps." Alternatively, you can use the direct close, where you straightforwardly ask for the sale, or the choice close, giving the prospect options to move forward based on their preferences. These techniques help create a sense of momentum and make it easier for the prospect to make a decision. Remember though, any hesitancy means that your client is not ready to close yet so needs more of either extraction, engagement or excitement. Head back there, overcome the objection and start the Ending again. Immediately after closing, initiate proactive follow-up to reinforce the prospect's decision and offer any additional support they may need. Your prompt and personalized follow-up demonstrates your dedication to their success and ensures a smooth transition towards implementation. This follow-up could include a thank-you note, a summary of the next steps, or a welcome package that provides further information about your product or service. By maintaining this level of engagement, you build trust and show that you are committed to their long-term success.

Recognize that buyer's remorse is natural, but your thorough understanding of their needs and effective communication have set the stage for confidence in their decision. Reaffirm the value and benefits of your solution, using testimonials and case studies to validate their choice. For example, you might share a success story of a similar client who achieved significant results with your product. Your proactive approach ensures they feel supported every step of the way and helps mitigate any doubts or concerns they might have. Celebrate your success by cultivating advocates who enthusiastically promote your product or service. Encourage referrals and introductions to other potential clients who could benefit from your offering. Your dedication to excellence and customer satisfaction fosters long-term relationships built on trust and mutual success. Consider implementing a referral program that rewards clients for referring new business to you. This not only incentivizes them to spread the word but also demonstrates your appreciation for their support.

By exceeding expectations and delivering exceptional value, you've not only closed a deal but also earned a loyal advocate. Your commitment to customer success inspires confidence and loyalty, turning satisfied clients into enthusiastic champions within their networks. Celebrate this achievement—it's a testament to your skills and dedication! Regularly check in with your clients to ensure they are happy with your product and to address any issues that may arise. This ongoing relationship management is key to maintaining their advocacy.

Imagine closing a deal for a cutting-edge CRM solution with a major client. Your proactive follow-up and personalized support ensure a seamless onboarding process, delighting the client with immediate results and ongoing support. As a result, they not only endorse your solution but also refer several industry peers, solidifying your reputation as a trusted advisor and expert in your field. This real-world example highlights the importance of follow-up, support, and relationship-building in turning clients into advocates. Congratulations once again on mastering the ending phase of the sales process! By utilizing effective closing techniques, proactive follow-up strategies, and a commitment to customer satisfaction, you've paved the way for long-term success and advocacy. Celebrate your achievements and embrace the role of a trusted partner who continues to exceed expectations and drive meaningful results. Your journey doesn't end here—it's the beginning of a thriving relationship and future opportunities for growth and success. Embrace this ongoing journey with confidence and dedication, knowing that each satisfied client is a stepping stone to greater achievements.

All in all, you should have been able to see the sales process of the 5 E's unfold. It started as you asked them to sit in your lobby and read over your testimonials. Then it ventured into reciprocity as you offered a bottle of water. You shook hands firmly with a clear look in your eye that says I am here to help you. They sat, you sat and you began to build rapport. What can you tell about them based on what you know from previous conversations, the car they drive, the clothes they wear, etc.? As they begin to let their guard you give the firm intent of the meeting to ensure we meet the target we are looking for.

You begin to ask questions, never asking if they want your solution rather you are there merely to help them find the right answer. You dig deeper and deeper until you can create a real root cause analysis as to why this client is currently sitting in your office and what they believe is the solution. You then begin to discuss how your solution could solve the pain points of the client and even what it means if they don't find the solution they are after. The client comes to the determination through your subtle inception that your solution is the right solution for them. Agreeingly, you start to get them hyped up with testimonials and stories and any and everything you can to lock them into their decision to work with you. You then use the assumptive close to write up the paperwork and ensure that your new advocate feels comfortable and is excited about their idea and decision. Great job! You have just overcome the salesman's paradox.

Part Seven

Mastering Productivity

&

Peak Performance

30/30/30/10 Rule Meets Pareto's 80/20

In the dynamic world of sales, mastering efficiency is essential for achieving consistent success. The 30/30/30/10 rule provides a structured framework to optimize your daily activities, while Pareto's Principle (the 80/20 rule) offers strategic insights into prioritizing tasks based on their impact. The 30/30/30/10 rule divides your workday into segments, each dedicated to specific types of tasks to ensure a balanced and productive approach. The first 30% of your day should focus on high-impact activities that directly contribute to your sales goals. This could include closing deals with key clients, conducting strategic planning sessions, or nurturing relationships with top prospects. By prioritizing these tasks when your energy and focus are at their peak, you set a proactive tone for the day and maximize productivity. For example, imagine you're a real estate agent aiming to close a major property deal. Spending the first 30% of your day preparing and meeting with potential buyers or sellers aligns with this rule, ensuring you allocate prime time to critical revenue-generating activities.

The second 30% should be allocated to essential but less urgent tasks that support ongoing sales efforts. This might involve following up on client inquiries, updating CRM records, or preparing detailed proposals for upcoming presentations. These tasks maintain momentum and operational efficiency throughout your day. Consider a software sales representative who spends the second 30% of their day responding to customer queries, refining product demos, and updating sales pipelines. These activities support ongoing client engagement and ensure all interactions are timely and well-managed.

The third 30% should be dedicated to learning and development to enhance your sales skills and industry knowledge. This could include attending webinars, reading industry reports, or participating in sales training sessions. Investing in continuous improvement strengthens your abilities and keeps you competitive in a dynamic sales environment. For instance, a pharmaceutical sales manager might use this time to study new medical research, refine their product knowledge, and participate in professional development workshops. These efforts equip them with updated information and advanced techniques to better serve their clients and achieve sales targets.

The final 10% should be reserved for unforeseen tasks or urgent matters that require immediate attention. This buffer allows flexibility to address unexpected challenges without disrupting your overall productivity or sales objectives. Imagine an insurance broker who dedicates the final 10% of their day to resolving urgent client issues, handling administrative tasks, or attending impromptu meetings. This strategic allocation ensures they can manage unexpected demands while staying focused on their primary sales goals.

Applying Pareto's Principle in sales complements the 30/30/30/10 rule by emphasizing the importance of focusing on tasks that yield the most significant results. According to Pareto's Principle, approximately 80% of outcomes come from 20% of efforts. In sales, this means identifying and prioritizing activities that drive substantial results, such as closing high-value deals, nurturing key relationships, or exploring new market opportunities. For example, a technology sales executive might focus on nurturing relationships with top clients who generate the majority of revenue. By prioritizing these key accounts and tailoring their sales strategies accordingly, they maximize their impact and achieve substantial sales growth. Optimize time allocation by dedicating a significant portion of your time (the first 30%) to high-impact activities. This strategic approach minimizes time spent on low-value tasks and maximizes productivity throughout your day. Consider a marketing manager who applies Pareto's Principle to streamline campaign strategies. By focusing on the 20% of marketing activities that generate 80% of leads or customer engagement, they optimize their budget and resources effectively, driving higher ROI and campaign success.

Regularly assess your tasks and activities to ensure they align with Pareto's Principle. Identify any inefficiencies or low-impact tasks that may detract from your overall sales goals. Delegate, automate, or refine these tasks to prioritize activities that drive revenue and business growth. For instance, a sales team leader might review monthly performance metrics to identify top-performing strategies and areas for improvement. By leveraging data insights and adjusting their sales approach accordingly, they enhance team efficiency and achieve sustainable sales success.

Integrating the structured approach of the 30/30/30/10 rule with strategic insights from Pareto's Principle empowers sales professionals to optimize productivity and achieve consistent results. By prioritizing high-impact activities, investing in continuous learning, and refining sales strategies based on data-driven insights, you create a pathway to sustained success in sales. Embrace efficiency, focus on what matters most, and elevate your performance to drive growth and exceed your sales targets.

Min Time Wasting: Max Productivity

In the dynamic world of sales, time is your most valuable asset. How you manage it can make all the difference between average performance and extraordinary success. It's about more than just ticking off tasks—it's about optimizing every minute to achieve meaningful results and build lasting relationships. Efficient time management in sales requires a keen understanding of your priorities and the ability to focus on activities that drive the most significant impact. We all have them—those little things that eat away at our day without adding much value. It could be excessive meetings that could be condensed, or distractions like constantly checking emails. Recognizing these time wasters is the first step in reclaiming your focus and productivity. Think about your day—are there tasks that drain your energy but don't move the needle forward? By identifying and minimizing these distractions, you free up valuable time to concentrate on what truly drives your success—closing deals, nurturing client relationships, and strategic planning.

To maximize your impact, prioritize tasks that have the highest ROI potential. Use the 30/30/30/10 rule: dedicate 30% of your time to revenue-generating activities like client meetings and negotiations, another 30% to strategic planning and goal setting, and 30% to personal development and relationship building. The remaining 10%? That's for unforeseen challenges or opportunities—flexibility is key in a dynamic sales environment. This structured approach ensures that you are consistently focusing on activities that contribute directly to your sales objectives and professional growth. Delegate non-essential tasks to your team or automate processes wherever possible. This not only frees up your time but also empowers your team to grow and excel in their roles. Effective time blocking is another game-changer—chunk your day into focused intervals for specific tasks, ensuring you stay on track and minimize distractions. By creating dedicated time slots for high-priority activities, you enhance your ability to concentrate and achieve more in less time.

In sales, relationships matter just as much as results. Allocate time for personalized client interactions, follow-ups, and team collaboration. Strong relationships build trust and loyalty, essential for long-term success. Make every interaction count—whether it's a client call or a team meeting, approach each with genuine interest and a focus on adding value. Nurture your network through regular check-ins and proactive communication. Remember, people buy from those they trust and connect with on a personal level. Building and maintaining these relationships requires consistent effort and attention to detail.

To truly optimize your efforts, leverage data and analytics to track performance metrics and customer feedback. Identify what's working and what isn't, then refine your approach accordingly. Continuously evaluate and adjust your sales strategies to stay ahead of the curve and deliver exceptional results. Use customer relationship management (CRM) systems to organize and analyze data, helping you make informed decisions and identify new opportunities. Ultimately, efficiency in sales isn't just about doing things faster—it's about doing the right things at the right time. Embrace a proactive mindset, harness technology to streamline processes, and prioritize activities that drive meaningful outcomes. By mastering time management and focusing on high-impact tasks, you'll not only boost your productivity but also elevate your sales performance to new heights. Imagine a day where every minute counts, where your efforts are strategically aligned with your goals, and where relationships are nurtured and results are consistently achieved. This is the power of effective time management in sales—a tool that transforms your approach, maximizes your potential, and propels you toward sustained success.

Identifying Toxicity to Thriving Positivity

Navigating toxic work environments is crucial in sales careers, where a positive workplace culture can significantly impact performance and well-being. Toxicity manifests in various forms that undermine teamwork, productivity, and job satisfaction. Examples include micromanagement, where supervisors excessively control tasks and lack trust in their team's abilities. Another sign is a lack of transparency, where important decisions are made without consulting or informing the team, leading to confusion and frustration. Office politics and favoritism create divisions and undermine trust, while high turnover and low morale signal dissatisfaction and poor leadership. Hostility or conflict, whether overt or passive-aggressive, disrupts teamwork and undermines collaboration.

Even if you aren't the official boss, you can play a huge role in ensuring a positive work environment and the overall success of the team. Every individual has the power to influence the workplace culture positively. You have what is called referent power or power bestowed upon you by peers based on personal characteristics, charisma, and the respect and admiration you inspire in your peers. Start by leading through examples. Demonstrate integrity, fairness, and empathy in all your interactions. When you embody these qualities, you inspire others to do the same, fostering a supportive and collaborative atmosphere.

To avoid toxic environments, thoroughly research potential employers, seek insights from current employees, and assess company culture. Positive indicators include transparent communication, opportunities for growth, and a supportive team atmosphere. When faced with toxic dynamics, adapt your communication style to foster better collaboration and minimize conflicts. Document specific incidents and seek support from trusted colleagues or mentors for advice. Engage with HR or management to address concerns professionally, presenting constructive solutions for improvement. Advocate for initiatives that promote transparency, fairness, and respect, such as team-building activities and conflict resolution workshops.

In your daily interactions, encourage open communication among team members and set clear expectations to minimize misunderstandings. Recognize and celebrate individual and team achievements to boost morale and motivation. Implement initiatives that prioritize work-life balance and mental well-being, supporting flexible work arrangements and wellness programs. Toxic behavior involves actions that undermine trust, create conflict, and hinder productivity. Examples include gossiping, undermining colleagues, refusing to take responsibility, and fostering a culture of fear or competition. In contrast, behaviors that promote a positive work environment include collaboration, open communication, constructive feedback, and mutual respect for diverse perspectives. Building a supportive culture requires consistent effort to address toxicity promptly and foster a workplace where everyone can thrive.

Imagine stepping into a workplace where positivity isn't just encouraged—it's celebrated as the cornerstone of success. It's a place where every interaction, from the morning greetings to team meetings, radiates with genuine enthusiasm and support. This is the essence of the positive ideal workplace—a haven where productivity thrives, creativity flourishes, and success becomes not just a goal but a natural outcome.

In his book "Work Rules!", Laszlo Bock, former Senior Vice President of People Operations at Google, emphasizes that creating a positive workplace isn't just beneficial—it's essential for organizational success. Bock advocates for fostering an environment where employees feel valued, respected, and empowered. This resonates deeply with companies like Google, where transparency, trust, and open communication are core principles that contribute to a positive workplace culture. At the heart of Bock's insights lies the importance of empowering employees through autonomy and trust. When employees feel empowered to make decisions and take ownership of their work, they become more engaged and motivated. This empowerment fosters creativity and innovation, driving the organization forward. Google's famous "20% time" policy, where employees are encouraged to spend 20% of their work hours on projects of personal interest, is a testament to this principle, leading to groundbreaking innovations like Gmail and Google News.

Bock also emphasizes the significance of continuous learning and development. He advocates for providing employees with opportunities to grow professionally and personally, which not only enhances their skills but also fosters a culture of learning and curiosity. Google's robust learning and development programs, including mentorship opportunities and internal courses, empower employees to constantly evolve and adapt to new challenges and opportunities. Diversity and inclusivity are also central themes in Bock's approach to creating a positive workplace. He highlights the importance of building diverse teams and creating an inclusive environment where every individual feels valued and respected. By embracing diversity, organizations like Google leverage different perspectives and experiences to drive innovation and better serve their diverse global audience.

Walking into a positive ideal workplace, inspired by Bock's principles, feels invigorating. There's a tangible sense of camaraderie and shared purpose, where colleagues support each other's growth and celebrate collective achievements. For example, companies inspired by Bock's insights create environments where employees are encouraged to express their unique personalities and contribute to a community built on trust and positivity. Identifying such a workplace is evident in the high levels of employee engagement and low turnover rates. Companies that embrace Bock's principles see higher retention rates and stronger employee loyalty. They excel in customer satisfaction, as happy employees naturally provide exceptional service and build lasting relationships with customers.

Maintaining positivity requires intentional effort and adaptability. Leaders play a crucial role in setting the tone and modeling desired behaviors, especially during challenging times. Companies like Patagonia have demonstrated resilience by staying true to their values and supporting their employees, ensuring that their positive workplace culture remains steadfast even in the face of adversity. Research consistently underscores the benefits of positive workplaces. Studies show that such environments lead to higher productivity, improved employee well-being, and enhanced innovation. Companies that prioritize positivity not only perform better financially but also attract top talent and maintain a strong reputation in their industries as employers of choice.

In conclusion, the positive ideal workplace, guided by Bock's insights in "Work Rules!", is not just a vision but a strategic imperative for organizations aiming for sustained success. By fostering a culture of positivity, respect, and support, companies can unleash the full potential of their employees and create a workplace where everyone thrives. Embracing Bock's principles isn't just about enhancing business outcomes; it's about creating a fulfilling environment where employees are inspired to do their best work, innovate fearlessly, and contribute meaningfully to the organization's success journey.

Navigating toxic work environments and fostering a positive workplace culture are two sides of the same coin in the pursuit of sales success. While it's essential to recognize and mitigate the impact of toxicity, it's equally crucial to build and maintain a workplace where positivity and productivity flourish. By identifying toxic behaviors and addressing them proactively, sales professionals can protect their well-being and focus on their goals. Simultaneously, by embracing the principles of a positive workplace, companies can cultivate environments that inspire employees to excel and achieve lasting success. Even if you aren't the official boss, your proactive efforts in promoting a positive work culture can transform your workplace into a beacon of success and well-being. Remember, every positive action counts and can create a ripple effect, uplifting the entire team towards greater achievements.

Fighting the Good Fight: Integrity through Adversity

In the fast-paced and competitive world of sales, the pressures to meet quotas and achieve short-term gains can often lead to losing sight of what truly matters: the well-being of your team. Yet, the true measure of a leader lies in their commitment to doing what's right, even when it's not the easiest path. This chapter, "Fighting the Good Fight," dives into the importance of advocating for the happiness and welfare of your subordinates and peers—creating a workplace where people come first. Many of us have experienced the frustration of working in environments where the focus on profits or quick wins comes at the expense of employee satisfaction. You may notice morale slipping, burnout rising, or key team members leaving due to high stress. You speak up, suggest changes to make the workplace more supportive and sustainable, but you're met with resistance. Senior leaders may see the suggestions as distractions or unnecessary expenses. But fighting for what's right—making sure your team is taken care of—must remain your priority.

Imagine you've identified that your company's high-pressure sales tactics are driving up stress among your team. You've noticed that these tactics are causing frustration, leading to turnover, and burning out your best people. You bring this to the attention of your leaders and propose a solution: a more balanced approach that values both sales results and employee well-being. Even when met with skepticism or pushback, you continue to advocate because you understand that long-term success comes from having a happy, engaged team.

It's easy to feel defeated when your efforts to create a better environment are ignored, but the real fight is for your people. When you stand up for the well-being of your subordinates and peers, you're doing more than improving your workplace—you're setting a standard that others will follow. Your leadership can create a ripple effect, inspiring others to take a stand for what's right. In fact, when employees see their leaders genuinely care for their happiness and balance, they are more likely to be loyal, motivated, and perform better. One of the most intriguing anomalies I have witnessed is that for most people it doesn't matter whether you win or lose the battle, what matters is that you were willing to fight for what's right and fight to take care of your people.

When you work in alignment with your values, especially around employee care, it brings a deeper sense of fulfillment. Studies have shown that employees who feel supported and valued are more engaged and productive. By fighting for their happiness, you're creating an environment where people can thrive. Take, for example, a sales manager who noticed that aggressive targets were demoralizing the team. Instead of pushing harder, they advocated for realistic goals and a more supportive management approach. The result? Happier employees, better retention, and sustained performance improvements.

One real-world example of fighting for the happiness of employees comes from companies like Patagonia, which focus not only on their mission but on creating an employee-centered culture. They provide flexibility, support for work-life balance, and make sure that employees feel valued. This doesn't just happen in forward-thinking companies—it happens when leaders step up and consistently advocate for what's right for their teams. Another example could be someone in your own workplace—a leader who constantly pushes back when their team is overwhelmed, making sure that workloads are balanced and their team has the resources and time they need to succeed. They may not be saving the world, but they are doing something equally important: ensuring their people are happy and engaged.

When you fight for your employees' well-being, the results often speak for themselves. Teams with strong support systems and leaders who prioritize their happiness tend to outperform others, not because they're being pushed to the brink, but because they feel valued, supported, and motivated to do their best work. This isn't about being a soft leader—it's about being a smart one. Statistics underscore this point. Companies with engaged and happy employees are 21% more profitable, with 17% higher productivity and 41% lower absenteeism, according to Gallup. Furthermore, research published by Harvard Business Review reveals that organizations with highly satisfied employees outperform their peers by 2.3% to 3.8% in annual stock returns. Deloitte's findings align with this, showing that businesses with strong employee well-being cultures experience 2.5 times greater productivity. Engaged employees are less likely to leave, more likely to innovate, and ultimately contribute to a more successful and sustainable organization. Your fight isn't just about immediate results; it's about creating an environment where people want to stay and succeed long-term.

Fighting the good fight means prioritizing people—your peers, your subordinates, and your team's happiness. It's about building an environment where everyone can thrive, not just hit numbers. By standing up for what's right in your workplace, you can build a legacy of respect, care, and trust. And remember, when you take care of your people, success naturally follows.

4-Hour Workday - Work Smarter not Harder

Imagine a workday where you achieve your sales goals and complete all necessary tasks in just four focused hours. This concept of a 4-hour workday isn't about working less, but working smarter and more efficiently. In sales, where time is money and productivity is key, mastering this approach can lead to significant gains in performance and work-life balance. Let's delve into how to transform this vision into reality, ensuring that every minute of your workday is productive and impactful. The foundation of a productive 4-hour workday starts with setting clear priorities. Begin each day by identifying the most important tasks that align with your sales goals. Prioritize activities that directly contribute to revenue generation, such as prospecting, client meetings, and closing deals. Use tools like Eisenhower's Urgent/Important Principle to categorize tasks and ensure you focus on what matters most. By clearly defining your priorities, you create a roadmap for your day that keeps you on track and focused on high-impact activities. Consider starting your day with a quick review of your goals and tasks. Ask yourself: What are the top three things I need to accomplish today to move closer to my sales targets? By honing in on these key tasks, you set a clear direction for your efforts and eliminate the noise of less critical activities.

Efficiency hinges on optimizing your workflow. Leverage technology and automation tools to streamline repetitive tasks like email follow-ups, CRM updates, and proposal generation. For instance, CRM systems like Salesforce offer automation features that can schedule emails, track customer interactions, and streamline data management, saving valuable time and enhancing productivity. Imagine automating your email follow-ups. Instead of manually sending reminders to prospects, use your CRM to set up automated follow-up sequences. This ensures consistent communication while freeing up your time to focus on more strategic activities. Additionally, consider integrating tools like calendar apps to automate scheduling and avoid the back-and-forth often involved in setting up meetings.

Allocate specific time blocks for different tasks throughout your 4-hour workday. Time blocking helps maintain focus and minimizes distractions. For example, dedicate one hour for prospecting calls, another for client meetings, and a final block for administrative tasks. Use techniques like the Pomodoro Technique to work in focused intervals with short breaks in between, optimizing productivity and mental clarity. By segmenting your day into dedicated blocks, you create a structure that promotes deep work and minimizes the cognitive load of switching between tasks. During each block, commit to working exclusively on the designated activity. This level of focus not only increases efficiency but also enhances the quality of your work.

Effective communication is crucial in a condensed workday. Clearly communicate expectations with clients and team members to minimize misunderstandings and maximize efficiency. Utilize concise emails, agenda-driven meetings, and clear call objectives to ensure productive interactions that respect both your time and theirs. For instance, before a client call, outline a clear agenda and share it with the client. This sets expectations for the conversation and ensures that both parties come prepared. During meetings, stay on topic and address key points efficiently. After the meeting, follow up with a summary and next step to reinforce clarity and commitment.

To maximize your efficiency in a 4-hour workday, minimize non-productive activities such as excessive socializing or unnecessary meetings. Stay focused on your tasks and avoid getting drawn into conversations that do not contribute to your sales objectives. By staying disciplined and avoiding distractions, you can accomplish more in less time and enjoy the benefits of additional free time. Evaluate your daily activities and identify any patterns of wasted time. Are there meetings that could be condensed or handled via email? Are there moments in your day when you find yourself procrastinating? By addressing these inefficiencies, you create more space for productive work.

In sales, data-driven decision-making is essential for optimizing performance. Utilize analytics tools to track key metrics like conversion rates, pipeline progression, and customer feedback. Analyzing this data helps identify trends, refine strategies, and prioritize activities that yield the highest return on investment within your limited work hours. Set up regular reviews of your sales metrics to gain insights into your performance. Identify which activities are driving the most significant results and double down on those. Use data to refine your approach, adjust your strategies, and continuously improve your efficiency.

Stay agile and adaptable in your approach. In the Air Force we used to say flexibility is the key to airpower, you can adopt it if it's a mantra of the greatest Air Force in the world, right? You also must continuously learn from successes and challenges, and be willing to adapt your strategies based on feedback and evolving market conditions. Attend industry webinars, read relevant publications, and engage in professional development to stay ahead of trends and refine your sales techniques. Make continuous learning a part of your daily routine. Dedicate time each week to explore new sales strategies, industry developments, and emerging technologies. By staying informed and adaptable, you ensure that your approach remains effective and relevant.

A 4-hour workday isn't just about productivity—it's about achieving a healthy work-life balance. Use your non-work hours for personal growth, relaxation, and activities that recharge your energy. Setting boundaries and disconnecting from work during off-hours ensures you return to your sales role refreshed and ready to perform at your best. Set clear boundaries for your workday and stick to them. When your 4-hour workday ends, make a conscious effort to disconnect from work-related tasks. Engage in activities that bring you joy and relaxation, whether it's spending time with family, pursuing hobbies, or simply unwinding. This balance enhances your overall well-being and keeps you motivated and energized.

Mastering a 4-hour workday in sales requires discipline, strategic planning, and a commitment to continuous improvement. By setting clear priorities, optimizing workflows, leveraging technology, and maintaining effective communication, you can maximize productivity and achieve your sales targets efficiently. Embrace a data-driven approach, stay adaptable, prioritize work-life balance, and avoid non-productive activities to create a sustainable and successful sales career that thrives within a condensed workday framework. The key is not to work harder, but to work smarter, ensuring that every minute of your workday is impactful and aligned with your goals.

Part Eight

Conclusion

Your Ultimate Sales Transformation

Comprehensive Review of Key Concepts

"Salesman's Paradox: How to Actually Sell Without Selling" is an insightful and transformative guide that elevates salesmanship to an art form. This book is not just a manual for closing deals; it's a journey through the psychological and emotional aspects of sales, designed to empower sales professionals with the tools and mindset necessary for true mastery.

The book begins by redefining the essence of a sale. It's not merely a transaction but a catalyst for change in someone's life. Through vivid anecdotes and practical examples, the author illustrates how a sale can spark a ripple effect, creating lasting impacts far beyond the initial transaction. This foundational concept sets the stage for understanding sales as a process of nurturing desires and instilling confidence.

One of the most compelling aspects of this book is its emphasis on breaking the negative stereotypes associated with salespeople. The author advocates for a shift towards ethical practices, focusing on building genuine relationships and providing real value to clients. This approach not only enhances trust but also fosters long-term loyalty and repeat business. The book's insights on authenticity and integrity are particularly impactful, highlighting how these qualities can transform a salesperson into a trusted advisor.

The book delves deeply into the psychological aspects of sales, presenting concepts like mental jiu-jitsu, energy dynamics, and the power of storytelling. These chapters are rich with techniques and strategies for mastering the subtle art of influence and persuasion. The discussion on personality types and how to engage different personas effectively is especially valuable, providing a nuanced approach to tailoring sales pitches based on individual client needs and behaviors.

The book's emphasis on building authentic rapport is a standout feature. Practical steps for creating unbreakable bonds with clients are provided, from the initial greeting to the final handshake. The strategies for mimicking body language, reading micro-expressions, and managing energy dynamics are presented with clarity and backed by psychological research, making them both accessible and highly effective.

"The Salesman's Paradox" doesn't shy away from the challenges inherent in sales. The author addresses common obstacles like buyer's remorse, handling objections, and maintaining optimism in the face of rejection. His advice is grounded in real-world experiences and reinforced by data, offering readers a robust toolkit for navigating the ups and downs of a sales career.

The structured approach of the 5 E's—Entry, Extraction, Engagement, Excitement, and the Ending—provides a comprehensive framework for mastering the sales process. Each phase is explored in detail, with actionable tips for creating impactful first impressions, extracting valuable insights, engaging with purpose, generating excitement, and delivering memorable endings. This systematic approach ensures that no aspect of the sales journey is overlooked.

The author's insights into efficient work practices, including the innovative 30/30/30/10 rule meets 80/20 and the concept of the 4-hour workday, are game-changers for productivity and work-life balance. These strategies are designed to maximize efficiency without sacrificing quality, enabling sales professionals to achieve their goals while maintaining a healthy balance between work and personal life.

The book also emphasizes the importance of fostering a positive work environment. Strategies are provided for navigating toxic workplaces, promoting a culture of transparency and respect, and leading by example. Real-world examples and psychological principles underscore the benefits of a supportive and collaborative workplace culture.

"The Salesman's Paradox" concludes with a comprehensive review of key concepts and a call to action for continuous learning and growth. The author's passion for sales and genuine desire to help others succeed shine through, making this book not only a practical guide but also an inspiring journey towards sales mastery.

"The Salesman's Paradox: How to Actually Sell Without Selling" is a must-read for anyone in the sales profession. The blend of psychological insights, practical strategies, and ethical considerations makes this book a standout resource. It's a guide that resonates on a deep level, offering both novice and seasoned sales professionals the tools and inspiration needed to transform their approach to sales and achieve lasting success. This book is sure to leave a lasting impact and is highly likely to be referenced for years to come for its profound and actionable insights.

Conclusion: Your Journey to Sales Mastery

Embarking on the path to sales mastery is not just about closing deals; it's about transforming lives, including your own. The journey you've undertaken through this book has equipped you with the knowledge, strategies, and mindset to elevate your sales game to unprecedented heights. Now, it's time to put everything into action and realize your full potential. The principles and techniques discussed in these chapters are designed to help you understand and leverage the transformative power of sales. By viewing each interaction as an opportunity to ignite change and foster growth, you can create meaningful connections that go beyond mere transactions. Remember, every sale is a spark that can light the way to a brighter future for your clients and for you.

You've learned the importance of breaking negative stereotypes and embracing F.I.T. practices. Upholding integrity and building genuine relationships not only differentiates you from others but also establishes a foundation of trust and loyalty. Your clients will see you as a trusted advisor, someone who truly cares about their success and well-being. The psychological insights into mental jiu-jitsu, energy dynamics, and storytelling provide you with powerful tools to influence and persuade effectively. Understanding personality types and tailoring your approach to engage different personas will enhance your ability to connect with diverse clients, ensuring that each interaction is personalized and impactful.

Building authentic rapport and managing energy dynamics are skills that will serve you well in every aspect of your career. These techniques, grounded in psychological research and real-world experience, are your keys to creating unbreakable bonds with your clients. When you master these skills, you become more than just a salesperson; you become a catalyst for positive change. You've also gained valuable strategies for overcoming challenges and maintaining resilience. By addressing common obstacles with data-backed advice, you can navigate the ups and downs of a sales career with confidence and optimism. Remember, every rejection is a step closer to success, and every challenge is an opportunity to grow stronger.

The structured approach of the 5 E's—Entry, Extraction, Engagement, Excitement, and Ending—provides a comprehensive framework for mastering the sales process. This method ensures that you leave no stone unturned in your quest for excellence, enabling you to create impactful first impressions, extract valuable insights, engage with purpose, generate excitement, and deliver memorable endings. Efficiency and work-life balance are critical components of sustainable success. The innovative 30/30/30/10 meets 80/20 rule and the concept of a 4-hour workday offer you a blueprint for maximizing productivity without sacrificing your personal life. By working smarter and more efficiently, you can achieve your goals while enjoying the journey.

Fostering a positive work environment is essential for personal and professional growth. By navigating toxic workplaces, promoting transparency and respect, and leading by example, you can create a culture of collaboration and excellence. Your efforts will inspire others, creating a ripple effect that uplifts the entire team. Your journey to sales mastery is a continuous process of learning, growing, and evolving. Embrace every opportunity to expand your knowledge, refine your skills, and push your boundaries. Stay curious, stay resilient, and stay committed to your goals. Your dedication to excellence and your unwavering integrity will set you apart and drive you to unparalleled success.

As you move forward, remember that you are not just a salesperson; you are a beacon of integrity, a catalyst for change, and a trusted advisor. Your commitment to ethical practices, genuine relationships, and continuous improvement will leave a lasting impact on your clients, your team, and your industry. This is your journey to sales mastery. Embrace it with passion, determination, and unwavering confidence. The world of sales is full of opportunities waiting to be seized. Go forth and transform those opportunities into lasting success. Your future is bright, and your potential is limitless. Keep fighting the good fight, and let your journey inspire others to follow in your footsteps. If you have mastered the concepts of this book then you have in fact mastered the Salesman's Paradox.

Additional Resources to Continue Learning

Expand Your Knowledge in Sales, Leadership, and Personal Growth

Books on Sales and Influence:

- **Influence: The Psychology of Persuasion** by Robert B. Cialdini
  A deep dive into the principles of influence and how to harness them for sales success.
- **How to Win Friends and Influence People** by Dale Carnegie
  The timeless classic on building relationships and influencing people through empathy and communication.
- **No B.S. Grassroots Marketing** by Dan Kennedy
  Practical, no-nonsense advice for implementing powerful marketing strategies.
- **The Psychology of Selling** by Brian Tracy
  Learn the art of selling by mastering the psychological aspects behind every deal.
- **The Millionaire Real Estate Agent** by Gary Keller
  A comprehensive guide for salespeople, especially in real estate, focusing on building a successful business through proven models and strategies.
- **Selling For Dummies** by Tom Hopkins
  A straightforward guide packed with techniques and strategies to help anyone excel in sales, regardless of experience.
- **The Millionaire Messenger** by Brendon Burchard
  How to turn your life story and expertise into a profitable business.

Personal Development and Success:

- **Eric Thomas, The Hip Hop Preacher - "How Bad Do You Want It?"**
  Eric Thomas' motivational speech emphasizes the intensity and commitment needed to achieve success. It's a must-listen for those pushing their limits.
  Link: Eric Thomas - How Bad Do You Want It?
- **Think and Grow Rich** by Napoleon Hill

A foundational book for understanding the mindset and principles behind accumulating wealth and achieving success.
- **The 7 Habits of Highly Effective People** by Stephen R. Covey
A comprehensive guide to personal and professional effectiveness through timeless habits.
- **Grit: The Power of Passion and Perseverance** by Angela Duckworth
Discover how perseverance and resilience contribute to long-term success.
- **Awaken the Giant Within** by Tony Robbins
A guide to taking control of your emotions, finances, relationships, and life in general.
- **Unlimited Power** by Tony Robbins
Robbins' first book, focusing on the principles of success and self-mastery.
- **Personal Development For Dummies** by Gillian Burn
Covers a variety of personal growth topics including goal setting, emotional intelligence, and building self-confidence.
- **The Motivation Manifesto** by Brendon Burchard
A rallying cry for personal freedom and the courage to live your best life.

Positive Psychology, Spiritual Growth, and Mind Expansion:

- **The Alchemist** by Paulo Coelho
A beautiful parable about following your dreams, discovering your personal legend, and the pursuit of happiness.
- **The Book of Joy** by The Dalai Lama and Desmond Tutu
A heartwarming exploration of joy, based on a week-long conversation between two of the world's greatest spiritual leaders.
- **The Secret Series** by Rhonda Byrne:
    - **The Secret**: Introduces the law of attraction and how positive thinking can shape your life.
    - **The Power**: Focuses on the power of love and positive energy in manifesting desires.
    - **The Magic**: Offers 28 practices to help harness gratitude and improve your life.
    - **Hero**: Guides readers on a journey to discover their own inner strength and purpose.

- o **The Greatest Secret**: Expands on the ideas of the original book, focusing on inner peace and lasting happiness.
- **The Gateway Tapes from Hemi-Sync**
  A series of guided audio sessions using brainwave synchronization technology to explore expanded consciousness, altered states of awareness, and out-of-body experiences.
- **Centerpointe Holosync Series**
  A program designed to enhance meditation and self-awareness by using sound technology to stimulate brainwave patterns, resulting in deeper states of relaxation and personal growth.
- **Mindfulness For Dummies** by Shamash Alidina
  An excellent introduction to mindfulness, meditation techniques, and how they can enhance everyday life.

Leadership and Personal Growth:

- **Dare to Lead** by Brené Brown
  Learn how to lead with courage and vulnerability to foster innovation and trust in teams.
- **The Power of Vulnerability** by Brené Brown
  A deep exploration of how embracing vulnerability can strengthen relationships, inspire leadership, and transform personal and professional life.
- **The Culture Code** by Daniel Coyle
  A guide to building highly effective teams and cultures through trust, cooperation, and leadership.
- **Turn the Ship Around!** by L. David Marquet
  A leadership guide based on Marquet's experience transforming a Navy submarine crew by giving them control and fostering accountability.
- **John C. Maxwell Books**:
  - o **The 21 Irrefutable Laws of Leadership**
  - o **Developing the Leader Within You**
  - o **The 5 Levels of Leadership**
  - o **The 15 Invaluable Laws of Growth**
  - o **Leadership Gold**

- **Sometimes You Win, Sometimes You Learn**
- **Work Rules!** by Laszlo Bock
Insights from Google's approach to transforming leadership and productivity.
- **Good to Great** by Jim Collins
How great companies emerge from good ones through leadership and disciplined strategy.
- **Built to Last** by Jim Collins
Explores why some companies thrive for decades and remain industry leaders while others do not.
- **Leadership For Dummies** by Marshall Loeb and Stephen Kindel
A practical guide to effective leadership, covering topics like team building, communication, and decision-making.
- **Prosci - Leading Your Team Through Change**
A guide to navigating organizational change effectively, focusing on leadership and team dynamics during transitions.
- **Lean Six Sigma Green Belt Training**
A detailed training resource for mastering Lean Six Sigma principles and becoming proficient in process improvement.

Microexpressions and Neurolinguistic Programming:

- **What Every BODY is Saying** by Joe Navarro
A former FBI agent's guide to reading body language to enhance communication and influence.
- **Introducing NLP** by Joseph O'Connor and John Seymour
Learn the fundamentals of neuro-linguistic programming to influence and understand behavior.
- **Emotions Revealed** by Paul Ekman
A guide to understanding emotions through facial expressions and improving emotional communication.
- **NLP For Dummies** by Romilla Ready and Kate Burton
Provides an accessible overview of NLP techniques and how to use them for personal and professional development.

These resources span sales strategies, leadership principles, personal development, and motivational frameworks, as well as mindfulness and consciousness-expanding techniques. Together, they offer comprehensive insights for growing both personally and professionally, helping you sharpen your skills, enhance your leadership, and stay motivated for success.

Happy reading and continuous learning!

Psychodynamic Marketing: Campaigning to the Consumer's Mind

Joey Poltor
Capella University
Summer 2012

ABSTRACT

In this paper, the writer looks at the theory of psychodynamic marketing, product development within the mind of the consumer. Through a compilation of traditional and modern methods, the psychodynamic marketer is able to lower costs by implementing guerila insurgency tactics to compete with corporate conglomerate counterparts. Small businesses simply do not have the budget of the large competitors and this theory can be considered a tactic which levels the playing field. The writer looks at the reasons behind marketing measures and how the consumer responds.

Table of Contents

1. **Chapter One**
   - Area of Practice
   - Significance of Psychodynamic Marketing
2. **Chapter Two: Literature Review**
   - Literature Review
   - History of Marketing Psychology
   - Theoretical Background
   - Best Practices
   - Significance and Relevance to the Knowledge Base of Psychology
   - Professional Standards
3. **Chapter Three: Method**
   - Purpose of Study
   - Research Design
   - Target Population and Participant Selection

- Procedures
    - Marketing Methods – Campaign Implementation
    - Conversions
    - Individual Branding
    - Research Questions and Hypotheses
    - Data Analysis
4. **Chapter Four: Expected Outcomes**
    - Goals
    - Time Tracking
    - Investment Tracking
5. **Chapter Five: Discussion**
    - Hypotheses
    - Further Research
    - Conclusion
6. **References**

Psychodynamic Marketing: Campaigning to the Consumer Mind

Introduction

In today's rapidly evolving marketplace, the small business fails time and time again due to over-restriction imposed by government and lack of market profitability due to corporate conglomerations. Cronin-Gilmore (2012) suggests that up to 50% of small businesses fail due to improper marketing and that eight out of ten small businesses fail within the first five years. For example, if one hundred small businesses open in January 2013, eighty will fail by 2018. Of that eighty, forty will fail due to improper marketing techniques. However, one may assume that 40% of all small businesses fail due to improper marketing techniques. America is supposedly built on the backs of small business. Therefore, it would be wise to incorporate an increase in the development of marketing strategies and understanding among small businesses which will further develop this great nation. A theoretical 40% increase in economic development would vastly improve American culture and way of life.

Area of Practice

To state the problem, there are too many small business failures due to a lack of proper marketing techniques. Grocery stores, convenience stores, and superstores have put the small businesses out of business. Dunham (1991), among other scholars, acknowledged this trend over two decades ago, yet America is convinced that small business still leads the crowd. The writer hypothesizes that this nostalgic belief system stems from a need to be different, a need to feel independence in American daily life rather than actuality. The small business association considers a small business to be one that employs less than 500 employees (sba.gov, 2012). However, this paper considers small businesses with less than 5 employees and a low level of marketing capital to be the target demographic. At 500 employees, a company is hardly a small business, yet society bases its understanding on skewed perception such as this. The research strategy undertaken in this paper is an attempt at understanding how to develop self-promotion from within the mind of the consumer. Psychodynamic assumes development within the mind thus psychodynamic marketing assumes the development of necessity and branding of a product within the mind of the consumer. While there are many ways to do this, relationship building is a main premise of the paper. The writer intends on using relationship building to promote products or services for a much lower cost than corporate conglomerate competitors. The very small business simply cannot reach the consumer on a major scale so must create a formidable relationship in any way possible. Scholarly articles have been investigated, copious amounts of time have been spent researching, successful small and large business techniques have been considered, and this paper develops the techniques which are needed to succeed in psychodynamic marketing.

Significance of Psychodynamic Marketing

Psychodynamic marketing is a new field of marketing that looks at traditional marketing methods and combines those with modern marketing methods. These methods include brand building and relationship building to newer sciences such as neuromarketing and internet marketing in the global marketplace. Khosla (2010) suggests that there is a base level six-step process that the consumer goes through: problem recognition, information search, evaluation of alternatives, purchase decision, purchase, and post-purchase satisfaction. Psychologists have found that through marketing these steps can be highly influenced. Mental triggers such as color variations, headline sales copywriting techniques, visual aids, interesting arousal techniques, and others all assist the marketer in easing the consumer through the process. While large companies have capital to shock and awe their consumers, small businesses must allocate resources to accomplish the same goals. By understanding the process of psychological marketing, the small business is able to compete with its corporate conglomerate counterpart through guerilla insurgency methods such as psychodynamic marketing. A small business simply cannot beat a large business in marketing funds and efforts. Large businesses have the ability to lose profits simply to ensure the failure of the small business competitor and keep market share. Psychodynamic marketing encompasses these guerilla insurgency tactics to capture the consumer at the source.

Chapter 2: Literature Review

History

The ultimate culmination of every marketer's goal is to know exactly what the target market wants and exactly when they want it. Through neuroscience, marketing is becoming less about the conscious and more about the unconscious decisions that we make. Lovell (2008) posits that through neuroscience the marketer is able to appeal to the rationalizing creature in the consumer rather than the rational decision-maker that people pretend to be. The theory was developed with the developments of the MRI and CT scan in the 1970s and 1980s with little research until recent years (Trend #5, 2010). The role psychology plays in marketing is often overlooked by small businesses, though major corporations such as Pepsi and McDonald's have been on the forefront of this type of marketing advancement for years.

Theoretical Background

This paper assumes that the small business is unable to enlist the services of a neuromarketing agency to understand the needs of their client base at its optimum level. Instead, a level of understanding must be attributed to the small business' strengths in branding, relationship building, storytelling, and other important aspects of marketing on a low level of capital. Through generations, storytelling has been a captive way of passing knowledge from one to the next. People relate to each other in stories and have been proven to be an asset in the psychology of marketing. Woodside, Sood, and Miller (2008) propose that the use of the anthropomorphic approach is a sound way of promoting the products within their business. The five propositions are central to the use of storytelling in marketing. First, people think narratively, next a significant amount of data stored in memory is episodic, thirdly, telling stories enables individuals to relive experiences, then brands are associated with the story of the brand, and lastly, individuals seek clarity through storytelling. The writer considers the fourth point to be further clarified in the example of the Pepsi versus Coca-Cola taste test in which Pepsi is generally enjoyed more so than Coke, though Coca-Cola continually outsells Pepsi. When one closes their eyes to consider the branding of Coca-Cola, one can imagine the Christmas scenes that have been playing for as long as most can remember on television. It is that story and other branding stories that people enjoy, relate to, and the cause of the continuous outselling of its major competitors.

Shabbir, Reast, and Palihawadana (2009) published an article which considers the development of psychology and marketing over the past twenty-five years. What can be drawn from their observation is the developmental process of psychology and marketing. The article takes the reader through classic conditioning methods, methods of postmodernism, domain-specific categories, and other factors such as intrinsic and extrinsic. The article fails to look at the impact that the internet has played in the psychology of marketing and newer sciences such as neuromarketing. The writer hypothesizes that through mediums such as the internet the small business is able to compete with larger organizations.

Best Practices

By understanding a psychodynamic promotional method, a method that develops within the mind of the consumer, a small business can play an even greater role to that consumer than a large competitor due to the level of intimacy that can be reached between the consumer and the small business. A small business fluent in psychodynamic marketing is able to help the consumer to build a relationship with the small business with little capital investment. An understanding of how the unconscious mind works and responds to different stimuli as can be seen in neuromarketing applies heavily. Understanding branding, from color choice to emails, from eye line to copywriting, and different types of propaganda are some of the attributes of what this echelon of marketing involves. The idea behind psychodynamic marketing is to help the consumer decide that the small business' products or services are so necessary and that any price would be a price worth paying and that consumer becomes a lifetime advocate for future purchases and testimonials.

There is great value in every aspect of marketing for the small business. Even logo design carries with it values that go far beyond the naked eye. Logo design considers intrinsic and extrinsic value as well as color, typeset, and other factors. Hynes (2009) postulates that logo color using the traditional warm colors such as yellows, oranges, and reds, can stimulate appetite and even make you angry. Consider the McDonald's logo. Cool colors can induce a calming effect that can be associated with the company. The shape of the logo can also induce a subconscious understanding and needs to be fully utilized. For example, the Nike swoosh signifies movement which is highly extrinsic in sales marketing. Using an octagon shape and a color red would signify a stop sign and when incorporating that theme into a logo can help to draw attention.

The writer postulates that developing advocacy is a function of relationship building. Consider star-crossed lovers and how a small business can incorporate that same type of feeling in their client base. Shakespeare's play, *Romeo and Juliet,* is where two people were willing to die for their love of one another. That love is the love that one wants to instill in his client base for the small business to thrive through psychodynamic marketing. Fortunately, death is not necessary to create a following of devoted customers. A thorough understanding of the psychology of marketing and implementation are needed.

To further delve into the best practices of psychodynamic marketing, the writer brings attention to the widely used internet marketing campaigns which have given small businesses the opportunity to sell in a global economy. Jie and Daugherty (2009) go into how the development of social media and the internet are being used to develop companies. With a social network campaign, the small business is able to develop a following of repeat clients who offer a vote of social proof to new customers. When considering the use of the internet as a media for small business, not only do new marketing venues play roles such as social media marketing but also traditional sales copywriting, branding, etc., all come into play. In the coming pages, the paper is going to give a checklist of procedures that can be followed and implemented to increase success levels in psychodynamic marketing.

Significance in Psychological Knowledge Base

Berger and Milkman (2012) examine nearly 7,000 New York Times articles to determine how emotional aspects play roles in the virality of online content. Virality is the level at which a particular content piece is shared around the internet. They found that arousal-type information, content that gets people angry or motivated to be highly successful at virality. While some would assume that negative content would be passed around more than positive content, positive content has a higher level of virality. This is because people like to be known as the person who passes around positive information or seem knowledgeable of the content. As one can tell, there could be an innumerable amount of factors to be understood and considered in developing a psychodynamic marketing campaign.

There have been great amounts of research completed which have considered traditional theories from the Gestalt principle to modern technologies such as neuroimaging in the psychology of marketing. Little research has been applied to the practicality of the small business' implementation procedures of said techniques. Often, it would seem that the studies performed are based on data results rather than overall results in productivity and profitability per the business. If a small business were to hire a specialized marketing agency to determine demographical information using neuroimaging technology, the small business may have to spend a year's profitability margin to complete the task, in turn becoming the cause of failure to the business. As stated above, the paper looks at a multitude of techniques, data, and hypothesizes to the implementation of guerilla insurgency tactics to lower capital investment which increases profit margins.

Professional Standards

It is imperative that the utmost caution be taken in the development of psychodynamic marketing techniques and practices. Lovell (2008) discusses the fear that comes with over-anxious marketing companies learning to control the subconscious through neuromarketing and the dangers that could be involved. By teaching a compilation of the most intricate mind-bending techniques to the small business owner, it is a concern that the charlatans of the marketing world would take advantage of the procedures. As a standard practice, professionals who adhere to the APA Code of Ethics and treat this information and their clients with nonmaleficence should be the main proponents of the techniques (APA, 2008). Currently, there are no licensing requirements for a marketing psychologist, though professionals should adhere to the APA Code which is assumed to be standard ethical practice in the field.

Chapter Three: Method

Purpose of Study

The purpose of this study is to investigate the outcomes of psychodynamic marketing campaigns on the success of small business development and marketing. The goal of this study is to create a valuable system which small businesses can implement which will increase the marketing conversion success rate while lowering the closure rate of companies overall. Up to 40% of small business failures can be attributed to the failure to properly market. Most small businesses are created and fielded by individuals who are professionals of their trade rather than professionals of marketing (Cronin-Gilmore, 2012). Therefore, many small business owners overlook the vital role marketing plays in the business development and growth due to this oversight.

One key issue to marketing is the cost involved. Small businesses do not have the capital of major corporate conglomerates. Therefore, the necessity for an inexpensive yet applicable marketing device is high. This device would need to be inexpensive, highly adaptive, easily configured and implemented, as well as convenient. Small business owners must have time to run their businesses as well as work their marketing campaigns.

Research Design

The design to be employed in this study is a case study. The writer solicits a small business with less than five employees to engage in the study and implements the psychodynamic marketing method into a marketing campaign. The intensive study of working with the data and outcomes of this case represent the case study (Flyvbjerg, 2011). The case study lasts for six months and the researcher meets with the business owner daily during the research term. The writer postulates that intensive case studies of multiple small businesses in multiple genres would give the reader a stronger level of validity and reliability as to the marketing method's strengths and weaknesses. To fully develop this study, the research design of case studies should be replicated over multiple businesses and genres as well as tracking be completed over years of research to understand the full implications of value that are associated with the psychodynamic marketing method. As a longitudinal study, the study should follow at least ten small businesses for at least five years to determine the long-term developments of the company. The current study is a case study of one company implementing the psychodynamic marketing method over the course of six months. Additional marketing research and studies should be conducted to further the validity and reliability of the findings.

Target Population and Participant Selection

The sample that will be used in this study is one that will include a small business where the small business owner can represent the brand of the company. This study will encompass a fitness and nutrition coaching company where the coach has books, DVDs, coaching calls, and other various products for sale. Being that this is a case study, the researcher would only consider this to be one study of the many in a longitudinal study. The company currently has a shotgun approach to marketing where they try different things, capture a sale and move forward to another sale. Psychodynamic marketing builds a relationship with buyers and attempts to create a necessity within the consumer's mind to ensure repeat business.

The coaching business, the study sample in this group, has a client base which mostly consists of mothers in their late twenties to early thirties who are physically fit and are into fitness. There is an annual household income of $65,000-$125,000, an average of two kids per household and the target audience is either employed part-time, full-time, or self-employed. The children of the target client are generally one school-aged and one toddler. The demographic is mostly Caucasian women but has a 20% variance of mixed minorities. These women hold between some college to an undergraduate level of education.

Procedures

The psychodynamic method will be assessed in a variety of different aspects. Ultimately, increased profits and long-term repeat customer base are the goals of the marketing method. The initial gathering of the minds will determine the precise components of the marketing campaign. In this ever-rapidly increasing global market, psychodynamic marketing relies heavily on using the internet to develop branding. Dou, Lim, Su, Zhou, and Cui (2010) postulate that there can be a high level of success when using the internet to develop branding and brand awareness of a company. This can be especially true among less tech-savvy users. While a tech-savvy individual may understand that search engine optimization or pay-per-click ads can move a company website to the top of the search results, a lay person may think that the top ad is more important than those below it. While there is a high level of internet marketing that the method depends on, offline marketing such as mailings, phone calls, and personal contacting are also used in an inexpensive and convenient manner.

Marketing Methods – Campaign Implementation

After signing all of the appropriate documentation and explaining the marketing process, the case study participant and the researcher come to a documented agreement and the process begins. The purpose of psychodynamic marketing is to help the consumer develop the brand without much input on the part of the business. The first step is in gaining traffic through online media sources. Once a budget and time allotment have been agreed upon by the researcher and study sample, the team agrees upon sources of media to build traffic upon. This list could include:

- Being seen as an expert on forums
- Pay-per-view marketing

- Blogging
- Article directories
- Pay-per-click ads
- Audio podcasts
- Video marketing
- Press releases
- Rented email lists
- Guest writing, blogging, interviews
- Question site answering and commenting
- Social bookmarking
- Offline marketing
- Affiliate programs
- High traffic community sites creating pages and groups (Skrob, 2011)

For this case study; social bookmarking, blogging, offline marketing, guest blogging, forums expert, video marketing, audio marketing, article marketing, and pay-per-click ads are all within budget and time constraints and opted to be incorporated into the campaign. A schedule is then created on how often to post, the content, and the costs and time involved. These limits are based on what the sample actually could afford in time and money to ensure that the assessment is as close to actual as possible for a traditional small business.

Conversion

The sample develops a couple of websites around the internet. In all, with this type of marketing, there could easily be 100 content submissions to create a daily increase in brand awareness; building backlinks, search engine optimization, and keyword strength throughout the internet. Within a matter of days, there is the chance that the sample may result in a daily increase of over 100 visitors to the site. About twenty percent of these visitors opt into an email list in exchange for a free widget. The widget could be a DVD, a report, or something of value. These opt-ins are then considered conversions and they begin to receive autoresponder emails from the company. The emails can be in the form of a story, as storytelling helps to build the brand through relating to the consumer (Woodside, Sood, & Miller, 2008). Soon the consumer is looking forward to the story emails and has forgotten that the company is trying to sell them things. Every couple of emails in, the company offers a new deal within the email to entice the consumers to buy.

Some of the visitors purchase immediately and those that leave the page are retargeted with cookies placed in their computer cache so that they see ads for the sample for the next couple of weeks on all of the other sites that they visit. This retargeting method serves as a great reminder of what the company has to offer. The immediate purchasers are sent through a sales funnel which up-sells and down-sells the consumer to maximize profitability and they are also entered into another email autoresponder system to further develop the relationship and brand.

Individual Branding

The last aspect which is tested is the effect of branding on the individual consumer versus branding at the macro level. This method is much more cost-efficient and may have a higher probability of success. The consumer has opted in and is receiving the automated email stories; they have been retargeted so that a cookie in their cache continues to show the company ads making it seem as if they are everywhere. The company is also seen on niche forums as an expert and in social media as an expert. The company has also used offline tactics such as a phone call or text messages asking if all questions were answered and postal mail sent as a reminder to keep interested. While this cost would be enormous if done to thousands of prospects, by utilizing psychodynamic marketing, the company seems overly large to the consumer though they are spending little time and effort by only marketing directly to interested parties. Jie and Daugherty (2009) give that this third-person effect that can be reached through the multiple media outlets aids in building brand awareness in the consumer. Not only is there a third-person effect reached in this method, there is also an illusion created within the consumer's mind of a bigger business that seems to be everywhere which aids in brand awareness, relationship building, and trust building.

Research Questions and Hypotheses

The main research question for the purpose of this research is how can a small business compete with a large business in marketing efforts? What does the small business have that the corporate conglomeration does not have? How can the small business seem as legitimate and as trustworthy as the large competitor without the expenses? How can psychodynamic marketing methods play a role in the furthered success of small businesses? Hypotheses for the research are as follows. Through a psychodynamic model, the small business is able to find the appropriate consumer, enter their lives and mind, and build a relationship through direct marketing at a fraction of the cost of large-scale interrupt marketing. The small business has the power of intimacy over the large corporations. This intimacy should be exploited in order to develop a strong relationship with the consumer. By using direct marketing targeted at a specific demographic, the small business is able to build legitimacy. Through facets of being seen as the expert on forums, social media, and other realms, legitimacy and trust are built. Through this process, the small business shall see measurable success. The null hypothesis is that the psychodynamic model will not increase marketing profits for the small business.

Data Analysis

The results of the campaign will be investigated and recorded throughout the course of the six-month study. Every month, traffic, conversion, response rate, sales, and repeat sales will all be tested and recorded. Minor ad tweaks will be done through split testing to ensure maximum response from the case study's target. Overall, profit margins are the ultimate in results data and if profits are up significantly with no major change in environment, then this study will have proven that psychodynamic marketing warrants further investigation and could be a new era of marketing for the small business. This could be a method closing the gap between small and large business overall. Complete statistics will be drawn from this qualitative study and analyzed for further reliability and validity statistics.

Chapter Four: Expected Outcomes

Goals

The ultimate goal of the researcher in this study is to increase the level of success of small businesses by creating a marketing method that is inexpensive, lucrative, and convenient. The psychodynamic marketing method acts on the premise that through modern technology, direct response marketing, relationship building, and individual branding a company can develop in the mind of the consumer without going through the expensive and time-consuming stakes of conventional marketing and branding methods.

Time Tracking

As stated in the purpose of chapter three, the method has to be seen as one that can be implemented in the time allowable in addition to other small business duties. In a small business where there is only a small staff, one individual wears many hats. This axiom meaning that the small business owner must take on many roles tends to lend itself to the target sample of this research study. Every day, during the daily meeting, the researcher tracks the amount of time the business professional spends implementing the process which is tracked and plotted on a frequency distribution and using a line graph showing the correlation between time spent and increased results (Howell, 2008).

Ideally, the researcher will find consistent increases in results starting within the first twenty-one days and steadily climbing throughout the course of the study. The researcher will also track any losses in profit due to the amount of time the business has to take to implement the method which the writer posits will be significant in the beginning and will taper down throughout the first few months of the study. Ideally, the time spent on profits will decrease gradually throughout the study. The writer posits that there will be weeks that are more productive than others and the line graph will show the value of the different campaign techniques. There will be a direct correlation within the line graph from successful technique to time invested showing for the particular business where time was best spent.

Investment Tracking

One of the most important aspects of marketing is tracking return on investment, or ROI. In marketing methods, a company has to invest money into marketing expenses. These numbers will be tracked daily and displayed weekly in another line graph to display how the return is doing throughout the course of the study. These line graphs will serve as a control for future studies on different businesses as well as for small businesses in implementation. By measuring time tracking and return on investment, the study will prove to be lucrative, convenient, and inexpensive or it will prove the opposite.

Overall, frequency distributions will be created for each aspect of the marketing campaign techniques. These distributions will be compared to the small business' previous annual returns by using quarterly tax statements from which such data is drawn. Anomalies in the comparison data will be accounted for by requesting further clarification from samples thus creating a valuable baseline of marketing results. By examining these frequency distributions and using the SPSS database and ANOVA function, the researcher will be able to determine which of the hypotheses or null hypotheses are proven.

Each technique in the campaign will also be tracked with the goal of the return on investment steadily increasing throughout the study while the time invested steadily decreases. When comparing the distribution of different techniques used, the writer will plot a histogram and the most successful techniques will stay with the marketing method while the least useful techniques will be reexamined and either adjusted and reimplemented or removed. The findings here shall be exemplary in determining the value of the method as well as the use of this type of marketing theory.

Chapter Five: Discussion

In this section, the writer revisits the problem as well as the research hypotheses, null hypothesis and through scholarly research, highlights key potential results. The writer goes into logic behind postulation and recognizes the limitations of the study. The writer then determines potential questions still looming over the reader. The problem is that there are too many small business startups that fail due to inadequate marketing. As many as 40% of small business startups fail due to inadequate marketing (Cronin-Gilmore, 2012).

Hypotheses

Through a psychodynamic model, small businesses are able to find the appropriate consumers and market directly to them for a fraction of the cost of standard branding techniques. Varadarajan (2010) posits that through the advancement in marketing strategy, as a field of study, there have been numerous benefits. Many of those benefits have been to the business world as well as the field of psychology. Social network marketing, direct marketing, strategic marketing, neuromarketing, and now psychodynamic marketing are a small portion of an undeveloped new field of study. Miller (2012) showed there was an estimated $153.3 billion dollars spent on direct marketing campaigns in 2010 in the US which yielded an estimated $2 Trillion in sales. Psychodynamic marketing is a development of a more personalized direct marketing method using modern marketing techniques, thus the marketing outcomes may be comparable if not a bit more favorable to the marketer.

At first glance, the psychodynamic model appears to be a more personalized form of direct marketing methods with the development of online content, neuromarketing, and branding techniques. However, with the limited data research and testing, the outcomes of this paper seem to be very much anecdotal at best.

Further Research

Further research in the form of multiple case studies is necessary to further eliminate doubt and prove the hypotheses. By comparing data to previous annual returns the null hypothesis is proven false though economic and environmental factors play an outstanding role in the uncontrolled sample. Being that the sample is an actual business with active worldly clients, it is inherently difficult if not impossible to amass data that is unaffected by outside factors.

Conclusion

As stated above modern marketing technologies are a somewhat new field of study in psychology which warrants further investigation. Basing that the psychodynamic model incorporates an infusion of multiple methods that have worked for decades along with newer proven marketing methods such as direct marketing and neuromarketing, the writer postulates that the psychodynamic method should be further tested on multiple genres of business, sizes, and markets.

Understanding how the method works on multiple business platforms will allow for the proving of the hypotheses and solving of the problem. The most vital potential question looming over the reader is whether or not the marketing method works for the small business. The answer, though anecdotal, is the method needs more research to be determined valid and reliable.

References

American Psychological Association. (2010). American Psychological Association ethical principles of psychologists and code of conduct. Retrieved online at http://www.apa.org/ethics/code/index.aspx

Berger, J., & Milkman, K. (2012). What Makes Online Content Viral?? Journal Of Marketing Research (JMR), 49(2), 192-205. doi:10.1509/jmr.10.0353

Cronin-Gilmore, J. (2012). Exploring Marketing Strategies in Small Businesses. Journal Of Marketing Development & Competitiveness, 6(1), 96-107.

Dou, W., Lim, K. H., Su, C., Zhou, N., & Cui, N. (2010). BRAND POSITIONING STRATEGY USING SEARCH ENGINE MARKETING. MIS Quarterly, 34(2), 261-A4.

Dunham, W. W. (1991). Survival by the numbers. (Cover story). Nation's Business, 79(8), 14.

Howell, D. C. (2008). Fundamental Statistics for the Behavior Science (6th ed.). Belmont, CA: Thomson Wadsworth.

Flyvbjerg, B (2011) Case Study. Sage Handbook of Qualitative Research. 4th Edition. Thousand Oaks, CA.

Jie, Z., & Daugherty, T. (2009). Third-Person Effect and Social Networking: Implications for Online Marketing and Word-of-Mouth Communication. American Journal Of Business (American Journal Of Business), 24(2), 53-63.

Khosla, S. (2010). Consumer Psychology: The Essence of Marketing. International

Journal Of Educational Administration, 2(2), 219-225.

Lovell, C. (2008). Is neuroscience making a difference?. Campaign (UK), (39), 11.

Miller, R. K., & Washington, K. (2012). CHAPTER 74: DIRECT MARKETING. In, Consumer Behavior (pp. 419-422). Richard K. Miller & Associates.

Sba.gov. (n.d.) Citing Websites. What is a Small Business? Retrieved Online http://www.sba.gov/category/navigation-structure/contracting/contracting-officials/eligibility-size-standards

Shabbir, H., Reast, J., & Palihawadana, D. (2009). 25 years of Psychology & Marketing: a multidimensional review. Psychology & Marketing, 26(12), 1031-1065.

Skrob, R. (2011) The Official Get Rich Guide to Information Marketing. 2nd Entrepreneur Press. Entrepreneur Media, Inc.

TREND # 5: Marketing to the Human Brain. (2010). Trends Magazine, (85), 29-32.

Varadarajan, R. (2010). Strategic marketing and marketing strategy: Domain, definition, fundamental issues and foundational premises. Journal Of The Academy Of Marketing Science, 38(2), 119-140. doi:10.1007/s11747-009-0176-7

Woodside, A. G., Sood, S., & Miller, K. E. (2008). When consumers and brands talk: Storytelling theory and research in psychology and marketing. Psychology & Marketing, 25(2), 97-145.